ECONOMIC DEVELOPMENT
AND THE PRICE LEVEL

ECONOMIC DEVELOPMENT
AND
THE PRICE LEVEL

BY

GEOFFREY MAYNARD

LECTURER IN ECONOMICS IN THE UNIVERSITY COLLEGE
OF SOUTH WALES AND MONMOUTHSHIRE, CARDIFF

LONDON
MACMILLAN & CO LTD
NEW YORK · ST MARTIN'S PRESS
1963

MACMILLAN AND COMPANY LIMITED
St Martin's Street London WC2
also Bombay Calcutta Madras Melbourne

THE MACMILLAN COMPANY OF CANADA LIMITED
Toronto

ST MARTIN'S PRESS INC
New York

PRINTED IN GREAT BRITAIN

PREFACE

The theme of this book was suggested to me by Professor Simon Kuznets during my tenure as Fellow in Political Economy at the Johns Hopkins University, Baltimore, in the academic year 1957/8. Some preliminary work carried out at Johns Hopkins enabled me to read a paper on inflation and growth at a Conference on Economic Development sponsored by the Department of Economics and The Institute of Latin American Studies of the University of Texas in April 1958; and in the course of the next two years the substance of this paper was expanded into its present form.

I am greatly indebted to Professor Kuznets for his kindness towards me, and for his help in my work, during my stay at Johns Hopkins. I have also received constant encouragement and assistance from Professor Brinley Thomas who read an early draft of the book. Professor Phelps Brown was kind enough to read and criticise a paper setting out some of the arguments now appearing in Chapter VI; and Mr. Esra Bennathan of the University of Birmingham made some valuable suggestions, as well as drawing attention to some useful sources of information.

I am also indebted to the University of Texas Press for allowing me to reproduce the substance of a paper 'Inflation in Economic Development' published in *Economic Growth: Rationale, Problems, Cases* (Proceedings of the University of Texas Conference on Economic Development, edited by Eastin Nelson), and to the Editors of *Oxford Economic Papers* for allowing me to include certain passages and statistics from my article 'Inflation and Growth: Some Lessons to be drawn from Latin-American Experience' appearing in the June 1961 issue of the journal.

GEOFFREY MAYNARD

University College
Cardiff

ACKNOWLEDGMENTS

The author wishes to acknowledge his indebtedness to the following, who have kindly given permission for the use of copyright material: Messrs. George Allen & Unwin, Ltd., for the sentence from *The Theory of Economic Growth*, by W. A. Lewis; the American Economic Association, for the extract from 'Factor Proportions in Japanese Economic Development', by G. Ranis, in *American Economic Review* (September 1957); Messrs. Basil Blackwell & Mott, Ltd., for Table 54 from *British Industry 1700–1950*, by W. Hoffman, and Table 26 from *British Overseas Trade*, by W. Schlote; Messrs. Bowes & Bowes Publishers Ltd., for various Tables from Vols. II, III and V of their *Income and Wealth* series; the Clarendon Press, Oxford, for extracts and a chart from *The Growth and Fluctuations of the British Economy, 1790–1850*, by Gayer, Rostow and Schwartz, the extract from *The British Economy in the Nineteenth Century*, by W. W. Rostow, and the substance of the article on 'Inflation and Growth: Some Lessons to be drawn from Latin-American Experience', in *Oxford Economic Papers*; the editor of *Economic History Review*, for the extract from 'Prices and Industrial Capitalism in France and England 1540–1640', by J. U. Nef; Martinus Nijhoff, The Hague, for extracts from *Public Finance and the Less-Developed Economy*, by P. A. M. Van Philips; the National Bureau of Economic Research, Inc., and Princeton University Press, for extracts by Holzman and R. P. Powell from 'Financing Soviet Economic Development' in *Capital Formation and Economic Growth* (1955); Princeton University Press, for the extract and statistical material from Tables 2, 3 and 8 from *The Economic Development of Japan*, by W. Lockwood, (1955); Messrs. Routledge & Kegan Paul, Ltd., for extracts from *Soviet Economic Development Since 1917*, by M. Dobb; Mr. Miyohei Shinohara, for Figure 4 and Table 6 from *The Growth Rate of the Japanese Economy Since 1878*, by Miyohei Shinohara, K. Ohkawa and others; The University of Chicago Press, for various statistical series appearing in Table 1 of the Appendix to S. Kuznets' 'Quantitative Aspects of the Economic Growth of Nations', in *Economic Development and Cultural Change*, Vol. V, No. 1 (October 1956), and the extract from S. Okita's article 'Savings and Economic Growth in Japan', in *Economic Development and Cultural Change*, Vol. VI, No. 1 (October 1957); the University of Minnesota Press, for the sentence from *Savings in the Modern Economy*, edited by Walter W. Heller, Francis M. Boddy, and Carl L. Nelson, (Copyright 1953 by the University of Minnesota); and the University of Texas Press, for extracts from 'Inflation in Economic Development', from *Economic Growth: Rationale, Problems, Cases*, edited by Eastin Nelson.

CONTENTS

Chapter I

INTRODUCTORY

In this book we shall examine the connection between economic development and the behaviour of the price level. It is clear that we may approach the task with two questions in mind. On the one hand, we may set out to provide an answer to the question, so often raised in discussions of economic development, 'Is some inflation a stimulant for economic growth?' Alternatively, we may simply seek an explanation of the behaviour of prices in the course of growth, without concerning ourselves explicitly with whether growth would have been faster or slower if prices had behaved differently. But these questions cannot really be separated. We cannot arrive at an answer to the first until we have some good idea of why prices should rise at all: and in looking for an explanation of price behaviour, we must necessarily concern ourselves, to some extent at least, with the nature and causes of economic growth. Indeed, as the following chapters will show, the answer to the first question largely depends on the nature of the answer to be given to the second. Nonetheless, it is worth distinguishing between them at the outset, if only to bring out more sharply the relationship between the two.

One way of setting about finding an answer to the first question is to examine the record of history. Is it typically the case that faster economic growth went hand in hand with rising prices? Some historians would certainly subscribe to this view. For instance, it seems to be generally agreed that substantial economic progress occurred in England, France and, to a lesser extent, Spain, in the sixteenth and seventeenth centuries when prices were rising fairly continuously, at a compound rate in England of about 1 per cent per annum. The early part of the Industrial Revolution in the second half of the eighteenth century was also accompanied by rising prices, in England, again, at a rate similar to that which had occurred earlier. Looking elsewhere, Japan's very high rate of economic growth that began at the end of the 1860's was associated with almost continuous inflation, right through to the end of the

1930's: in the course of sixty years, prices rose by about 350 per cent. It is well known, too, that massive economic growth in Soviet Russia in the 1930's was accompanied by equally massive inflation. And coming to more recent times, the 1940's and 1950's have witnessed considerable inflation, in developed and undeveloped countries alike; and in the former, at least, production has boomed — in stark contrast to the early 1930's, when production stagnated and prices fell.

But, of course, as one might expect, history is very equivocal. Britain's most rapid economic growth in the whole of its history probably occurred in the first half of the nineteenth century, after the end of the Napoleonic Wars. In general, prices were falling at this time. Again, the last quarter of the nineteenth century, now recognised as a period of substantial economic growth in Britain, particularly if real income *per capita* is taken as the criterion, has been given the name of the Great Depression, largely because prices fell. Certainly, economic growth from 1870 until the end of the century was at a faster rate than during the following fifteen years when prices were rising. Indeed, growth in this latter period may have been at an even slower rate than in the 1920's when again prices were falling.[1] As far as the United States is concerned, an analysis of growth and price behaviour also reveals no consistent pattern: faster-than-average rates of economic growth are found both when prices were rising and when they were falling. Even in the case of Japan where, as we have said, inflation was almost continuous, growth was probably slowest when prices were rising fastest, namely, in the period immediately before the First World War. And, of course, in very recent times, many under-developed countries have suffered from chronic inflation without seeming to benefit much in the way of growth, although others, it is true, have developed with inflation. It is clear, in other words, that mere reference to the facts of history does not prove the matter one way or another.

The apparent ambiguity of historical evidence, however, may arise largely through a misinterpretation of the nature of some of the great price movements of history. For a long time it was customary to explain the long term trends of prices — sometimes upward, sometimes downward — that have marked the growth of many present day developed countries in terms of changes in the

---

[1] If real income *per capita* is taken as the measure of growth. See Chapter VII.

quantity of money relative to the quantity of goods coming forward to be purchased, or to the volume of transactions taking place. The quantity of money itself was often seen to be linked to the available supply of precious metals, largely gold and silver, on which, to a greater or lesser degree, the circulating medium of exchange was based; and the supply of precious metals available for monetary use was dependent on the extent to which precious metals were absorbed by non-monetary uses and on gold and silver discoveries. Neither of these things was under the control of government and both could vary independently of what was happening to prices and production. Sometimes (according to the theory), the supply of precious metals in monetary use, and with it the quantity of money, increased relatively to the flow of production and transactions; and, in a manner not always clearly specified, monetary demand and prices would therefore rise. Moreover, the effect was to stimulate production and investment, and therefore promote economic growth, especially if, during the course of inflation, wages lagged behind prices. Contrariwise, when the quantity of money tended to lag behind the growth of production and transactions, prices were forced down. Production and investment were therefore discouraged, and growth retarded.

An explanation of this sort has been advanced to account for the association, that we have just noted, between rising prices and economic expansion of England and France in the sixteenth and seventeenth centuries, and again in the latter half of the eighteenth. The distinguished historian, Professor E. J. Hamilton, has stressed the importance of the opening up of the New World, which led to an influx of gold and silver into Europe, causing prices to rise for almost 200 years.[1] Similarly, in the latter half of the eighteenth century, the rise in prices is attributed to an expansion of Mexican silver output and Brazilian gold discoveries. In the course of these inflations money wages lagged well behind prices — Hamilton's data seems to suggest, for instance, that real wages fell by almost a half during the sixteenth and seventeenth centuries — from which Hamilton concludes that profits must have been inflated, to the benefit of saving, investment and growth. Keynes gave his theoretical support to this interpretation of history. In the *Treatise on Money*, he wrote, 'It is the teaching of this Treatise that the

[1] E. J. Hamilton, 'American Treasure and The Rise of Capitalism', *Economica*, 1929.

wealth of nations is enriched not during Income Inflations but during Profit Inflations — at times, that is to say, when prices are running away from costs.'[1] On the basis of data used by Hamilton, Keynes went on to calculate price-costs ratios for the sixteenth, seventeenth and eighteenth centuries, to illustrate the extent to which prices must have run away from costs during these periods of rapid economic growth.[2]

The inadequacies of the Quantity Theory of Money — as the theory to which we have been referring is usually described — to explain short run, or cyclical, changes in the price level have long been recognised; but, until recently, the theory has been held adequate to account for the longer swings of prices (particularly the so-called 'secondary secular movements' in the nineteenth and twentieth centuries) that have characterised the economic development of the United Kingdom and other capitalist countries.[3] As far as the nineteenth century is concerned, the empirical basis of the theory largely rests on the coincidence between each of two big rises in gold output, namely at the end of the 1840's and the middle of the 1890's — and an upturn in the secular trend of prices. The precise manner in which the former produced the latter, however, is not made clear. The most likely mechanism would seem to be a fall in the long term rate of interest, reflecting the abundance of money, which would encourage spending. But the facts are otherwise: we have the so-called Gibson paradox in history, that is, the long term rate of interest seemed to rise when prices were rising, and conversely. Moreover, if the phase of rising prices had purely reflected a fall in the value of money brought about by an increase in its supply we should expect to find that all prices, factor as well as commodity, rose proportionately. In fact, they didn't, and this also needs to be explained. There is further considerable theoretical and empirical doubt about the connection between changes in the monetary stock of gold and the quantity of money. The former was only a proportion, perhaps no more than 50 per cent, of the total stock of gold, and there seems no good

---

[1] J. M. Keynes, *Treatise on Money* (Macmillan), Vol. II, p. 154.
[2] Ibid., pp. 159–61.
[3] See S. Kuznets, *Secural Movements in Production and Prices*; W. W. Rostow, *British Economy in the Nineteenth Century*; and *The Process of Economic Growth*. According to Rostow, prices rose from 1793 to 1815; fell from 1815 to 1848; rose from 1848 to 1873; fell again 1873 to 1896; rose from 1896 to 1920; and fell from 1920 to 1935. Since then they have been rising.

reason why this proportion should remain unchanged when the total stock changed. Finally, the available data do not show any close correlation between changes in the monetary stock of gold and changes in the quantity of money in the hands of the public — and not all of the latter, of course, would be held in active balances.

A number of strong objections can, in fact, be set against the Quantity Theory as an explanation of the secular swings in prices in the nineteenth century, or indeed of price movements at other times as well.[1] Certainly, fortuitous gold discoveries cannot be held to account for the seventy years inflation in Japan, or the severe inflation in Soviet Russia in the 1930's. Thus doubt is cast on the supposed relationship between rising prices and rate of economic growth. But price movements did occur and have to be explained; and it is not satisfactory to dispose of one theory without replacing it by another. Fortunately, as we shall show, other interpretations of price behaviour in the nineteenth century and in other periods are possible, which throw more revealing light on the connection between growth and prices.

It is obvious from what we have said that if the facts of history are to throw light on the question, 'Is inflation conducive to economic growth?', then they require interpretation. This necessarily involves us in a prior *theoretical* discussion of the nature and causes of price behaviour during economic growth. Moreover, in tracing out the causes of price behaviour, we must indicate their connection with the rate of economic growth: the two questions to which we referred in our opening paragraph must, as we then said, be answered together. It will also be necessary to distinguish between a rise in prices which is deliberately and consciously produced by governments or monetary authorities, and one which is not so deliberately produced by them. In fact probably few inflations are the result of deliberate government intention: usually they arise as the by-product of faulty development policies or inadequate control over the financial system; and sometimes they stem from causes over which governments have no real or direct control. Even so, there are theoretical grounds for thinking that a deliberately contrived inflation might accelerate economic growth in under-developed countries at least, and it is possible that some

[1] See E. H. Phelps Brown and Ozga, 'Economic Growth and the Price Level', *Economic Journal*, March 1955, for a discussion of these and other points.

governments have intentionally pursued inflationary policies with this in mind.

In the next chapter we shall explore in some detail the conditions required for inflation successfully to speed up growth. Briefly, it can be said that inflation may help in this direction by breaking two deadlocks that are said to be characteristic of many under-developed areas. The first, and relatively minor one, is associated with the difficulty of guiding purchasing power into the hands of potential entrepreneurs. It is often argued that the absence of a suitable financial mechanism for transferring purchasing power from the hands of savers to entrepreneurs is a severe obstacle in the way of utilising a country's current saving for productive investment. Those sections of the population who are able to save are often reluctant to relinquish control over their wealth in exchange for paper titles: they prefer to invest it in ways that leave it more under their direct control, but which are often not very productive in terms of *social* income and wealth. It takes time, which under-developed countries can ill afford, to develop suitable financial intermediaries, and also experience to manage them which is not readily available. But if governments are willing to create money, the problem of transferring purchasing power is short circuited: purchasing power can be directly channelled into the hands of potential entrepreneurs (who may include the government itself) without other people being forced to give up control of theirs.

Usually, however, the contribution of inflation towards economic development is regarded as more fundamental than this. The more important obstacle that under-developed countries have to overcome is a deficiency of real saving. When *per capita* real income is low then the amount of saving that tends to be voluntarily forthcoming to finance productive investment is also low. But if investment is tied to the current level of voluntary saving, then the growth of real income will be retarded; saving will remain low, and so therefore will investment. Low saving, in other words, tends to perpetuate itself; and economic growth, particularly when measured in *per capita* terms, remains insignificant. It may even be negative, if population is increasing fast. Inflation is seen as a way of breaking this deadlock by forcing saving. To do so, however, rising prices must redistribute real income away from sectors of the economy in which the propensity to save is low towards sectors where it is high; and this, in turn, implies that the former sectors must be unable to increase their money incomes, or their money expenditure on consumer goods, in the same proportion that prices are rising. We shall give considerable attention to this aspect of the matter in the next chapter.

It is also argued that rising prices may increase the rate of capital formation in under-developed countries by raising the inducement to invest: it is said that entrepreneurs will have greater assurance that investment undertaken and brought to fruition during an inflation will turn out profitable in purely financial terms. But it doesn't follow that it won't be misdirected: indeed, as we shall indicate in Chapter II, one of the dangers of inflation is that it will lead to speculative types of investment rather than to additions to real capital in productive industry. Lack of inducement to invest, however, is largely a problem of private enterprise economies, and does not arise in completely 'socialised' economies where investment decisions are taken without regard to private profit, but rather according to priorities laid down by some planning body. Even so, investment decisions cannot be taken without some attention to the pattern of consumers' demand, otherwise other difficulties are likely to arise. And, of course, socialised economies, as well as under-developed private enterprise ones, are faced with the problem of deficient real saving when income is low — although their political set-up may permit them to adopt a more ruthless solution.

Whilst it is true that attempts to add to productive capital at a greater rate than voluntary saving alone would permit tend to produce a rising price level, it will be emphasised in later chapters that inflation in under-developed countries (or for that matter in developed countries as well) does not stem only from a lack of balance between investment and saving, deliberately contrived at by government monetary policies. In Chapters III, IV and V, we shall indicate other forces that tend to produce a rise in prices in the course of economic growth, one of the most important being a lack of balance between the development of agriculture and the development of industry. Nonetheless, the analysis in these chapters enables us to show that whilst few governments *deliberately produce* inflation *in order to accelerate* growth, many may be faced with a rather similar problem, namely, the dilemma of *permitting* some inflation, produced by forces not entirely within their effective monetary or fiscal control, or of adopting policies that will tend to *slow down* growth. In either case, therefore, the choice may turn out to be either faster economic growth or no inflation. Much of this book is concerned with outlining possible causes of this dilemma.

Chapters II, III, IV and V are largely theoretical; but in the later chapters we look at the actual price and growth experience of a number of countries, with a view to illustrating the *a priori* arguments developed. It must be emphasised that neither the theoretical chapters nor the empirical ones provide an exhaustive analysis or account of the problems of economic growth. The theoretical chapters are concerned with only one small aspect of the wide field of theory dealing with economic growth, namely, the behaviour of the price level. Correspondingly, the empirical chapters are included merely to illustrate the arguments of the earlier ones: they by no means constitute a full account of the economic development of the countries concerned. Although these chapters are therefore necessarily selective, it is hoped that they will not thereby prove greatly misleading.

PART I

SOME THEORETICAL CONSIDERATIONS

Chapter II

INFLATION AND CAPITAL FORMATION
IN UNDER-DEVELOPED COUNTRIES

The case for employing inflation as a means of promoting or accelerating economic growth in under-developed countries arises largely from two circumstances that are said to be typical of many of them. First, it is said that the level of real income is so low that voluntary saving by itself would be insufficient to finance the rate of capital accumulation required for *per capita* real income to grow. Second, the fiscal apparatus is not efficient enough, nor can easily be made so, to enforce the required amount of saving; moreover, although other methods of coercion are no doubt available, these are not easy to apply within a democratic framework. Therefore money must be created to finance spending on investment projects, and rising prices must be relied on to divert resources from consumption. In addition, inflation is sometimes recommended as a means of encouraging investment when the inducement to invest is lacking in a more stable price environment — although the danger here is that the wrong sort of investment, for example, speculative rather than productive, will be encouraged. But lack of inducement to invest and maldistribution of investment are not likely to be great dangers in an economy in which the government is playing a leading and decisive role in development. The required level of investment, and its distribution among the various sectors of the economy, are likely to be determined within the framework of some central plan, and the government is therefore more concerned with achieving the necessary real saving. If this should necessitate some inflation, then the government must decide on how much inflation it will — or can — tolerate in order to achieve its investment target. But when capital formation is being left to the dictates of private entrepreneurs, then the effect of inflation on the latters' decisions must be taken into account. Governments must consider not only what inducements, in the form of liberal but perhaps inflationary credit facilities, etc., it must offer private producers in order to get them to invest at all, but also whether the kind of investment which entrepreneurs are likely to carry out in an inflationary climate is desirable or not from the point of view of growth. In practice, no doubt, these two viewpoints shade into one another, since, in most under-developed countries, even when they remain basically private enterprise, governments are likely to intervene to some extent; and investment decisions are likely to be shared between government bodies and private entrepreneurs. The important thing is to establish the kind of price behaviour — absolute as well as relative — which will prove most conducive to economic growth, taking into account all likely effects on saving and investment. Too rigid an insistence on stable prices may result in a level of investment and saving too low for satisfactory growth, whilst, on the other hand, too free a resort to credit creation and inflation may have undesirable repercussions on the character of investment (and perhaps on saving as well), which also retard growth. The balance has to be struck between the two.

Quite apart from the danger that inflation may have undesirable effects on the distribution of investment, the desirability or otherwise of allowing prices to rise must be judged in the light of other considerations. There is always the danger that rising prices will get out of hand and hyper-inflation set in. This will happen if the community as a whole loses confidence in money as a medium of exchange and a unit of account. Nobody will be prepared to hold it, and as the speed with which it passes from hand to hand rises so will the speed at which prices are rising. Hyper-inflation must be avoided not so much because no real capital formation is possible when it occurs: the experience of Germany in the hyper-inflation of the 1920's shows that even when prices are rising astronomically a great deal of industrial expansion can take place:[1] but because it must eventually lead to the complete breakdown of the monetary and financial system. If there is a long tradition of monetary and financial stability and development, as in the case of Germany, the re-establishment of the system may well be possible; but if the financial system is still in an embryonic form, the consequences may be disastrous, and prevent, or at least delay, its future development. This would hardly be conducive to economic growth.

[1] F. D. Graham, *Exchange, Prices and Production in Hyper Inflation: Germany 1920–3* (Princeton 1930).

In the second place it might be argued that real investment should not be stimulated so much by inflation that people living at already very low income levels have to accept yet a further cut in their standard of living. There is not only the moral question concerning the extent to which present generations should be made to suffer for the benefit of those that follow: there is also need to maintain a minimum level of physical well-being of the population in order that they can play their part in development. Inflation is hardly very discriminatory in allocating the sacrifices necessitated by a higher rate of capital formation, and it is not certain that those who can most afford it will suffer the most.

Finally, the effects of inflation on the country's international balance of payments cannot be ignored. Most under-developed countries are to an appreciable extent dependent on foreign trade. Foreign demand for an important export is often a major stimulant to early development, and the foreign exchange which is earned pays for vital imports of capital goods which cannot be produced at home. Potential export goods therefore must not be priced out of the world market. Moreover, domestic inflation can precipitate a flight of capital abroad; saving, which could be more usefully employed at home, is used to purchase foreign assets. Continual depreciation of the exchange rate is no answer to the problem raised by inflation. Even if export prices in terms of foreign currency are kept competitive, rising import prices in terms of home currency put further pressure on the domestic price level, and the danger of hyper-inflation, associated with a constantly depreciating exchange rate, increases. It must not be overlooked, of course, that balance of payments problems may arise quite independently of domestic inflation. A shift from consumption to investment, for example, tends to raise the demand for imports no matter what happens to the overall level of money incomes, since, in the early stages of development, the import-content of investment goods tends to be greater than that of consumption goods; and on the other hand, fluctuations in foreign trade prices may inject inflation into the domestic economy as well as disturb the balance of payments. It remains true, however, that balance of payments considerations may well be crucial in determining whether or not inflation should be used to promote growth.

Whilst these qualifications are clearly important they will be largely ignored in what follows: attention will be concentrated on the manner in which inflation affects saving and investment. We shall begin by examining the process by which inflation increases real saving — if it does — and indicate the conditions that will determine the efficiency of inflation in achieving this end. For this purpose, the efficiency of inflation will be judged in terms of the relation between the extent to which prices rise, and the given rise in real saving expressed as a proportion of national income or output. Thus the more prices have to rise, to bring about a rise in the realised ratio between saving and national income, the less efficient is inflation; and the less they have to rise, the more efficient it is.[1] Although, as we have indicated earlier, inflation may also affect the inducement to invest and the kind of investment that is actually carried out, as well as the actual volume of saving, considerations of this sort will be left until later. Instead the inducement to invest and the desired level of investment will be taken as given, and attention will be focussed on the relative success of inflation in bringing about the necessary realised saving-income ratio.

I

INFLATION AND SAVING

The manner in which inflation is able to bring about a rise in saving is well known. In some circumstances a 'money illusion' can be created so that even when individual money incomes are rising no more than in proportion to prices, a larger proportion of current money, and therefore real, income is saved. But money illusion can hardly be relied on except in the early stages of inflation, and it quickly disappears once people realise that their real income is remaining unchanged. Essentially, if inflation is successfully to force a higher level of saving, it must cause a shift in real income away from people who tend to save a small or negligible proportion of their incomes to people who tend to save a larger proportion. In turn, this implies that the money incomes of the former group must rise in less proportion than prices whilst that of the latter group must rise in greater proportion. Unless the low savers have financial assets on which they can draw they must reduce their

---

[1] Alternatively, the efficiency of inflation could be judged from the social point of view, that is, in relation to the decline in real consumption of those who lose in inflation relative to the increase in real saving and investment: the latter is usually less than the former because some people whose real income rises in inflation are able to increase their consumption as well as their saving.

consumption by as much as their real income has fallen; whilst even if the consumption of the high savers rises it is unlikely to rise by as much as the decline in consumption of the low savers. The aggregate level of consumption then falls, and resources are released to satisfy investment demand.

The rise in prices itself is produced by excess demand pressures appearing in the economy as a whole or in important sectors of it. When spending on investment increases, a multiplier process is set up in which money incomes experience a cumulative rise. The increase in spending may at first be met by a fall in existing stocks, but eventually, if resources and materials are available, production will rise and so will factor incomes. The rise in the latter causes further increases in spending on consumption goods and perhaps on investment goods as well and the cumulative process continues. It may be, however, that a general shortage of resources or bottle-necks in the supply of particular materials, equipment or labour, will prevent any significant rise in output. Thus the increase in spending on investment can only be satisfied in real terms if resources are withdrawn from other employment. Competition for them tends to raise the general price level. The prices of scarce raw materials may at first lead the way, but as they are withdrawn from other production, the output of at least some goods will fall, and they, therefore, become scarcer in relation to demand. The rise in prices, in consequence, may soon become general. No doubt profits will receive the initial benefit from the general rise in the price level, but wages may also be affected if labour feels the general competition for resources, or if labour organisations are strong enough to force up wages in sympathy with prices. In any case, the rise in money incomes will lead to further spending on consumption goods, and the rise in prices and incomes will be both sustained and accelerated.

The questions that now arise are: first, under what circumstances will a new price and income equilibrium be achieved?; second, what determines the extent to which prices and incomes have to rise before this equilibrium is achieved?

Let us suppose that we are considering an economy in which, initially, the level of investment expenditure is running at a rate equal to a proportion a of national income; and that this invest-ment ratio corresponds to the proportion of national income that would be *voluntarily* saved at this given level of real income.

Thus if b is the average propensity to consume, then $a = 1 - b$.[1] Suppose now that the government (or the private enterprise sector as a whole) proposes to raise the level of investment to the proportion x of national income (i.e. $x > a$); and assume that this is a real target in the sense that it will not be eroded away by price inflation. In other words, assume that after its initial rise, investment expenditure rises in the same proportion as prices and national income. Finally, assume that *real* national output cannot be increased in the short run (more pertinently, over the life of the multiplier process), and that all prices are flexible and move to keep equilibrium between supply and demand.

A formula for the rise in money national income may then be derived. If ΔY is the increase in money national income, Y its initial level, and b' the marginal propensity to consume (i.e. the relation between the change in national income and the consequential change in spending on consumption), then

$$\Delta Y = \frac{Y(x - a)}{1 - b' - x} \qquad (2)$$

This formula tells us that ΔY has a finite value (i.e. national income will reach a new, but higher, stable level) provided that $b' + x$ is less than 1. This condition is not likely to hold, however, unless during the course of the multiplier process a change in the distribution of income has occurred to produce a fall in the average propensity to consume. This follows from the fact that since $a + b = 1$ and x is greater than a, then b' must be less than b if $b' + x$ is to be less than 1. In other words, the *marginal* propensity to consume must be lower than the *average* propensity. Whilst this is not unlikely in a situation of *rising real income* when the distribution of income remains unchanged, it would imply money illusion

---

[1] The complications of government expenditure and foreign trade are here ignored.

[2] This formula is derived from the fact that the increase in national income equals (*a*) the increase in spending on investment goods plus (*b*) the increase in spending on consumption goods. (*a*) equals the initial increase to raise investment from a proportion *a* of national income to a proportion *x* plus the consequential change in spending to keep investment a constant proportion of income as the latter rises; and (*b*) equals the increase in income multiplied by the marginal propensity to consume. Thus:

$$\begin{aligned}
\Delta Y &= \Delta I + \Delta c \\
&= Y(x - a) + \Delta Y . x + \Delta Y . b' \\
&= \frac{Y(x - a)}{1 - b' - x}
\end{aligned}$$

on the part of at least some people in the community if the rise in income was monetary rather than real.

Ignoring this problem for a moment, however, the proportionate rise in money incomes and prices can be calculated, and will be equal to:

$$\frac{x-a}{1-b'-x} \qquad (1)$$

that is to say, prices will rise more, the larger is the difference between x and a, and the larger are both x and b'. Thus if $x=0·05$, $a=0·04$ and $b'=0·9$, then prices and money national income rise by 20 per cent. The *efficiency* of inflation (e) in forcing an increase in real saving can then be defined as the ratio between the rise in real saving, expressed as a proportion of income, and the proportionate rise in prices.

$$\text{i.e.} \quad e=\frac{(x-a)}{(x-a)/(1-b'-x)}=1-b'-x.$$

The larger this value is, the greater will be the efficiency of inflation, and the smaller it is the less it will be. Maximum efficiency will be obtained when b' (i.e. the marginal propensity to consume) is zero and minimum efficiency when $b'+x$ approaches unity.

The use of this conventional multiplier formula, however, is not very satisfactory in the analysis of inflation, largely because it does not take explicit account of changes in the distribution of income. It requires the assumption of a constant marginal propensity to consume; and whilst this would be quite compatible with changes in income distribution, provided the propensities to consume of all income recipients were the same, this is not likely to be the case. Nor is the distribution of income likely to remain unchanged during the course of inflation since factor prices cannot be relied upon to move proportionately. Indeed if it were not for disproportionate changes in factor prices and differing marginal propensities to consume inflation could not be successful in forcing saving.[2] Of particular importance is the relationship between price changes and wage changes, for this affects the distribution of income

[1] The proportionate rise in money income and prices equals $\frac{\Delta Y}{Y}$ which in turn equals $\frac{x-a}{1-b'-x}$.

[2] Except in the unlikely case of money illusion being important.

between wages and profits which then has considerable influence on the course of development, profits being the most important source of productive saving. However, the simple multiplier formula can be modified to some extent to take account of wage-price relationships, and therefore can be made to throw somewhat more light on the connection between inflation and forced saving. Here we shall assume that only two sectors exist in the economy: the wage sector and the profit sector.

When suitably modified, the income (or price) multiplier formula expressing the proportionate rise in income or prices becomes:

$$p = \frac{x - a}{1 - [r\gamma(u - v) + v + x]}$$

and the *efficiency* of inflation is measured by

$$1 - [r\gamma(u - v) + v + x]$$

where p = the proportionate rise in prices or money national income

a = the initial ratio of investment to national income

x = the desired ratio of investment to national income

u = the marginal (and average) propensity to consume of wage earners

v = the marginal (and average) propensity to consume of profit earners

r = the wage-price co-efficient, i.e. the proportionate change in wages divided by the proportionate change in prices

and γ = the initial ratio of wages to national income.

Once again, we are assuming that investment is raised in real terms from a proportion a of national income to a proportion x, whilst total output is fixed.[1]

It follows from the formula that a new, stable price and income

---

[1] The formula is derived as follows:
If Y is initial national income, then
$$Y = Y\gamma u + Y(1 - \gamma)v + Ya$$
and $Y(1 + p) = Y\gamma(1 + rp)u + [Y(1 + p) - Y\gamma(1 + rp)]v + Y(1 + p)x$
Subtract Y from both sides
$$pY = \gamma Yrpu + vYp - v\gamma Yrp + Y(x - a) + Ypx$$
so that
$$p = \gamma rpu + vp - v\gamma rp + (x - a) + px$$
$$= \frac{x - a}{1 - [\gamma r(u - v) + v + x]}$$

equilibrium is possible provided that $r\gamma(u-v)+v+x$ is less than 1. We are therefore enabled to discover what maximum value of the wage-price coefficient is compatible with an eventual equilibrium of prices and incomes, assuming that we have some knowledge of the other variables.

Suppose, for example, we are given the following values: $\gamma=0.8$, $u=1$, $v=0.8$, $a=0.04$ and $x=0.05$. A new price and income equilibrium would then only be possible if r is less than 0.9375. If r were just below this critical level, say 0.93 (i.e. in every price round, wages rise 93 per cent of the rise in prices) then a new equilibrium would be attained, but prices would have to rise by 833 per cent before this happened. In other words, there would have occurred very considerable inflation before sufficient real saving had been forced to finance the desired level of investment. The rate of inflation must, of course, be judged against the time period over which the multiplier works itself out; but, clearly, even if the period was a year or more, a rise in prices of this magnitude would almost certainly lead to hyper-inflation and the complete breakdown of the monetary system. When confidence is lost in money as a store of value, neither of the consumption propensities incorporated in the formula can be expected to remain stable, and the formula then becomes completely inappropriate for predicting the course of inflation.

The extent to which prices rise as a result of a rise in real investment clearly depends on the values of x, $(x-a)$, u, v and r, that is, it depends on the absolute size of the desired investment-income ratio as well as on its size relative to the initial level, on the marginal propensities to consume of wage and profit earners, and on the wage-price coefficient. The larger all these things are, the more will prices rise. In the following tables we set out for illustrative purposes calculations of the price rise that would result from various combinations of the above variables. In all cases we assume that the marginal propensity to consume of wage earners is unity (i.e. $u=1$) which is unlikely to be far from the truth in under-developed countries.

It would seem from the tables that the values of v, $(x-a)$ and r are of prime importance, which, of course, is readily understandable. The size of r determines the success with which inflation brings about the necessary redistribution of income: if r is equal to 1, then redistribution cannot occur. v determines the success of

income redistribution in bringing about a rise in saving;[1] and
$x - a$ determines the required rise in real saving. If both r and v are
low, i.e. if wages rise considerably less than prices in each round,
so causing a rapid redistribution of income, and if profit earners
save a substantial proportion of the increase in their real income,
then a substantial rise in real investment can be brought about with
very little rise in prices. For example, if $r=0.1$, $v=0.6$, then increasing investment from 8 per cent to 9 per cent of national income raises prices by only about 4 per cent. Even doubling investment from 8 per cent to 16 per cent of national income raises prices
by only 38 per cent. But if v was 0.8, then doubling investment
would raise prices by 285 per cent, even if r is equal to 0.1. Equally
crucial is the size of r. If investment is doubled from 8 per cent to
16 per cent of national income when $v=0.6$, then if r is greater than
about 0.7, no price stability is possible; if v was as high as 0.8, then
price stability would require r not to be higher than about 0.3. The
tables make clear that high wage-price coefficients, unless accompanied by low marginal propensities to consume of profit earners,
quickly lead to unstable price multipliers, as the investment target
is raised. The absolute size of x also plays a part, but its importance
is perhaps less than that of the other variables. For example,
raising investment from 4 per cent to 5 per cent of national income,
when $r=0.1$ and $v=0.8$, raises prices by about $7\frac{1}{2}$ per cent. If the
initial ratio of investment to income was 8 per cent, then raising it
to 9 per cent still only raises prices by about 11 per cent, given the
same values of r and v as before. But the importance of the absolute
size of x increases with larger wage-price coefficients.

The conclusion to be drawn is obvious. Inflation cannot be relied
on to raise real investment unless r and/or v are low. If both are
high, prices are likely to rise a great deal and loss of confidence in
money becomes a great danger. Moreover, if wages rise in the same
proportion as prices, then real saving cannot be forced no matter
how far prices rise, *unless* wage earners or profit earners or both
suffer from money illusion. Real wages and real profits would
remain unchanged so that unless the average propensity to consume fell, which is unlikely, real consumption would also remain
unchanged. No resources would be released for extra investment.
In the circumstances postulated by the model we have used here,

---

[1] More strictly, it is the difference between u and v that is important, but we
have assumed $u=1$.

there would have to be a cut in real wages and in wage earners' real consumption for saving to be forced. Real profits would then rise, and assuming no *rise* in the average propensity to consume of profit earners, real saving would be produced.[1] Of course, if profit earners' marginal propensity to consume was smaller than their average propensity—which need not be ruled out if their *real* incomes are rising—then the redistribution of income would have greater success in forcing real saving on the community, and the rise in prices would also be less.

This brings us to a further, interesting implication of the model we have been using, namely that the fall in wage earners' real income and consumption, associated with a rise in real investment, does not depend on the size of the wage-price coefficient. Let us suppose for example, that during the course of inflation, wages rose in a smaller proportion than prices in each round of the wage-price spiral. Suppose that the wage-price coefficient had a value that made a new price equilibrium only just possible, given the values of the other pertinent variables. If $a=0.04$, $x=0.05$, and $v=0.8$, then $r=0.93$ would be just below the critical value ($=0.9375$), and prices would eventually settle down at a new stable equilibrium level. In the new position of price equilibrium, real wages and wage earners' real consumption would have fallen by about $6\frac{1}{2}$ per cent on average,[2] and resources would have been released equivalent to about 5 per cent of the national product. Of this, however, only one fifth (i.e. 1 per cent of national product) would have been used for extra capital formation, the remainder being used to augment profit earners' real consumption. On average, the real consumption of each profit earner would have risen by about 25 per cent. Thus, although inflation has succeeded in forcing a

[1] When total output is fixed, no permanent rise in the ratio of investment to national product is compatible with eventual price stability unless there is a permanent fall in the share of wages and in the level of real wages. It may be, however, that although institutional pressures in the labour market are strong enough to keep wages rising until they have risen in the same proportion as prices, the speed at which they rise may be less than the speed at which prices are rising. In this case, whilst inflation continues, real wages will tend to be lower than initially, thereby providing room for some extra capital formation. But there can be no end to the inflation until total output rises or until money illusion reduces the propensity to consume of wage earners or profit earners. Money illusion itself is not independent of the movement of prices. It is not likely to be significant if prices are rising fast, and it is likely to become less so the longer the time during which prices are rising. Hence, quite apart from the effects of temporary or permanent shifts in the distribution of income, the propensity to consume and the behaviour of prices are likely to be interconnected.

[2] Prices would have risen by 833 per cent, and wages by about 775 per cent.

Table I

Estimated Percentage Price Increase for Various Values of a, x, u, v, r and γ

A. Let $\gamma = 0.8$, $u = 1$, $v = 0.8$, $a = 0.04$

Value of r	$x = 0.05$ $(x-a=0.01)$	$x = 0.06$ $(x-a=0.02)$	$x = 0.07$ $(x-a=0.03)$	$x = 0.08$ $(x-a=0.04)$	$x = 0.09$ $(x-a=0.05)$	$x = 0.1$ $(x-a=0.06)$	$x = 0.11$ $(x-a=0.07)$
0.1	7.5	16.2	26.1	38.4	53.2	71.4	94.6
0.2	8.5	18.6	30.6	45.4	64.1	88.2	120.0
0.3	9.9	21.8	36.6	56.0	80.5	115.2	166.6
0.4	11.6	26.4	45.4	71.4	108.5	166.6	269.2
0.5	14.3	33.2	60.0	100.0	166.6	300.0	700.0
0.6	18.5	45.4	88.5	166.6	357.1	1,500.0	∞
0.7	26.3	71.4	166.6	500.0	∞	∞	∞
0.8	45.4	166.6	1,500.0	∞	∞	∞	∞
0.9	166.6	∞	∞	∞	∞	∞	∞
1.0	∞	∞	∞	∞	∞	∞	∞

B. Let $\gamma = 0.8$, $u = 1$, $v = 0.6$, $a = 0.08$

Value of r	$x = 0.09$ $(x-a=0.01)$	$x = 0.1$ $(x-a=0.02)$	$x = 0.11$ $(x-a=0.03)$	$x = 0.12$ $(x-a=0.04)$	$x = 0.13$ $(x-a=0.05)$	$x = 0.14$ $(x-a=0.06)$	$x = 0.15$ $(x-a=0.07)$	$x = 0.16$ $(x-a=0.08)$
0.1	3.6	7.4	11.2	16.1	21.0	26.3	32.1	38.4
0.2	4.0	8.5	13.2	18.5	24.3	30.6	37.6	45.4
0.3	4.6	9.8	15.4	21.7	28.7	36.5	45.4	55.5
0.4	5.5	11.6	18.5	26.3	35.2	45.4	57.3	71.4
0.5	6.6	14.3	23.0	33.3	45.4	60.0	77.7	100.0
0.6	8.4	18.5	30.6	45.4	64.1	88.2	120.0	166.6
0.7	11.6	26.3	45.4	71.4	108.7	166.6	269.2	500.0
0.8	18.5	45.4	88.2	166.6	357.1	1,500.0	∞	∞
0.9	45.4	166.6	1,500.0	∞	∞	∞	∞	∞
1.0	∞	∞	∞	∞	∞	∞	∞	∞

Table I (continued)

C. Let $\gamma = 0.6$, $u = 1$, $v = 0.8$, $a = 0.08$

	Value of x							
Value of r	$x=0.09$ ($x-a=0.01$)	$x=0.1$ ($x-a=0.02$)	$x=0.11$ ($x-a=0.03$)	$x=0.12$ ($x-a=0.04$)	$x=0.13$ ($x-a=0.05$)	$x=0.14$ ($x-a=0.06$)	$x=0.15$ ($x-a=0.07$)	$x=0.16$ ($x-a=0.08$)
0·1	10·2	22·7	38·4	58·8	86·2	125·0	184·2	285·0
0·2	11·6	26·3	45·4	71·4	108·7	166·6	269·2	500·0
0·3	13·5	31·2	55·5	90·9	147·0	250·0	500·0	2,000·0
0·4	16·1	38·4	71·4	125·0	227·3	500·0	3,500·0	∞
0·5	20·0	50·0	100·0	200·0	500·0	∞	∞	∞
0·6	26·3	71·4	166·6	500·0	∞	∞	∞	∞
0·7	38·4	125·0	500·0	∞	∞	∞	∞	∞
0·8	71·4	500·0	∞	∞	∞	∞	∞	∞
0·9	500·0	∞	∞	∞	∞	∞	∞	∞
1·0	∞	∞	∞	∞	∞	∞	∞	∞

NOTE: γ = initial share of wages in national income
u = marginal and average propensity to consume of wage earners
v = marginal and average propensity to consume of profit earners
a = initial ratio of investment to national income
x = desired ratio of investment to national income
r = wage-price coefficient
∞ = infinity

higher rate of real saving on the community (assuming no loss of confidence in money) it has done so at what might be considered as considerable social cost: the real consumption of the poorer section of the community would have been reduced whilst that of the better-off would have risen. The interesting thing to note however is that this apparently unnecessary redistribution of income does not depend on the size of the wage-price coefficient. Suppose, for example, that the rise in wages was only one-tenth of the rise in prices, i.e. $r = 0.1$. The rise in prices is then very moderate, about $7\frac{1}{2}$ per cent and wages would have risen by only $\frac{3}{4}$ per cent. Nonetheless, the real consumption of wage earners as a whole still declines by about 5 per cent of the national product, whilst the real consumption of profit earners rises by 4 per cent. If r were equal to 0.5 then prices would rise by about 14 per cent, but once again the fall in wage earners' consumption is the same as before.

This result is purely the consequence of the particular model of the economy we are using, which may or may not be strictly valid, but is sufficiently appropriate to yield useful conclusions. In this model, real saving depends only on the distribution of real income — since we are assuming unchanged saving propensities of both wage earners and profit earners. In equilibrium, the distribution of income must be such as to bring about real saving equal to the desired level of investment. When the propensity to consume of wage earners is unity, then profit earners must receive that share of real income that will induce them to save an amount equal to investment, given their propensity to consume. If the latter is 0.8 (i.e. the propensity to save is 0.2) then profit earners must receive one quarter of national income if they are to save an amount equal to 5 *per cent* of it. Thus it follows that the size of the wage-price coefficient determines only the extent of the inflation but not the effect on wage earners' real consumption. The social cost of inflation, in these circumstances, remains high even if the rise in prices is moderate.

Both the social cost and the extent of inflation would, of course, be less if the average propensity to consume of profit earners fell during inflation, i.e. if their marginal was less than their average propensity to consume. As we have said, this is not beyond the bounds of possibility provided the wage-price coefficient is less than unity. From the point of view of social justice it would probably be preferable if profit earners' real consumption fell rather than rose — assuming them to be initially better off than wage earners — so reducing or even eliminating completely the burden on wage earners. If, however, the aim of maintaining wage earners' real consumption was pursued by tying wages to prices (i.e. making r equal to unity) then, in the absence of further government intervention, it is most unlikely that profit earners' average propensity to consume would fall. If it didn't the price situation would then be completely unstable and saving would not be forced. One possibility would be to impose a sufficiently high rate of tax on profit earners' *marginal money incomes*, so that their *disposable* money income rose in less proportion than prices. Even so, it is more likely that profit earners would reduce their real saving rather than their real consumption. Hence, tying wages to prices is no solution to the problem of maintaining the real consumption of poorer sections of the community in the course of inflation. If wage earners' living standards are already too low to permit further reduction then it is clearly better not to allow inflation in the first place. The alternative is to reduce the real consumption of wealthier people by imposing a higher average tax on their existing incomes, when real investment is raised. But of course the problem remains to ensure that consumption and not saving is reduced by the tax, else nothing is gained. Furthermore, adverse effects on the incentive to invest must be avoided. Unfortunately the difficulty of achieving both these things probably makes some inflation unavoidable. Inflation does become more justified if a reduction in the consumption of the mass of the people is considered feasible although impossible of achievement by the existing fiscal machinery — *always provided* that the wage-price spiral can be kept in check. On the other hand, if wage increases cannot be kept smaller than price increases, inflation will prove no more effective an instrument for forcing saving than is an inefficient tax system.

The model of the economy that we have used here presents a rather gloomy picture of the problem of capital formation in underdeveloped countries. This is because it assumes that total real output remains constant during the course of the inflation, so that an increase in the rate of capital formation necessarily involves a fall in the output of consumption goods and therefore a fall in someone's real consumption. In fact, however, some under-developed countries may be fortunate enough to have a 'hidden' reserve of

C

labour which can be used to create capital at no cost of a reduction in the supply of consumption goods. In this connection it is often said that an under-developed economy is characterised by having two, almost separate sectors: the capitalistic or market sector and the subsistence sector. The former sector is identified by the fact that reproducible capital is used in production, and further by the fact that money is extensively used as a medium of exchange.[1] The subsistence sector makes little or no use of reproducible capital and economic activity is carried out mainly for self-consumption or, at most, for limited, internal and barter exchange. The marginal productivity of labour in this sector is negligible, so that labour can be transferred to the capitalist sector with no loss of output. Provided this surplus labour is set to work on basic capital projects requiring but little other scarce resources (for example, irrigation), total output will in fact rise by as much as investment rises. Inflation is not thereby avoided since the newly employed labour in the capitalistic sector now have money incomes to spend, although the supply of consumption goods in this sector has not increased. Goods formerly consumed by the surplus labour in the subsistence sector have to be attracted into the capitalist sector, or those already being produced and consumed in the capitalist sector have to be redistributed in favour of the newly employed. Prices have to rise, therefore, not so much to force saving but rather to redistribute an existing supply of consumption goods. How far prices will have to rise depends, as before, on the ability of the potential losers in this process to protect themselves; but given this ability, prices will rise less when surplus labour exists than when a rise in investment has to be accompanied by a fall in consumption.

Moreover, the model ignores the possibility that yield from the *newly created* capital may affect the process of inflation. Basically it assumes that the multiplier process works itself out in a time period shorter than the gestation period of the new investment which set it going. Suitably chosen investment projects, however, may produce a quick yield of consumption goods which checks the rise in prices. But the effect is not likely to be great even if it be assumed that the new investment gives its full yield of consumption goods by the time that the multiplier process has exhausted itself.

[1] See W. A. Lewis, 'Economic Development with unlimited supplies of labour', *Manchester School*, May 1954; and Schatz, 'Inflation in Under-Developed Areas', *American Economic Review*, September 1957.

The model can be adapted to show this. (The existence of surplus resources is again ignored.)

Suppose we start with an initial situation in which total output is divided into investment good output and consumption good output in the proportions a and $(1-a)$ respectively. Further, suppose that investment good output is being used purely for replacement i.e. net investment is zero. Now let gross investment be raised to a proportion x of gross real output and be maintained at that proportion no matter what happens to prices and real output as a consequence. Suppose that total real output does begin to rise shortly after the increase in investment, the increase being related to the increase in the capital stock by the marginal capital-output ratio (α), which we shall take to be the same as the average ratio (i.e. when real investment rises by ΔI, gross real output rises by $\Delta I/\alpha$).

Then, initial gross investment, I, equals aY_0^m, where Y_0^m is the monetary value of initial gross national income; and, the increase in gross investment in money terms

$$= xY_0^m - aY_0^m + \Delta Y^m x$$

$$= Y_0^m(x-a) + \Delta Y^m x$$

Therefore the *increase* in gross national income (in *money* terms), ΔY^m,

$$= \frac{Y_0^m(x-a) + \Delta Y^m x}{1-b}$$

$$= \frac{Y_0^m(x-a)}{1-b-x}$$

where b is the marginal propensity to consume related to *gross*, not *net*, income (we assume, for the sake of simplicity, that wages and prices move proportionately, leaving the distribution of income unchanged). In equilibrium, the final level of gross *money* income will be

$$Y_0^m + \frac{Y_0^m(x-a)}{1-b-x}$$

$$= Y_0^m \cdot \frac{1-b-a}{1-b-x}.$$

Once again, it is obvious that the marginal propensity to consume must be lower than the average if there is to be a new equilibrium of income and prices, but this is not so implausible as it would have been in our earlier example, since here real income and output are rising. Writing Y_0^R for the initial level of aggregate real output and ΔY_0^R for the *increase* in real output, arising from the increment of investment, and α for the marginal (and average) capital-output ratio, then

$$Y_0^R + \Delta Y^R = Y_0^R + \frac{Y_0^R (x - a)}{\alpha}$$

$$= Y_0^R \frac{(\alpha + x - a)}{\alpha}.$$

Writing p for the proportionate rise in the price level then

$$1 + p = \frac{Y_0^m + \Delta Y^m}{Y_0^R + \Delta Y^R}$$

which equals

$$Y_0^m \frac{1 - b - a}{1 - b - x} \cdot \frac{1}{Y_0^R} \frac{\alpha}{\alpha + x - a}$$

and, since Y_0^m and Y_0^R are money and real (gross) national income respectively at the base period, and therefore may be put equal to 1, this may be written

$$1 + p = \frac{1 - b - a}{1 - b - x} \cdot \frac{\alpha + x - a}{\alpha}.$$

We can substitute appropriate values in this equation and test the effect of investment yield and varying capital-output ratios on the rise in prices.

Suppose for instance, that we have $a = 0.1$, $x = 0.15$, and $b = 0.8$. If the yield of the increment to the capital stock is ignored then the rise in prices would amount to 100 per cent. (This is derived from the equation $1 + p = \frac{1 - b - a}{1 - b - x}$ or $p = \frac{x - a}{1 - b - x}$.) If now the yield is taken into account and a marginal capital-output ratio of 4 is chosen, then the rise in prices would amount to about 98·7 per cent. Even if a very low capital-output ratio is chosen, for example, 1 (which is much lower than typically found in developed or under-developed countries alike), the rise in prices still amounts to 95 per cent. It is clear, therefore, that the yield from the increment of investment does not much affect the degree of inflation, given plausible values of the capital-output ratio.

However, the yield from the increment of capital is not unimportant. Indeed it provides the justification for using inflation to promote capital formation when other ways are not easily available. As Professor Lewis has put it, 'Inflation for the purpose of promoting capital formation is essentially self-destructive.'[1] There are three stages to the process. In the first, prices are likely to rise quite sharply whilst capital is being created. Provided, however, that income is being redistributed in such a way as to bring about a rise in voluntary saving, a second stage will be reached when prices become reasonably stable. Thereafter they will fall as extra output, stemming from the increment in capital stock, comes on to the market. But, of course, as Professor Lewis admits, the first stage may be 'dangerous and painful'. It is 'dangerous' because if prices rise too swiftly, confidence may be lost in money, and elastic price expectations may be set up. People will be more reluctant to save, even if they are able to, so that distributional changes in income prove abortive. Spending and price increases both accelerate and inflation begets its own internal dynamic. At what point hyper-inflation sets in, cannot be said *a priori*. There is considerable evidence that prices can rise at a considerable rate and over a considerable period of time before the usefulness of money as a medium of exchange and as a store of value is destroyed.[2] But the critical point is no doubt lower in under-developed countries, in which the money system may still be very primitive, and in which indeed, the mass of the population may only just be accepting money as a medium of exchange. The first stage is also 'painful' because, it usually involves a decline in consumption of those sections of the population least able to bear it — if it does not, it can hardly succeed in promoting capital formation. The sooner the third stage appears, the greater are the chances of preventing runaway inflation: hence the vital need for appropriately chosen investment projects which, in quick time, can produce substantial increases in the supply of consumption goods, rendering inflation both less dangerous and less painful. It is im-

---

[1] W. A. Lewis, *The Theory of Economic Growth* (Allen and Unwin), p. 217.
[2] A. J. Brown, *The Great Inflation* (Oxford), Chapter VIII.

portant, then, to consider what effects inflation will have on investment — whether it will stimulate investment in desirable projects,
thereby promoting both growth and eventual price stability, or
whether, as has often been argued, it will cause investment to take
an unproductive form, and thereby lead to a slower rate of growth
than would have occurred if more orthodox monetary and fiscal
policies had been used.

II

INFLATION AND INVESTMENT

The effect of inflation on investment decisions is, of course, not
predictable: a lot will depend on the type of expectations set up in
the minds of entrepreneurs. If expectations that prices will continue to rise for a long time into the future are held with considerable certainty, then this would seem to have a stimulating effect on
the level of investment. There is not only the psychological effect
that a climate of rising prices will have on the minds of entrepreneurs (particularly if some important costs of production, like
wages, are lagging): there is also the important economic fact that
the *real* rate of interest will tend to be lower than when prices are
stable or falling. This assumes, of course, that the money rate of
interest is unaffected by inflation or at least rises by less than the
expected rate of increase of prices. But where inflation is the deliberate result of government policy this assumption seems
reasonable, for it seems likely that the government will keep the
money supply reasonably elastic to prevent interference with the
aims of its policy. Not only is the level of investment stimulated by
the lower real rate of interest, but also investment projects with an
expected longer economic life, or production processes employing
capital rather than labour, are encouraged relatively to others. In
other words, capital intensive processes of production are promoted, whether the intensity is measured in relation to output or
to quantities of other factors combined with capital.

Are these effects desirable from the point of view of economic
growth? If investment is being left mainly in the hands of private
entrepreneurs, and the incentive to invest is lacking, then it is
clear that the stimulating effect of inflation on investment may be
highly desirable. The importance of optimism among entrepreneurs for overall economic growth can hardly be overstressed.

But if optimism and inducement is not lacking then inflation may be more of a disadvantage. Excessive investment plans may be made, which owing to particular bottlenecks of important materials, or immobility of resources, cannot be fulfilled. Too many projects can be started and, in consequence, none fulfilled, whereas had fewer been concentrated on, more would have been realised. The delayed fulfillment of investment plans is equivalent to a lengthening of the gestation period of investment, which is probably very undesirable, both because the check to inflation and the stage of falling prices are postponed, and because quick yields may be desirable to maintain living standards when population is increasing fast.

The encouragement which correctly anticipated inflation seems to give to capital intensive processes of production also raises the question of what investment criteria should be laid down for maximising economic growth. This subject has had considerable airing in the literature in recent years, and only brief reference can be made here to the various arguments that have been deployed. Unfortunately, no firm conclusions have as yet been established.

It has been strongly argued that investment projects should be chosen that will lead to processes of production in which capital rather than labour will play the most important part.[1] The grounds on which this argument is based are as follows. *First*, production processes which employ a high ratio of capital to labour lead to a larger share of the resulting income going to profit earners and a smaller share to wage earners. Since profit earners have a higher propensity to save than wage earners, saving rather than consumption is encouraged, and a larger proportion of the yield of the initial investment becomes available for further investment. In other words, capital intensive processes of production have high reinvestment coefficients. Growth is thereby accelerated; and although less labour is currently offered employment than if more labour intensive processes had been employed, in the *long run* more labour will be absorbed since growth will be faster. *Second*, if in the interests of maximising employment in the short run, labour intensive processes are employed, an anti-mechanisation attitude of mind among the people may be promoted which, later on, will

---

[1] See Galenson and Leibenstein, 'Investment Criteria, productivity and economic development', *Quarterly Journal of Economics*, August 1955.

impede the adoption of mechanised processes. *Third*, industrialisation usually implies urbanisation, and therefore causes social capital requirements to compete with those of productive capital for the country's limited supply of saving. It is better, therefore, to reduce the need for social capital by pulling in as little labour as possible into urban areas. *Fourth*, the emphasis on capital intensive processes tends to favour the development of capital goods industries rather than consumption good industries. Emphasis on the former lengthens the time before the mass of the population receives the benefits of economic development: on the other hand, it provides the basis of a much faster expansion in living standards later on. *Fifth*, highly capital intensive production processes generally imply longer lived capital goods; depreciation can therefore be spread over a longer period of time. Hence a smaller proportion of gross investment resources in the near future will be required for replacement purposes, and a larger proportion becomes available for *net* capital formation.[1] Future growth may therefore be accelerated. It should be noted, of course, that if capital intensive processes are associated with high capital-output coefficients, then growth of output in the early stages of development will be retarded.

It is certainly a valid point to make that investment criteria should take into account the *disposal* of the yield of investment, that is, the effect different projects have on the distribution of income and on the rate of saving. It does not necessarily follow, however, that the choice of capital intensive processes of production will automatically maximise the rate of investment in the future. Even if such projects ensure that a large proportion of their yield (income) is directed into the hands of high savers, total saving may be less than if less capital intensive processes had been used. Saving probably depends on the total level of income as well as on its distribution, and the former will not be maximised if the wrong factor proportions are used. It could be argued therefore that the aim should not be to maximise either the marginal or the average product of labour by employing as much capital as possible. In conditions of labour surplus, for example, the maximisation of total output (and therefore of total income) would require combining capital and labour until the marginal productivity of the latter was

---

[1] See E. D. Domar, 'Depreciation, Replacement, and Growth,' *Economic Journal*, March 1953.

zero; that is, it would require the spreading of as little capital as possible over as much labour as possible, so maximising the average product of the former. At the same time output per head of the population, whether employed or not, would be maximised.

If saving were independent of the distribution of income and depended solely on its level, then production processes involving higher ratios of capital to labour and capital to output than need be the case, can only be defended to the extent that they involve lower replacement requirements in the future and therefore make possible a higher rate of net capital formation. But saving is clearly not independent of income distribution, nor is it made generally by the mass of the population. Instead, it comes largely from entrepreneurial profits. Moreover, the tax collecting powers of the government may be greater when income is concentrated in a few hands rather than when widely distributed. Thus in some circumstances a higher volume of saving, both private and public, may be achieved with lower than optimal levels of income and sub-optimal methods of production. Hence to the extent that an inflationary climate redistributes current income towards high savers, and favours the development of capital intensive industries, it raises the rate of current and future saving. To this extent it may speed up growth. But the emphasis on capital intensive industries may heighten the danger of inflation. If it is true that capital good industries are favoured relatively to consumer good industries, and if it is further true that some current output is sacrificed to get both a higher rate of gross saving and a higher rate of net capital formation in the future, then the enjoyment by the mass of the population of the fruits of economic development is postponed. Not only may this result be undesirable from a humanitarian point of view, particularly when population is increasing fast, it may increase the difficulty of keeping wage and other incomes stable, and therefore increase the likehood of accelerated price inflation.

The influence that inflation may have on the level of investment and the nature of investment decisions, depends largely on the certainty with which expectations as to the rate at which prices will rise are held. Clearly, if a rising price level is to encourage an entrepreneur to undertake or increase the number and scale of his investment projects, the entrepreneur must hold his expectations with reasonable firmness. The firmness with which expectations are held, however, depends largely on the character of inflation itself; and as important as anything will be the rate at which prices have been rising in the past and the length of time for which the upward trend has continued. Suppose that prices had been rising at 3 or 4 per cent per annum for some considerable time in the past, with no tendency for the pace to accelerate. It would not be un-reasonable for producers to assume with confidence the continu-ance of this moderate sort of inflation, and to plan their investment accordingly. But if prices are rising rapidly and have been so in the past with an accelerating trend, or if the country has a history of rapid or hyper inflation, then expectations must be held with far less confidence. The horizon of expectations of future inflation becomes very short. Businessmen know full well that governments cannot allow inflation to get out of hand, so precipitating loss of confidence in money. Steps must therefore be taken to check inflation, and these steps usually imply, in the first stages at any rate, checks to trade and economic growth as well. Even if the steps fail, or even if the government is incapable of taking steps in the first place, then accelerating inflation eventually brings itself to an end through the destruction of the monetary and financial system which must initially have a discouraging effect on trade and pro-duction. Hence the character of investment decisions is likely to be quite different when taken in the light of an actual or anticipated *rapid* rise in prices from when they are taken in the light of a more moderate one. No doubt, it is the fact that inflation in under-developed countries is difficult to restrain and to keep moderate which causes many influential economists to oppose the use of inflationary methods of promoting growth, on grounds that, even if saving is successfully forced, inflation brings about the wrong sort of investment.

In this connection it has been strongly argued that inflation causes saving to be directed into non-productive forms of invest-ment, such as the hoarding of gold, precious stones, foreign securities and similar assets, and the acquisition of real estate and inventories of goods and materials. Gold, precious stones and foreign assets in general are attractive to savers since they provide an effective hedge against the depreciation of the external value of the currency. Investment in real estate, in the construction of luxury apartment blocks and other buildings is encouraged not only by the low real rate of interest (they have a high capital-output ratio) but also by the fact that, during inflation, income and wealth may be shifting in favour of the upper income groups. A sure appreciation in their value can therefore be expected. Merchants prefer to hoard materials and stocks of finished goods, looking for quick speculative gains, rather than steady income. The essential characteristic of these types of investment is that they are highly liquid and offer the prospect of capital gain. Furthermore, the assets so acquired can be used as collateral for borrowing and are generally and easily accepted by banks for this purpose. Nor, or so it is thought, does this investment require particular business ability or skill which investors must certainly have if successful investment in agriculture or industry is to be undertaken; and the latter is further discouraged by the shift of income away from the low income groups which, in the longer run, must provide the markets for economic growth. Finally, investment in export industries is discouraged by inflation particularly if the exchange rate is held stable; whilst if the exchanges are not kept stable, direct investment in foreign assets becomes even more profitable.

It is more than probable, however, that the danger of such maldistribution of saving and investment becomes serious only when prices have been rising at a rapid rate; for, as we said earlier, under these conditions expectations of further rapid inflation must be limited. If prices were expected with *absolute* certainty to rise *for ever*, then, no matter what the rate of increase is, investment in longer life assets would be relatively more profitable than in those with shorter life. Nor would investors be anxious to keep their wealth in liquid form. The fact is that investors know full well that the life of a very rapid inflation must be limited, and will be brought to an end either by deliberate government policy or by internal collapse. Hence in rapid inflation, investors look for ways of accumulating wealth that will appreciate in terms of money but at the same time will be quickly realisable. They must be prepared to get out before the boom bursts. A slow inflation need not set up such anticipation of collapse; hence it should encourage investment decisions to be taken more rationally with income yield rather than capital appreciation considerations in mind. Furthermore, if the rate of inflation is being kept at something less than the current money rate of interest, speculative gains disappear, and the danger of a flight from money and monetary assets is correspondingly much reduced.

III

CONCLUSIONS

The case against inflation may therefore be summarised in three counts: first, it may have very adverse effects on habits of *voluntary* saving, whilst its ability *to force* saving is limited, and indeed in certain circumstances may be non existent; second, that it leads to very unproductive forms of investment, as outlined above; and third, that it gives rise to considerable social costs, quite out of proportion to the favourable effects it might have on capital accumulation. There is obviously considerable substance in the case, and it is certainly advanced by an authoritative body of experts, including some of those in the various United Nations organisations concerned with problems of growth.[1] Even so, the case for and against inflation must be examined in a wider context and not be determined regardless of particular circumstances. With regard to voluntary saving, for example, if this is already very low even when prices are stable, then opposition to credit creation and inflation seems somewhat beside the point. The fault may, of course, lie in the absence of suitable financial inter-mediaries to collect the savings of the community; and an urgent priority in these circumstances is to create such institutions. No proponent of inflation would deny this. But if the shortage of voluntary saving is mainly due to low real income or, as Professor Lewis has argued, to the absence of an entrepreneurial class and a profit sector, then credit creation may be required to break the bottleneck. It enables purchasing power to be placed directly into the hands of potential entrepreneurs (or the government planning authority) and the resulting inflation may redistribute income in favour of the expanding entrepreneurial sector. Similarly, it is beside the point to criticise inflation for promoting unproductive investment if more fundamental causes are preventing saving from

---

[1] See, for example: *Methods of Financing Economic Development*, United Nations, 1949, p. 19; and various *Economic Surveys* prepared by the United Nations' Economic Commission for Latin America, particularly that for 1955. Also see: E. Bernstein, 'Financing Growth in Under-developed Countries', in *Savings in the Modern Economy* edited by Heller, Boddy and Nelson (Minneapolis 1953); Patel, 'Inflation in relation to Economic Development', *International Monetary Fund Staff Papers*, November 1952; F. Pazos, 'Economic Development and Financial Stability', *International Monetary Fund Staff Papers*, October 1953; and R. Nurkse, *Capital Formation in Under-Developed Countries* (Oxford 1953).

going into agriculture or industry. 'Deep seated institutional causes hold down personal saving and divert them from productive investment.'[1] Savers in under-developed countries seem to be reluctant to lose direct control over their wealth, and prefer to invest it in a manner which leaves it in their possession. Here again, as Professor Lewis has argued,[2] the basic cause of unproductive investment may well be the absence of an entrepreneurial or capitalist class which thinks in terms of 're-investing its income productively', for future income rather than capital gain. Inflation may raise additional barriers against voluntary saving and productive investment; on the other hand if these barriers are already so great as to prevent growth, credit creation and inflation may contribute to the initial breaking of the deadlock.

It can hardly be denied that inflation is a wasteful method of forcing saving: the loss in real consumption of those who tend to lose in the process tends to be greater than the gain in capital formation, and some sections of the population are unnecessarily made better off. One author, Van Philips, has argued that the social cost of inflation alone provides sufficient justification for avoiding inflation. He maintains that satisfactory economic development necessarily implies, among other things, that 'an absolute decrease in the numbers of those living at some minimum level of income' must take place. 'An inflationary development is incompatible with this conception of growth because capital accumulation then takes place at the expense of the consumption of the poorest.'[3] Whilst the sentiment underlying this argument cannot be denied, nevertheless it tends to overlook the fact that economic development must at first involve sacrifice on some people's part. It would be nice if this sacrifice could be confined to those best able to bear it, but the fiscal and administrative machinery available to the governments of many under-developed countries is not developed enough to ensure this. Furthermore, even if it could be ensured, the consequential rise in real saving may still not be sufficient to bring about satisfactory growth, and sacrifices may have to be extended lower down the scale. Exem-

---

[1] E. Bernstein, 'Financing Growth in Under-developed Economies', in Heller, Boddy and Nelson, *Savings in the Modern Economy* (University of Minnesota Press).

[2] W. A. Lewis, *The Theory of Economic Growth*, Chapter V.

[3] Van Philips, *Public Finance and the less developed Economy* (The Hague), p. 61.

plary fiscal and monetary policies may only produce stagnation, and at best confirm the country in its poverty: at worst, if population is growing fast, individual poverty may increase. In such a situation it may be best to bring about some artificial reduction in or check to living standards in the short run, to prevent even greater inroads into these standards in the long run.

There is of course an ideal case for using inflation to promote growth, but its existence depends on the conjunction of a number of favourable conditions. These conditions include:

  (i) the existence of surplus labour which can be used to produce capital goods with no real cost in terms of consumption goods,
 (ii) the presence of 'money illusion' in the labour supply and saving schedules,
(iii) high saving propensities in groups which tend to gain in the course of inflation,
 (iv) general agreement, explicit or implicit, as to the desirable distribution of real income and real consumption,
  (v) the choice of investment projects with quick and appropriate yields,
 (vi) strong monetary authorities or other administrative machinery capable of checking and controlling prices when inflation threatens to get out of hand.

It is obvious that we cannot expect to find all these conditions in every under-developed country. On the other hand, if they are all absent, then the outlook for stable growth cannot be great. Perhaps the most important of these conditions is reasonable agreement as to the distribution of sacrifices and gains arising from development; and in practice this may involve some conscious policy concerning wages, profits and prices. It might be objected that most of the older, already developed, countries achieved their growth without having an explicit policy relating to income distribution, yet few of them suffered from serious inflation. In many respects, however, the difficulties facing present day under-developed countries are greater than was the case for older countries at a corresponding stage of their development. There is no doubt, for instance, that the climate of political opinion is different. Politicians and the educated elite in many under-developed countries are greatly influenced by the equalitarian policies and 'welfare state' ideology that have developed in the older countries in the later stages of their growth. The people themselves are probably more aware of the higher living standards and of the greater power of the ordinary person in richer countries in the political and economic life of their countries. In consequence, effective labour organisations more quickly take root: often they have close ties with political parties right from the start, so that even when the economic climate is not propitious to wage bargaining, political pressure may prove decisive. This means that in a free market environment, the wage-price spiral is a much greater danger, and the shift towards profit earners and savers more difficult to achieve. It does not follow that labour organisations must be banned or stagnation accepted. But it probably means that 'planning' must play a larger role, and that any major investment programme must have the agreement and support of labour unions. Conscious efforts have to be made to ensure a more equalitarian distribution of the burdens of early economic development than in fact occurred in the early stages of the development of the older countries.

When all is said, however, it is clearly not easy to arrive at a definite conclusion concerning the use of inflationary methods for promoting growth in under-developed countries. As is true in the case of many economic questions of crucial importance, an *a priori* decision is impossible, and even discussion seems inconclusive. We can list the *pros* and the *cons*, but it is not easy to strike the balance. Nonetheless, if one had to arrive at a conclusion, then it might be maintained with some confidence that *moderate* inflation is helpful to growth; and in later chapters some evidence will be considered in support of this view. But, of course, the question remains open. 'Can inflation be kept moderate?' The answer naturally depends on particular circumstances in particular countries; and on the answer itself depends the decision about the use of inflation. There is, however, one important factor which, if the experience of many under-developed countries is anything to go by, plays a crucial role in determining whether inflation can be kept moderate. This factor is the supply of food. If it is lagging behind demand, food prices tend to rise: money wages then become difficult to restrain and a wage-price spiral in the industrial sector quickly develops. In these circumstances saving is not easily forced, and either the investment target in industry must be lowered or the food supply situation must be increased. In the next chapter therefore we shall look more closely at the inflationary impact of lagging agricultural development, with a view to emphasizing the manner in which it can provide an independent source of inflationary pressure, quite apart from the fiscal and monetary policies pursued by governments.

In concluding this chapter we must point out that we have been largely concerned with the connection between inflation and capital formation in under-developed countries; but in principle at least, the connection remains the same in the more developed countries as well. Thus, if inflation redistributes income in favour of large savers, in particular in favour of the profits of corporate industry, and if it induces more investment to be undertaken, then capital formation and growth will benefit. But in fact it is much less likely that the growth of the richer, developed countries will be held back by a deficiency of saving, or that, even if it were, inflation would have to be resorted to in order to produce more.[1] A large part of income already comes within the control of corporate industry, and more or less of it may be distributed to shareholders, depending on the level of investment to be financed. There is also more scope for voluntary saving, which can often be raised by increasing the attractiveness of the return to savers or by propaganda campaigns, at no great cost to consumers. And finally the fiscal system in developed countries is an efficient weapon for forcing saving and can easily be supplemented by other controls, for instance hire purchase regulation, when the need arises.

On the other hand, in the place of a deficiency of saving, developed countries may suffer from a lack of inducement to invest. The willingness and the ability to save then goes to waste and the economy stagnates. Perhaps this danger has been over-rated, but it is doubtful whether it can be ignored; and it is as incumbent on governments to make sure that sufficient investment is undertaken as it is on them to produce the necessary saving. The governments of most advanced, developed countries today do in fact pursue conscious full employment policies, and the expectation of the maintenance of full employment is no doubt an important factor encouraging business investment. But full employment policies

---

[1] Exceptional circumstances, such as wars, might involve a decline in real consumption greater than can be easily achieved through normal fiscal methods or controls, so that inflation has to be relied on to do the job.

may also create the danger of inflation[1]: if they do create some inflation, then it could be argued that in this sense inflation is necessary
for growth. But there are more important reasons for thinking that
inflation may raise the rate of investment in developed economies.
In a private enterprise economy investment will only be undertaken
if the expected rate of return on capital is expected to be equal to
or greater than the supply price of risk capital. The latter itself is
normally considerably higher than the pure rate of interest to be
obtained on riskless government bonds, both because of the greater
risk that savers run in putting their money into business enterprise
rather than into government bonds, and because of the lower
liquidity of business equities. Inflation can both raise the expected
rate of return on capital, and lower the supply price of risk capital
by inducing savers to prefer equities to bonds. It may therefore
raise investment and stimulate growth. In this way inflation can be
shown to be good for growth in the developed countries, as well as
in the under-developed ones.

Moreover, there is much more chance that inflation in a developed country, except in circumstances such as wars, will be,
and can be kept, moderate. The elasticity of supply of output, for
instance, tends to be much higher in the short run than it is in
under-developed countries: there is a greater cushion of stocks, so
that a rise in fixed investment is often met by disinvestment elsewhere, rather than by an immediate fall in consumption; and even
when prices and incomes begin to rise, they can be quickly restrained by government budgetary or monetary policy. Perhaps as
important as anything else, however, is the fact that prices tend to
be far less flexible than they typically are in under-developed
economies, and do not respond so readily to the forces of demand
and supply. The reason for this is that agricultural and primary
produce in general is a much smaller proportion of total output
than it is in the poorer countries, and therefore a smaller component
of output is priced in highly competitive markets. Manufacturers
of industrial products usually have greater control over the
prices they charge for their products than do the producers of
primary commodities, and do not immediately or readily adjust
their prices to changes in the pressure of demand even when the
latter is proving excessive in relation to their output. The importance of this is that when demand is rising and is exceeding the

[1] The reason for this we consider in a later chapter.

capacity of the economy to supply, prices often do not immediately rise. In other words the inflationary pressure is partially suppressed by the willingness of producers to add to their order books and/or ration their retail outlets. This gives time for production to catch up with demand, and the pressure on prices may be reduced before it becomes effective in raising prices. There are in fact a number of stabilisers in a developed economy which can be relied on to check inflation and keep it moderate. Nonetheless, developed countries do suffer from secular price raising pressures, moderate as they are; but it is doubtful whether, in normal circumstances, the cause is deficient saving and excess demand. Other pressures of an institutional nature are at work that tend to produce inflation in the course of development. We shall defer consideration of these, however, until a later chapter.

Chapter III

ECONOMIC DEVELOPMENT AND THE PRICE LEVEL IN THE BACKWARD ECONOMY

In Chapter II the problem of inflation and economic growth in under-developed countries was looked at from the point of view of fiscal and monetary policy. In effect, the question was posed: 'To what extent can inflationary methods of financing (i.e. those leading to a rising price level) promote economic growth?' The answer to this question largely turns on what happens to investment and saving, and it is fairly clear that both favourable and unfavourable effects can be expected. Hence no definite answer to the question can be given, since whether the favourable or the unfavourable effects will predominate depends on a variety of political, economic and sociological factors which clearly differ from country to country and from time to time, and about which little generalisation seems possible.

It would be a mistake, however, to think that expansive monetary and fiscal policies, aimed at the promotion of growth through forced saving, always lie at the bottom of inflation in under-developed countries: on the contrary, other factors, independent of the balance between the rate of capital formation and the capacity to save, are often at work. These inflationary pressures stem from certain structural features which typify many under-developed countries.

First, an under-developed country typically employs a very large proportion, probably between 70 and 90 per cent, of its total labour force in agriculture.[1] The reason for this is obvious: the level of labour productivity in agriculture is so low that the bulk of the population must be engaged in agricultural pursuits if the minimum basic needs of the population for food and clothing are to be satisfied. Moreover, when agricultural productivity is low, the real income of the people is also low. According to Engels Law, there-

[1] A developed country, on the other hand, would employ around 15 per cent of its labour force in agriculture, more if it is a net exporter of agricultural products, less if it is a net importer.

fore, a large proportion of income is spent on food and similar essentials; and only a small proportion of a small real income is spent on other goods. The market for these other goods is then limited, and little opportunity for the profitable employment of labour, capital and enterprise in the production of these goods is offered. In effect, low productivity in agriculture and Engels Law mutually determine the employment structure. At the same time, however, output per head outside agriculture tends to be higher than in agriculture: it may indeed be three times as much. This fact seems to offer the solution to economic development, since, if labour is shifted out of agriculture into other occupations, labour productivity in the economy *as a whole* would then rise. But such a solution clearly has to be accepted only with some qualifications. In the first place, the fact that output per person outside agriculture is higher than it is inside, does not necessarily imply a more favourable, i.e. lower, capital-output ratio. On the contrary, it may purely reflect a greater input of capital relatively to labour. Hence no quick conclusion can be drawn concerning the allocation of capital between agriculture and other sectors. In the second place, unless agricultural output per head of the population rises when labour is being transferred, the shift can hardly be self-sustaining, for, as we have said, the demand for other goods and services tends to be very limited when agricultural productivity is low. Moreover, to the extent that development in other sectors of the economy is being pressed forward despite backwardness in agriculture, strong inflationary pressures are set up which are difficult to contain by normal monetary and fiscal measures.

The second structural feature of many under-developed countries that often leads to monetary instability is a heavy bias towards the export of one or very few primary products. Inelasticity of demand for and supply of these products produces large swings in their prices, and therefore in export receipts. In turn, monetary instability is introduced into the monetary and fiscal system, particularly when, as is usually the case, both the supply of money and fiscal revenue are closely geared to foreign exchange earnings. Moreover, fluctuations in export receipts do not merely bring about fluctuations in domestic money incomes and prices: on the contrary (for reasons we shall mention later) they tend to produce a persistent pressure towards inflation.

In this chapter, therefore, we shall consider theoretically the inflationary pressures that may arise as a result of these structural characteristics; and we shall begin by analysing the monetary instability introduced by fluctuations in primary product prices.

I

FLUCTUATIONS IN THE TERMS OF TRADE OF
PRIMARY PRODUCERS

It is generally agreed that demand and supply elasticities with respect to primary product production tend to be rather low: moreover, the prices of primary products are normally determined in competitve international markets rather than by decree of individual producers. In consequence, discrepancies between world demand and supply tend to produce sharp movements in prices rather than in outputs; and the export receipts and terms of trade of primary producing countries therefore suffer from instability. Fluctuations in prices are particularly acute in the short run, since the supply of many primary products is subject to the vagaries of weather and disease, and demand varies with employment and output in the industrial countries. Moreover, movements in prices often tend to encourage speculative activity on the part of importers, who sometimes increase their stocks of primary products when they expect prices to rise or run them down with opposite anticipations in mind; and the rise or fall in prices is therefore made greater than it would otherwise be. Even in the longer run, the growth of demand and supply of primary products cannot be expected always to match. The rate of world demand is likely to vary over time, and although producers of primary products will be induced to vary their output in response to demand, usually this takes time to accomplish: moreover, for reasons we shall indicate in a later chapter, the response of output to demand may prove excessive, bringing about a later imbalance in the opposite direction. It is not surprising, therefore, that we find, in the nineteenth and twentieth centuries, for example, longish periods of rising primary product prices alternating with periods of falling prices. Naturally, primary producers tend to benefit from a long term expansion in the demand for their products; and they have more time and scope to adjust themselves to a long term fall. It is therefore the short run fluctuations in prices which occasion them most difficulty, and it is to the consequence of these that we now turn.

Let us begin by assuming that world demand is producing a favourable, that is, upward, trend in primary product prices and, therefore, in the export prices of primary producers. It is reasonable to assume that the net barter terms of trade[1] of the primary producers will also be moving favourably, since generally the elasticity of supply of manufactured good imports is higher than the elasticity of supply of primary product exports. We can immediately point to two consequences that will be favourable for economic growth. The first is that real *income* will be rising faster than real output. Whilst the benefit can be taken out in the form of a higher real consumption on the part of the mass of the population (or at least of some of them), the opportunity is presented for higher real saving and capital formation without further sacrifices in terms of consumption being necessary: higher real income can yield higher real investment rather than higher real consumption. The second consequence is that the capacity to import will be raised. This follows from the fact that when export prices rise in the circumstances we have assumed, export volume is more likely to rise than to fall. A rise in the capacity to import is usually of immense significance for under-developed countries, since, in the early stages of development, capital goods and equipment have normally to be obtained from abroad. Indeed, it may not be going too far to say that investment in under-developed countries depends as much on the capacity to buy capital goods from abroad as it does on the capacity to save. Once again, of course, the advantage need not be taken: the increase in foreign exchange earnings can be used to purchase consumption goods or foreign assets. But it cannot be denied that an improvement in the terms of trade and an expansion of export receipts at least provide the opportunity for speeding up growth.

Whether the opportunity will be taken depends mainly on what happens to incomes and prices in the domestic economy. If the exchange rate is kept stable, export profits and incomes receive the initial benefit; but the effects will not be confined to the export sector. The government itself is likely to benefit from a rise in taxes levied on the export sector, but whether this results in a rise in public or private investment or in expenditure on current ser-

[1] i.e. Export prices divided by import prices.

vices, naturally depends on policy objectives and the means of carrying them out. Some of the extra income will remain in the export sector to finance direct investment there, for the rise in foreign demand makes extension of production worthwhile. Some will be spent on the products of other domestic industries, setting up multiplier effects, which may then increase the inducement to invest in sectors of the economy other than the export. And some no doubt will be made available to finance investment in these other sectors. In brief, a combination of multiplier and accelerator effects are likely to ensue from the initial expansion of export demand, and incomes and activity in the economy as a whole will tend to rise.

However, the situation is likely to become inflationary if the rise in export prices and incomes is at all substantial. Wages are not likely to remain stable in the face of rising profits and demand: hence costs of production may tend to rise. At the same time, it is unlikely that imports can rise sufficiently to satisfy all the increase in money income and demand, whilst in the short run at least, the elasticity of domestic output will normally be low. But the improvement in the terms of trade does mean that real income will be rising to some extent, so that provided wages do not rise at a much faster rate than prices, some real capital formation can take place. The government can, of course, take steps to prevent the cumulative rise in money incomes and prices, for example, by allowing the exchange rate to appreciate when export prices rise, or sterilising the affect of rising export proceeds on the internal monetary supply: in the former case, rising profits and incomes tend to be confined to the import sector with but limited multiplier and accelerator effects, whilst in the latter case, greater activity in the export sector is offset by declining activity elsewhere. In either case the rest of the economy fails to enjoy the stimulating effects of rising monetary demand, and growth is not likely to be promoted.[1] Thus it is more probable that governments will permit money incomes and prices to rise, relying on the growth of real incomes to limit the course of inflation.

The beneficial effect of a rise in export prices and improvement in the terms of trade can, therefore, be summed up in the following way: real income is caused to rise faster than real output whilst, at

[1] In this case, the international currency reserves of the country receive the main benefit.

the same time, the growth of the latter is promoted by a rise in the capacities to save and to import, and in the inducement to invest. And to the extent that faster growth does take place, it will be accompanied by rising prices.

Naturally, these favourable effects are more likely to be enjoyed if export prices and incomes are receiving the benefit of a fairly long run rise in demand. They tend to be quickly dissipated if the rise in export prices is purely a temporary boom, to be followed by an equally precipitate slump. Unfortunately, as we have said earlier, short run instability of export prices seems to be the fate of many primary producing countries, which makes the path of their economic development the more difficult. The economy barely has time to adjust itself to a rise in its export receipts and incomes when the subsequent collapse forces re-adjustment. Perhaps the greatest difficulty arises from the fact that inflation becomes more difficult to control when export receipts and income fluctuate. We have just argued that when exports are enjoying a favourable boom, the general economic climate will normally be somewhat inflationary; that is, the general price level will be rising with export prices. It might be thought therefore that when export prices fall inflation would be automatically checked, and perhaps prices in general might even fall. Often this is not the case, however, and at least three factors can be relied on to exacerbate inflation rather than check it.

In the first place, worsening terms of trade bring about an immediate check to the growth of real income: indeed, real income is likely to fall in absolute terms if the export sector has very large weight in the economy. If real income does fall, it converts a rise in wages, incomes and prices which, when export prices were rising, served to redistribute real income *gains* throughout the economy, into a vicious spiral in which all sections of the community are attempting to maintain individual real income standards that are no longer jointly compatible. When the terms of trade were improving, real income gains could be made by some sections of the community without absolute loss to others: now, when export prices are falling, gains by any one sector, or even maintenance of its present position, implies absolute loss elsewhere. In these circumstances, the check to inflation is likely to be less, and the wage-price spiral becomes more vicious. Second, a fall in export prices and income often precipitates a rise in the government budget deficit (or a fall in its surplus). It is not easy for governments to disengage themselves quickly from expenditure commitments entered into when exports receipts and tax revenue were booming; and other sources of revenue in under-developed economies may not easily be tapped. Hence, credit creation puts further pressure behind the inflationary spiral. Third, a balance of payments crisis is often precipitated by the fall in export earnings, since here again it may be difficult to cut back imports quickly. If foreign exchange reserves have not been earlier accumulated against this contingency, exchange rate depreciation has to follow. Import prices now rise whilst the fall in export incomes (in domestic currency) may be somewhat checked: in any case the domestic cost of living is given a further fillip, increasing the difficulty of restraining the rise in money incomes. Thus the pressure behind inflation intensifies and the rise in prices accelerates. It is in these circumstances that all the unfavourable effects on investment and saving, discussed in the previous chapter, tend to come about; and it is unlikely that economic growth will continue as before. Moreover, the government itself has to take steps to bring the acute inflation to an end, and, in doing so, it will generally have to employ means which check growth as well.

It follows that short run fluctuations in primary product prices are a source of great monetary instability in under-developed countries, and smoother development would no doubt take place if they were eliminated. On the other hand, the elimination of fluctuations must not be achieved at the expense of getting rid of any longer term favourable trend, for, as we have seen, economic development as a whole may be favourably affected when export prices are showing a long term rise. Unfortunately, however, fluctuations cannot be got rid of by action on the part of primary producer countries alone: the industrial countries, who are the buyers of primary products, must also play a part. Agreement between buyers and sellers of primary products is not always easy to reach, for whereas the latter are interested in obtaining a long term rise in primary product prices, when fluctuations are eliminated, the former would clearly prefer a long term fall. Hence many agreements break down through differences on this point.

Thus it is that many under-developed countries see the way out of their dilemma in the reduction of their dependence on primary product exports, and in the overall diversification of their economies; and it is obvious that in most cases this is how their economic development must proceed. Unfortunately, if industrialisation, which in many cases is the ultimate solution to their problems, is carried out at too fast a rate relative to the growth of agriculture or to the ability to import, then monetary instability may not be removed. On the contrary, a potent source of inflationary pressure may be introduced which, in the end, will stultify their efforts to promote growth; and it is to the nature of these inflationary pressures that we now turn.

II

AGRICULTURE AND INFLATION

Whether economic development is taking place, is usually judged by reference to what is happening to the country's output of goods and services, i.e. its real national output or income. If this is growing over time then we recognise that some form of economic development is taking place. This criterion of growth is sometimes qualified by relating the increase in national output to the increase in population: only when output *per capita* is rising can true economic progress be said to be made. Further reference may also be made to the manner in which incomes are distributed: for if all the gains of development are accruing to a few, leaving many at the bottom of the income scale no better off, or perhaps even worse off, then some doubt may be cast on the nature of the progress. Quite apart from these qualifications it should be quite clear that growth of total output is not the only important factor: we need to consider what this output comprises. We could imagine a situation, for instance, in which, owing to the growth of the capital stock, the national output is showing a steady and persistent rise, yet the output of consumption goods (aggregate or *per capita*, depending on what definition of growth we employ) remains constant or even falls. This could happen if the extra capital stock was being used to produce military equipment and to fight wars; or, more pertinent from our point of view, if capital was being used solely to produce more capital. If the aim of economic activity is the satisfaction of consumer wants, then the indefinite prolonging of a policy which aimed solely at the accumulation of capital, to the exclusion of everything else, can hardly be said to constitute real economic progress. The rationale of a policy which gives great priority to capital accumulation is, of course, that in the long run consumers will be better off than if the fruits of economic development had been more equitably distributed over time. But if the advocates of such a policy often seem to overlook the somewhat pertinent fact that those who lose by the excessive concentration on capital accumulation are not necessarily, nor even likely to be, the same as those who eventually gain, yet they would certainly admit that the policy remains unjustified, and even incomplete, until the level of real consumption (aggregate and *per capita*) receives the benefit.

Nor must attention be focused solely on the quantity of consumer goods that are produced, important as this is. They must also be the sort of goods that people want. Whilst, perhaps, too much can be made of the virtues of a free market and of production carried on in accordance with free consumers' choice, nevertheless it is obvious that the pattern of output must largely correspond to the pattern of consumer priorities. It would not be very desirable, to take a rather extreme example, for a government to take massive steps to increase the output of television sets when the mass of the population lived in primitive housing conditions and still had too little to eat. The pattern of consumers' wants is, of course, not the same in every country; more important, it does not remain unchanged in any one country as economic development takes place. At low levels of economic development and low levels of real income, consumers' demand is primarily directed towards goods satisfying the basic needs: food, clothing, and shelter. As they become increasingly well off, the pattern of demand becomes more sophisticated and turns towards the output of manufacturing industry. It follows from this that the direction of investment and the nature of its yield must change through the course of economic development, so that whilst economic development stems directly from investment, the character and distribution of the latter is, or should be, affected by the stage of the former.

It can be argued that in a free market economy, where the distribution of investment and resources and the distribution of output take place according to the criterion of market profitability, the danger of persistent over investment or badly directed investment is not acute, although obviously, as the cyclical experience of the developed, free enterprise economies shows, it can take place. In the last resort the profitability of investment good industries depends on the profitability of consumption good industries; so that logically the development of the latter should precede, or at any rate keep pace with, the development of the former. But, as we pointed out earlier, at low levels of real income per head both the proportion of consumers' real income spent on, and the income elasticity of demand for, food are high. Hence in the early stages of the development of low income countries, the scope for other, non-food type, consumption good industries is very limited, and the rate at which they can profitably grow determined by the rates at which population and agricultural output per head grow. In other words, conditions of agricultural supply determine in large part the rate at which capacity in non-food consumer good industries can profitably grow, and therefore at one remove, the rate at which capacity in producer good industries can profitably grow. They therefore play a large part in determining the rate of growth of the economy as a whole.

The constriction that slow agricultural development places on overall economic growth and the fact that an agricultural revolution must precede, or at least accompany, the industrial one are both very well recognised.[1] The argument for prior agricultural development, however, usually emphasizes the need for raising labour productivity on the land, so that labour may be shifted into urban industry without causing a reduction in the supply of food to the population. It also recognises that, when a country is very over populated so that land is divided up into units too small for efficient farming, moving labour off the land may be a precondition for agricultural improvement. In such circumstances industrial and agricultural development must proceed together. The argument advanced in the preceding paragraph here is purely the obverse of this: it emphasizes the need for raising the output of food to meet the potential demand stemming from rising real income and population, in order that other consumer good industries may be profitably established. For if the demand for food cannot be satisfied then the market for other consumer goods will be limited. Moreover, if a government of an under-developed country attempts to speed up growth by forcing industrialisation — that is, by encouraging labour to move out of agriculture at a faster rate

---

[1] In the long run this constriction may be avoided by the country's becoming an exporter of manufactures in exchange for agricultural products. But the development of markets for manufactured good exports takes time; and in this analysis we shall be concerned with the interim period. See, however, Chapter IV.

than productivity growth permits — then it courts the rise of considerable inflation and the ultimate failure of its policy for growth.

The manner in which excessive emphasis on industrialisation in the very early stages of development can lead to inflation is easily demonstrated with the aid of a simple model.

Suppose we have an economy composed of two sectors only; the agricultural sector which produces food, and the manufacturing sector which produces both capital goods and manufactured consumer goods (we ignore agricultural input to the manufacturing sector). Capital goods are not bought by consumers, and we assume that the demand for them does not depend on current real income. Food and manufactured consumer goods are however bought by consumers, and correspondingly, the demand for them does depend on real income. Let total output be initially divided up as follows: food 70 per cent, capital goods 10 per cent, and manufactured consumer goods 20 per cent. Now suppose that the government pursues a policy to promote industrialisation, so that labour is drawn away from agriculture into urban industry; and assume that as a result of this policy, output in the manufacturing sector of the economy increases by 20 per cent in a given period of time, whilst agricultural output remains constant.[1] What may happen to prices? There are of course a number of possibilities.

The rise in output in the manufacturing sector could take the form of capital goods only, the output of which then rises by 60 per cent. Since total output is rising, total real income also rises, so that if there is no equivalent rise in saving from the marginal increment of income, there will be excess demand for consumer goods, both food and manufactured, the prices of which will tend to rise. We have in fact normal excess demand inflation. Moreover, if marginal saving is zero (or low relatively to the increase in income) and the income elasticity of demand for food is less than unity, manufactured consumer good prices will tend to rise relatively to food prices. For instance, if in our example the marginal ratio of saving to income is equal to the average ratio (i.e. $0 \cdot 1$) and if the income elasticity of demand for food is just below unity, say $\frac{6}{7}$, then the proportionate increase in the demand for manufactured consumer goods exceeds the proportionate increase in the demand for food, so

---

[1] It is also assumed, of course, that productivity in agriculture rises sufficiently to offset the relative loss of labour.

raising the prices of the former relatively to the latter. Alternatively, the rise in manufactured good output could take the form partly of capital goods, partly of manufactured consumer goods. Here again, if the rise in income does not lead to a rise in saving equivalent to the increase in investment, general excess demand appears. In this case, however, it is more likely that food prices will rise relatively to the prices of manufactured consumer goods — unless the income elasticity of demand for food is rather low — since now the supply of manufactured consumer goods, as well as the demand for them, is increasing. Thus, in our example, if the increment of manufactured good output is divided *equally* between capital goods and manufactured consumer goods, and if the marginal saving ratio is equal to 0·1 as before, then the income elasticity of demand for food would have to be below a half to cause the terms of exchange to move in favour of manufactured goods. The higher the income elasticity of demand for food and the larger the proportionate increase in the supply of manufactured consumer goods, the more likely it is that food prices will rise relatively to others.[1]

Another possibility is that when capital good output is increased the government is able to ensure that the amount of extra investment so being undertaken will be matched by an equal amount of saving from the increment of income. In other words assume that *ex ante* investment and saving are made to balance. If in these circumstances the *whole* of the increment of output in the manufacturing sector takes the form of capital goods (i.e. we are assuming that both food and manufactured consumer good output remain constant) then no excess demand or supply would appear and prices would remain stable. But if part of the increment of output in the manufacturing sector takes the form of consumer goods (food output still remaining constant), a contrived balance between *ex ante* saving and investment would necessarily involve an excess supply of manufactured consumer goods. There would not be *general* excess supply, however, since there would exist simultaneously excess demand for food: on the other hand, neither would there be *general* excess demand. But it does not follow that the *general* price level would therefore remain stable. For reasons

---

[1] It is even possible that demand for manufactured consumer goods will increase less than supply, thereby exerting a *downward* pressure on their prices. We consider this possibility in a clearer context in what follows.

we shall now consider, it is much more likely that in these circumstances prices in general will rise.

The factor likely to produce a rise in the general price level in a situation in which excess demand for food exists side by side with an excess supply of manufactured goods, is the greater sensitivity of agricultural prices to demand. The upward pressure in the food market is likely to produce a rise in prices much more quickly than a downward pressure in the manufactured good market produces a fall in prices. In the short run, therefore, the general price level rises,[1] whilst a relative rise in the price of food switches demand away from food to manufactured goods.[2] Now a lot depends on what happens in the labour market. If money wages are sensitive to movements in prices then they may begin to rise with very little time lag, and, as a consequence, money expenditure on food rises still further. Pressure on food prices is therefore maintained; furthermore, costs of production in manufacturing industry may also be affected.

What happens to manufactured good prices in the longer run depends on the initial, and developing, cost and profit position in industry: in a private enterprise economy, some minimum level of profitability in these industries must be maintained if their expansion is to continue. Much, therefore, depends on what happens to productivity in manufacturing industry. If, as is likely to be the case in an under-developed country, industrial output is rising because of a transference of labour from agriculture to industry, rather than because of a rise in the productivity of labour already employed, there may in fact be little room for a reduction in the price level of manufactured goods without impairing profit prospects in industry; and the situation is made worse if urban money wages rise with food prices. Any rise in costs of production in manufacturing industry ensures that the required improvement in agriculture's terms of trade will have to be brought about by a rise in food prices rather than by a fall in manufactured good prices, and hence ensures that inflation will continue. Inflation

---

[1] It is hardly likely that rigidity in the supply of money will prevent this, since the velocity of circulation is bound to be able to vary within limits. If interest rates then rise, it does not follow that investment or other demands will fall off either in the short run or in the long, particularly if the government is taking a leading role in capital formation.

[2] A low elasticity of substitution of food for manufactured consumer goods would imply a large relative rise in the price of food, making it more difficult to maintain general price stability.

would probably be somewhat less if the increase in output of the manufacturing sector stemmed from a rise in productivity there, since now there would be a greater chance of manufactured good prices falling if excess supply continued. But if money wages are responding very quickly to prices, particularly food prices, the beneficial effects of productivity growth on costs would be partly, perhaps wholly, offset, and manufactured good prices would not then fall. Once again the behaviour of food prices determines the change in the terms of exchange, in the context of a general rise in prices.

A major assumption of this example is that food output remains constant when manufactured good output increases; but we need not be so restrictive. The important thing is that food supply *per capita* does not increase at a rate appropriate to the increase in real income *per capita* and the income elasticity of demand for food. There is then an upward pressure on food prices which may trigger off a wage-price spiral. If, on the other hand, the relationship between real income growth, food supply and income elasticity is a more appropriate one, then, of course, there is greater chance of price stability. Indeed in such circumstances, an improvement in agriculture's terms of exchange could take place in an environment of falling prices: for instance, productivity may be rising so fast in manufacturing that in order for its output to be absorbed manufactured good prices must fall relatively to food prices. If there is little or no upward pressure on food prices owing to the satisfactory growth of food output, then the general price level will fall.

It is obvious that our explanation puts great stress on food prices, particularly as the prime mover in the wage-price spiral, but this does not seem unreasonable in a situation in which expenditure on food is still by far the largest item in total spending, i.e. the typical case as far as under-developed countries are concerned. Moreover, it is important to note that the type of inflationary pressure with which we are concerned does not stem simply from too high a rate of investment or from the *failure of the government sufficiently to restrict total consumption* (i.e. from the failure to provide the necessary saving). Rather it is the result of unbalanced development, which is forcing total consumption into a less desired pattern: the community is being forced to consume more industrial goods and less agricultural goods than its level of real income would normally lead it to do *at unchanged relative prices*. In a free consumer market, therefore, food prices have to rise relatively to other prices, and if this necessarily involves an absolute rise in food prices, then general inflation is the most likely consequence.

It follows from this argument that the government cannot easily offset this danger by employing conventional fiscal policy. Suppose, for instance, that, anticipating the excess demand for food, it tries to offset it by taxing incomes. It will then aim at limiting the increase in consumers' *disposable* incomes so that, given the income elasticity of demand for food, the increase in the demand for food is no greater than the increase in supply. But it is evident that if taxation were imposed at this rate, although equilibrium would be restored in the food market, the disequilibrium in the 'non-food' consumer good market would be made much worse. Excess supply would be larger and the need for a fall in prices would be greater. Thus in successfully checking an inflationary rise in food prices, the government would, at the same time, have reduced the scope for the profitable expansion of urban industrial production.

It is of course open to the government to use other methods of keeping down food prices and of preventing the wage-price spiral. For instance, food prices to urban industrial workers could be subsidised, or the farm sector could be forced to sell its output at prices below those that would rule in a free market. But such remedies require a system of rationing and a firm control over black market activities, both of which require considerable administrative machinery and expertise which tend to be lacking in under-developed countries; and the latter remedy runs the further risk of perpetuating the crucial obstacle to industrial growth since it offers the farmer no incentive to increase his output. Alternatively, the government could permit the inflation to run its course whilst subsidising the expansion of urban industry. Indirect taxes on food can be used to prevent the agricultural sector from taking the full benefit of rising food prices and the proceeds used to offset the rising production costs of urban industry. Economic growth then continues but in an increasingly unbalanced form, which the taxation of agriculture and subsidising of industry can hardly serve to correct. In the case of a country which must have some recourse to foreign trade, this course of action cannot last for long; for the internal inflation will soon put strains on the balance of payments which sooner or later have to be corrected, and this cannot be done whilst inflation continues.

E

It is therefore the need to maintain the profitability of urban industries, if their expansion is to continue, which presents the government of a basically private enterprise economy with an acute dilemma. If agricultural output is not rising, or rising but very slowly, then the terms of exchange between agricultural goods and industrial goods must move strongly in favour of the former, if demand for the latter is to make the continued expansion of output worthwhile to private entrepreneurs. As we have said, this is very difficult to achieve except in the context of a rise in the general price level.[1] Governments may therefore be forced to choose between on the one hand, allowing the rate of agricultural development to determine the overall rate of growth, and on the other, breaking the restriction by permitting inflation. The more sensitive industrial prices are to agricultural prices (for instance, through labour costs), the more difficult it is to bring about the necessary change in relative prices; hence the more severe will inflation be. On the other hand, if it is too severe, growth is not likely to take place for reasons mentioned in an earlier chapter.

In a completely socialised economy, in which production and investment decisions are taken in the light of some central economic plan and in which, since the means of production are publicly owned, the profit incentive is of no significance, part of the problem disappears. Industries may be developed which in a free market economy would not prove profitable; and lack of success in promoting agricultural development need not therefore inhibit the development of the economy as a whole. Even so, if food output per head of the population remains at a very low level, it is difficult to expand the output of non-agricultural manufactured consumer goods, if for no other reason than that it would be politically difficult to do so. To put the matter again in an extreme and no doubt exaggerated form, even the people of a totalitarian state would realise that a bad distribution of resources was taking place if they were asked to buy television sets when they had insufficient to eat. The difficulty can be avoided, however, if the state concentrates on the expansion of producer goods industries, justifying the policy

---

[1] Theoretically, if the expansion of industrial output takes place on the basis of rising productivity of labour employed, then the relative price changes between agriculture and industry can be brought about by a *fall* in industrial good prices. We are assuming here, however, that expansion of industrial output is mainly the result of labour moving from agricultural pursuits to industry, which as we implied earlier, is quite likely to be the case in the early stages of development.

on grounds of need, real or imaginary, to build up military strength, or on grounds of the much faster economic growth which would follow in the longer run. It is worth speculating, for instance, on the extent to which the relative failure of agriculture to develop in Soviet Russia in the 1930's contributed to the character of its industrial development.[1] No doubt the priority given to the expansion of producer good capacity as against the production of consumption goods reflected the determination of the government to attain a rapid transformation into a capitalistic economy, as well as to meet the threat of approaching war. But it may also be true that the failure of agricultural development put considerable difficulties in the way of more balanced growth, and that emphasis on producer good production and military preparedness was a necessary condition for a currently high rate of economic growth.

The important point to be made, however, is that if development in an under-developed country is taking an 'unbalanced' form with industrial development outstripping that of agriculture to such an extent that a shortage of food and agricultural raw materials develops, then it is most likely to be accompanied by severe inflationary pressure. It must be stressed again that neither the level of investment nor the rate of saving is at fault: it is simply the case that investment is failing to produce yield appropriate to the pattern of consumers' demand. The usual remedy of reducing the total level of consumers' demand is not really appropriate, since, as we have argued earlier, if it is carried far enough to produce equilibrium in the food market, it will create a deficiency of demand for industrial consumer goods, thereby removing the stimulus to growth. A more selective method is appropriate, but the required administrative machinery and skill may not be available. Hence in the last resort the government has to choose between slowing down the pace of early industrialisation and permitting inflation.[2]

We can therefore sum up this chapter in the following terms. Inflationary pressures often arise in under-developed countries as a result of a lack of balance in their economies. This lack of balance invariably takes the form of a large low productivity agricultural sector relatively to other economic activity, and it may also take the

---

[1] We consider inflation and growth in Soviet Russia in a later chapter.
[2] We have concentrated on the inflationary consequences of a policy which puts excessive emphasis on industrialisation, but of course even when this is not the case inflation can be produced by the mere occurrence of a bad harvest.

form of heavy dependence on primary product exports. This latter factor is a potential source of considerable monetary instability, rendering stable fiscal and monetary policies difficult to pursue. Moreover, it means that external economic events play a crucial role in the determination of the under-developed country's rate of growth. Hence there is a strong incentive for governments to promote the early diversification of their economies, to encourage manufacturing industry to grow relatively to agriculture, and to concentrate on domestically orientated industries rather than export ones. Paradoxically, however, as desirable as it is from the point of view of monetary instability, the early diversification of under-developed economies must not take place at too fast a rate; for if industrial development is promoted when agricultural productivity lags behind, the result is usually severe inflation, and indeed, long term industrial growth may then prove impossible. In the early stages, therefore, what is required is a balanced development of both agriculture and industry, until a broadly based market for exports is established, which then permits some specialisation of economic activity, and continuing economic growth.

This specialisation may eventually take the form of a heavy bias towards manufacturing output, a large part of which is exported in exchange for primary products and foodstuffs. Alternatively, a country may remain a large primary product producer and exporter, even when the manufacturing sector is relatively well developed. But it seems more appropriate to describe such an economy, whether biassed towards the export of manufactures or towards primary products as a 'specialised' economy rather than an 'unbalanced' one: clearly it is not comparable to the poorer, more backward countries with which we have been principally concerned in this chapter. Nonetheless, even these more developed economies do not always escape the dilemma of inflation or slower growth, although it usually takes a less acute form. In the following chapters, therefore, we shall go on to examine the problem in the context of the more developed economy.

Chapter IV

ECONOMIC DEVELOPMENT AND THE PRICE LEVEL IN THE MORE ADVANCED ECONOMY

The inflationary pressures considered in the previous chapter arise as a result of substantial and rapid improvements in the terms on which agricultural (more generally, primary) products exchange for manufactures or industrial goods, or as a result of severe fluctuations in them. The former appears when an under-developed country is attempting to diversify its economy through industrialisation at too fast a rate relatively to the the growth of agriculture or to its ability to import foodstuffs from overseas. The latter are generally introduced into under-developed, primary product exporting countries through fluctuations in the demand of the importing industrial countries. In this chapter, it will be argued that the price levels of even relatively well developed economies are subject to similar, although less severe and perhaps slower working pressures — namely those arising from changes in the net barter terms of trade between agriculture and industry. We shall be concerned first with an economy relatively well developed, so that agriculture by no means provides the most important part of national product; in which the manufacturing sector is at least as important as agriculture; but which is relatively self-sufficient, in that both exports and imports constitute a very small and insignificant part of total economic activity.[1] Indeed for the purposes of our analysis we shall regard the economy as a closed one. We shall then go on to consider the problem in the context of a more internationally specialised economy, which either exports a large part of its manufactured good output in return for agricultural

[1] The sort of economy we have in mind would be illustrated by the United States after 1870. In the last quarter of the nineteenth century agriculture and manufacturing each provided 17 or 18 per cent of national income, and imports and exports each represented at most 6 or 7 per cent of national product. Moreover, probably four-fifths of exports and one-half of imports were raw materials and foodstuffs: hence a change in the international terms of trade between manufactures and primary products would have but a negligible effect on national income.

and other primary product imports, or produces primary products on a substantial scale for export.

I

SECULAR CHANGES IN THE DEMAND AND SUPPLY
OF PRIMARY PRODUCTS

The overall rate of growth of an economy is determined by the rates of growth of its individual sectors and the relative importance of each. In what follows we want to concentrate attention on the relationship between agriculture and the rest of the economy: but partly as a matter of convenience, partly because the relationship between agriculture and manufacturing is of peculiar importance, we shall equate the manufacturing sector with the whole of the non-agricultural sector, although, of course it constitutes but a part. Where, however, it is necessary to make a distinction between manufacturing and the rest of the non-agricultural sector we shall do so explicitly.

In the course of economic growth we would not expect agricultural output to grow at the same rate as manufacturing output. Agriculture supplies the food and substantial part of the raw materials required for economic growth. Even if agricultural raw material input remained a constant proportion of final output in the rest of the economy, the demand for agricultural products would tend to grow at a slower rate than the growth of total output and real income. The income elasticity of demand for food is of course the crucial factor. If the income elasticity of demand for food remained equal to unity throughout the course of growth, then of course agriculture and manufacturing would have to grow at the same rate. If it were less than unity, but remained unchanged at this value, then agriculture would grow at a slower rate than manufacturing, but its rate of growth would not diminish provided the rate of growth of manufacturing remained unchanged.[1] None

---

[1] The formula for predicting the relative rates of growth of agriculture and manufacturing in these circumstances is:

$$\frac{u}{s} = k \cdot \frac{1 - \gamma\lambda}{\gamma\lambda + \alpha}$$

where s = rate of growth of agriculture
u = rate of growth of manufacturing
k = initial ratio of agricultural output to manufacturing output
γ = income elasticity of demand for food

of these suppositions is likely to be true. When real income *per capita* is very low, the income elasticity of demand for food is likely to be high: it could be equal to or greater than one: but as the former rises the latter is likely to diminish. Similarly, the ratio of raw material input to final product output is not likely to remain constant. Technological progress may enable final product to be produced with smaller raw material input; synthetic substitutes may be developed; and certainly the composition of non-agricultural output will not remain constant over time.[1] For all these reasons, therefore, the growth of agriculture is likely to be slower than the growth of manufacturing, and the difference will tend to increase over time.

It must be noted, however, that entrepreneurs tend to have less control over agricultural output than over manufacturing output. In the short run agricultural output is clearly at the mercy of climatic conditions: harvests may be good or bad irrespective of what is sown: and even in the long run, agricultural output and primary production in general are subject to a number of conflicting forces. The discovery of new areas of production, and their opening up and exploitation, cannot always be directly or closely related to the pressure of demand; and the exhaustion or spoliation of older areas of production can have significant effects on total supply. Hence forces can act on agricultural supply that are independent of demand, and thereby bring about long run imbalances between the growth of demand and supply. Admittedly, the growth of manufacturing output is subject to the forces of technological progress: these however are more likely to operate in the direction of accelerating growth rather than of retarding it, whilst other forces are likely to be much less significant.[2]

We want now to consider the effects on the general price level of a change in the rate of growth of agricultural output, produced by autonomous forces operating on the side of supply. In other words, we are not concerned with the case where agricultural growth slows down *because* of a prior slowing down in the growth

λ = initial ratio of food consumption to total income

and α = ratio of agricultural raw material input to manufacturing output.

It assumes that α and γ remain constant during growth.

[1] For instance, if service output comes to occupy a larger part of total output then the demand for raw material input will tend to grow at a slower and perhaps diminishing rate as compared with total output.

[2] Except for the effects that an autonomous slowing down in rate of agricultural growth are likely to have. We discuss these later.

of demand: rather we are partly concerned with how demand will react if the potential growth of agriculture is reduced by unfavourable supply conditions. We can imagine that agricultural output and non-agricultural output have been growing at just the right relative rates, so that, given the income elasticity of demand for food (more pertinently, the marginal propensity to spend real income on food) and the marginal requirements of manufacturing output for agricultural raw material input, the demand and supply for agricultural products have been in long run balance, without the need for relative price changes between agricultural products and manufactures. Now suppose that the growth of agricultural output is slowed down by an unfavourable supply factor. What happens to prices?

It will be more convenient if the analysis is conducted in *per capita* terms. The easiest assumption to make is that total population and its distribution between the various sectors of the economy remain unchanged as growth takes place. The latter assumption is, of course, unrealistic and, indeed, may be incompatible with growth, since experience shows that the latter is generally accompanied by significant shifts in the distribution of the working population. But when we are considering the case of a relatively advanced economy, it will not be misleading to assume that the shift of labour from agriculture towards other sectors of the economy has already largely been carried out, and we can therefore look on further shifts of this sort as being insignificant. It is also simpler if we assume that total product and total real income in each sector grow at the same rate as productivity per head and real income per head in these sectors. Moreover, we shall begin by assuming that money wages in each sector are rising at the same rate as productivity.

Given these assumptions, a decline in the rate of increase of agricultural output is associated with a decline in the rate of increase of both output per head of the agricultural labour force and output per head of the population. If real income *per capita* of the population continues to grow at the same rate as before,[1] then the consumption of food must now increase at a slower rate, whilst the consumption of non-agricultural goods must increase at a faster rate. The terms of exchange between agricultural goods and manufactured goods must move in favour of the former in order to

[1] Of course it may not do this. Later we shall consider reasons why it may not.

induce substitution of manufactured goods for food in the pattern of consumption over time. Moreover, the rate of growth of output of manufactured goods must rise. The terms of exchange may move in favour of food and agricultural products either as a result of a rise in agricultural prices or a fall in industrial prices — or perhaps as the result of a combination of the two. Obviously a lot depends on what happens to manufacturing costs. If, by chance, the rate of increase of productivity in the manufacturing sector rises just when the growth of agricultural output slows down, and if money wages in the manufacturing sector continue to rise at the same rate as before (that is, now at a slower rate than productivity) then, not only may the required increase in the availability of manufactured goods be brought about, but also its obverse — a fall in industrial costs and prices to produce the required change in the terms of exchange.[1] In these circumstances, since agricultural prices are remaining unchanged whilst manufactured good prices are falling, then the general price level would tend to fall.[2] But, of course, the conditions required to get this result are not likely to hold.

Thus if money wages in manufacturing begin to rise at a faster rate in sympathy with productivity, and/or if money wages in agriculture continue to rise at the same rate as before despite the decline in the rate of growth of productivity, then the required shift in the terms of trade would be brought about by a *rise* in agricultural prices relative to manufacturing prices. In other words the general price level would tend to rise as economic development proceeds. The process would not stop there, for the rise in agricultural prices would itself directly cause a rise in manufacturing costs of production at the raw material input stage. It might also have an *indirect* effect on manufacturing costs if money wages in manufacturing are at all affected by what happens to consumer good prices. If as a result of a rise in agricultural prices and in the general price level, money wages begin to rise at an even faster rate, that is, at a faster rate now than productivity in manufacturing,

---

[1] Throughout this argument it is assumed that manufactured good prices are cost determined. The existence of monopoly, which may reduce the *downward* flexibility of prices, is ignored, but we return to the problem later in this chapter and also more generally in Chapter V.

[2] It must be remembered that we are assuming that, initially, money wages are rising in each sector at the same rate as productivity is rising, prices being constant. With the decline in the rate of productivity growth in the agricultural sector, agricultural money wages are also assumed to rise at a slower rate.

then manufactured good prices begin to rise as well. Hence the rise in agricultural prices must be even faster to get the required shift in the terms of trade; and the general price level becomes subject to a cumulative process. Moreover, we have assumed that productivity in manufacturing (and therefore manufacturing output) begin to grow at a faster rate just when the decline in the rate of growth of agricultural output and productivity sets in.[1] If this does not happen (and there is no logical reason why it should), or if it happens but to an insufficient degree, then agricultural prices would begin to rise at the outset, even if for a time money wages in manufacturing continue to rise at the same rate as earlier; but the rise in the general price level might now affect money wages, and, as before, a cumulative process of rising agricultural and industrial prices sets in.

We could, of course, begin with the alternative situation in which money wages in all sectors of the economy remain constant when productivity rose, all our other conditions holding as before. In this case we should have an initial situation in which money incomes were constant, but prices were falling. Suppose now a decline in the rate of growth of agricultural output sets in. Once again, if, by chance just at this time, productivity in manufacturing begins to grow at a faster rate, money wages in manufacturing still remaining constant, then the rate at which manufacturing prices are falling will accelerate, and the required shift in the terms of exchange between agriculture and manufacturing will be brought about in the context of a more rapid fall in the general price level. If, however, productivity in manufacturing industry does *not* begin to rise at a faster rate when the growth of agriculture slows down, then the speed with which agricultural prices are falling will be checked. Because of the agricultural raw material input component of manufacturing output, the rate of fall of industrial prices will also be checked at the same time: hence, the rate of fall of agricultural prices must be further checked in order to get the required shift in the terms of exchange. If the decline in the rate of growth of agriculture is serious and sustained, then it is possible that the

---

[1] An increase in growth rate of manufacturing when growth rate of agriculture declines, assumes that manufacturing can make do with a smaller agricultural raw material input per unit of output. This may imply opportune technological change or a shift in the composition of manufacturing output: the latter may cast doubt on whether the required increase in rate of increase in productivity will take place.

movement of agricultural prices will be reversed: that is, they will begin to rise. Once this happens, the likelihood of manufactured good prices continuing to fall is greatly diminished, and they may soon begin to rise as well. The process may then become cumulative as before, if money wages now begin to rise in sympathy with the general price level.

We conclude that a slowing down in the rate of growth of agricultural output, produced by autonomous forces working on the side of supply, will, in a situation in which the general price level is falling, reduce the rate at which prices are falling: it might even reverse the direction of the price movement, causing prices to rise. If prices were initially stable or rising, then of course there is much greater likelihood they will now begin to rise, or rise at a faster rate than before.

Suppose, however, that the equilibrium between the rate of growth of manufacturing and rate of growth of agriculture is disturbed by an acceleration of the former. We could assume, for instance, that a sustained burst of technical progress raises the rate of productivity growth in industry, agricultural growth, however, remaining as before. How then would prices behave?

If we start with a situation in which money wages in all sectors are rising at the same rate as productivity, leaving absolute and relative prices unchanged, then, provided money wages in manufacturing do not begin to rise at a faster rate in sympathy with productivity, manufactured good prices will begin to fall.[1] But this fall may be checked somewhat by a rise in the price level of agricultural raw material input, the demand for which will now be increasing at a greater rate than before. Moreover, since real income *per capita* will be rising at a faster rate than before, the demand for food will also grow at a faster rate, although, owing to the relative decline in manufactured good prices, the pattern of consumers' demand may be shifting away somewhat from food to manufactured goods. Hence the required shift in the terms of exchange between agricultural products and manufactured goods will be produced by a fall in manufactured good prices and perhaps by some rise in agricultural prices; and there is a chance that the general price level will therefore be falling. On the other hand, if money wages in manufacturing industry immediately begin to rise

---

[1] Once again we abstract from the problem of monopoly and price rigidity, but return to it later.

at a faster rate when productivity growth increases, then naturally there will be much less chance of manufactured good prices falling, and correspondingly more chance that agricultural prices will rise. If the latter should happen, then it is possible that money wages will be further affected, so that they now begin to rise at a faster rate than productivity, in which case a cumulative rise in wages and prices may develop — even if the original imbalance between agricultural growth and manufacturing growth eventually disappears.

It must be obvious that a great deal depends on the mode of wage and price determination in the labour and product markets. When productivity rises, either prices of goods must fall or money wages and other incomes must rise, if the increase in output is to be absorbed. Which of these happens depends on the nature of the competition and the institutional arrangements in the two markets; and we examine these matters in more detail in the next chapter. But it is reasonably clear that the more organised labour is and the more monopolistic[1] industry is, the less likelihood there is that prices, in manufacturing industry at least, will fall: trade unions typically strive to keep money wages in line with productivity growth, and monopolistic industry seems to prefer to try to increase its sales by advertising, etc., rather than by cutting prices, even when costs fall. Hence, if the relative development of industry and agriculture is such as to necessitate an improvement in agriculture's terms of exchange against manufactures, this is much more likely to be achieved in the context of a rise in agricultural prices and in the general price level, and perhaps in manufactured good prices as well. The upward pressure on prices will be less in the case of an acceleration in manufacturing growth, and more in the case of a retardation in agricultural growth, but in both cases prices are likely to rise. If both labour and product markets were more competitively organised, however, then there is more chance that prices will fall in the former case although they would still be likely to rise in the latter.

The development most conducive to a fall in the general price level in the course of growth is an acceleration in the rate of growth of agricultural output which necessitates a *worsening* in agriculture's terms of exchange. If agriculture and industry have initially been

---

[1] Used here in a very wide sense to include monopolistic competition and oligopoly, etc.

growing at appropriate rates to leave the terms of exchange between them unchanged, an acceleration in agriculture's growth relatively to that of manufacturing must cause a fall in agricultural prices relatively to manufactured good prices. Agricultural prices are typically more flexible, in both upward and downward direction, than are manufactured good prices; and the pressure of potential excess supply will tend to cause agricultural prices to fall. Manufacturing industry will derive some benefit, *directly* as a result of a decline in agricultural raw material prices, and perhaps *indirectly* if money wages are at all influenced by the fall in food prices. If the market for manufactured goods is competitive, then manufactured good prices may fall as well; but even if they don't, the fall in agricultural prices lowers the general price level.

This explanation of the behaviour of the general price level during the course of economic growth emphasizes the relative *long term* or *secular* rates of growth of agriculture and industry.[1] It must be remembered however, that the economic growth of capitalist countries has not in fact proceeded in a smooth fashion, with output rising at a steady rate from year to year: on the contrary, it seems to have taken place in 'fits and starts', with investment and output rising steeply over the course of two or three years, and declining again, although usually not so sharply, in the following two or three years. We refer here, of course, to the cyclical fluctuations in output and income, the so-called trade cycle, experienced by most of the present day 'advanced' countries throughout most of their growth. Prices, as well as output, tended to rise and fall in the course of the trade cycle: hence any explanation of the behaviour of the price level in the long run which pretends to fit the facts must be consistent with an explanation of the shorter run fluctuations. Indeed, the trend of prices in the long run is nothing but the cumulative result of their movement in the short run. Thus what we really have to do is to explain why prices may rise and fall in the course of boom and slump yet behave in such a way that a discernible trend, either upward or downward, appears in the long run. In fact, however, our explanation can be

[1] It will be noted that no reference has been made to the quantity of money. The reason for this is the belief that, in the long run, the quantity of money is more likely to adjust to prices and to the 'needs of trade' than the other way round. In the short run, an inelastic supply of money may play a part in bringing booms to an end, although the community is usually able to economise in the use of its money, so that even an absolutely constant stock of money can support varying levels of income and prices.

made to fulfil this requirement. To show this, it will be useful to outline the forces that operate on prices in the course of a typical boom and slump.[1]

In the first place it must be noted that although output expands and contracts during boom and slump, the contractions must be less than the expansions, if long run economic growth is taking place. Generally, too, industrial output fluctuates more than agricultural output, rising more in the booms and falling more in the slumps (see Chapters VI and VII): but, if in the long run industrial output is growing at a faster rate than agricultural output, the percentage net increment of industrial output over boom and slump together will be larger than the percentage net increment of agricultural output; and the difference in each boom and slump will determine the relative growths of agriculture and industry over time.

With this in mind, let us suppose that because of more optimistic expectations on the part of business entrepreneurs, a rise in investment takes place, so producing an expansion of economic activity. Aggregate demand rises, bringing about an increase in production, incomes and spending. Some of the increase in spending will fall on agricultural goods, partly because agriculture is an important source of raw materials for industry, partly because, as money incomes rise, more will be spent on food. The elasticity of supply of agricultural output is, however, typically rather low in the short run so that prices of agricultural products may begin to rise quite soon in the boom.[2] If food prices share in this rise, then agitation in the labour market may begin to produce a rise in money wage rates even before full employment of labour is approached, and it will certainly add to the pressure on money wages once full employment is reached. In the early stages of the boom, productivity in industry will probably be rising very fast so that higher labour costs can be absorbed without prices of manufactured goods rising at the same time; but as full employment is reached, productivity growth begins to fall off and the rise in money wages accelerates, so that producers begin to raise prices generally in order to protect their profit margins. Moreover, bottlenecks in the

[1] We are not concerned here with the causes of fluctuations in economic activity, but simply with the behaviour of the price level.

[2] The size of the excess demand for agricultural products depends on the increase in industrial production relative to the increase in agricultural production, being greater the larger is the former relatively to the latter.

supply of particular intermediate materials may appear, causing their prices to rise; and producers generally may take the opportunity to enlarge their profit margins. A combination of factors, in other words, tends to produce a rise in the general price level in the course of the boom.

We can sum this up by saying that the magnitude of the price rise depends on three important short run supply elasticities: the elasticity of supply of agricultural output; the elasticity of supply of labour; and the elasticity of supply of non-agricultural output. The third elasticity depends partly on the other two, but mainly on the rate at which productivity in industry can rise when demand is increasing. If all elasticities are low, then prices begin to rise early on in the boom and may rise quite considerably before it comes to an end; and if the first elasticity is much lower than the third agricultural prices tend to rise relatively to manufactured good prices. The elasticity of supply of agricultural products is probably the most crucial, since if it is low, even a high elasticity of supply of labour will not necessarily prevent money wages from rising; in which case, a high rate of productivity growth in industry may be required to prevent an early and cumulative rise in prices. In any case, it is likely that prices will begin to rise well before full employment of labour and other resources is reached, and, for a time, output and prices will rise together. But once the economy does reach a point of maximum short run output (if it ever does) then of course there arises the danger that inflation will get out of hand. In fact, however, history seems to show that, in the more advanced capitalist economies at least, booms tend to come to an end before this point is reached, so that the rise in prices is checked and even reversed. Moreover, it does not seem to have been the case that prices stopped rising because saving had been forced up to match investment: rather, investment seems to have declined, producing a cumulative decline in output and activity.

We, however, are not concerned directly with the cause of the downturn, but rather with the subsequent price behaviour. So let us simply suppose that the boom comes to an end, say for instance as a result of a collapse of business profit expectations. Demand and production decline; but in a growing economy, industrial production does not decline by as much as it rose. Nor, therefore, does the demand for food and agricultural raw materials. Hence, if during the course of the boom, agricultural output had risen very little,[1] relatively to the expansion of industrial output, so that prices had been mainly affected, then it is possible that the subsequent decline in demand will involve little, if any, fall in prices; and in consequence the latter may not fall in the slump by as much as they rose in the boom. If food prices do remain higher towards the end of the slump than they were at the beginning of the boom, then, although a decline in demand for labour may cause some fall in money wage rates, it is likely that they in turn will not fall by as much as they rose.[2] A rigid element is then introduced into industrial costs, so that industrial prices, if they fall at all, will probably do so less than they rose.

In brief, a failure of agricultural output to rise very much in the boom, relative to the expansion of output in the rest of the economy, places a strong upward pressure on costs and prices in the boom; and, in the subsequent slump, it limits the extent to which prices fall. Naturally, the more productivity in industry rises in the boom, the more can rising costs of raw materials and labour be absorbed without a rise in industrial prices. On the other hand, given the elasticity of supply of agricultural output, then the greater is the increase in industrial output, the greater will be the rise in the price level of food and raw materials. In such circumstances, therefore, prices are likely to rise more in booms than they fall in slumps.

On the other hand, if in the course of the boom, agricultural output is able to rise substantially, relatively to the expansion of other output, then the rise in food and raw material prices is likely to be less, and so, too, therefore, will be the rise in industrial costs and prices. Moreover, the subsequent decline in demand, due to industrial contraction, may reduce demand for agricultural products well below the level to which output has grown in the boom. Hence prices will fall sharply, and may decline to a level lower than that ruling at the beginning of the boom.[3] As a result, a fall in demand

---

[1] See footnote 2 on page 70.

[2] Of course there are other forces, too, which set a lower limit to the fall in wages.

[3] Formally, the increase in agricultural output during the course of the boom involves a movement along a given supply curve *plus* a movement to the right of the supply curve itself, the latter being due to a long term growth factor affecting the potential supply of agricultural products at various price levels. The more important this growth factor is the less will agricultural prices rise in the boom; and the greater is the chance that they will fall back to, or even below, their pre-boom level, even though demand remains higher at the end of the slump than it was at the beginning of the boom.

for labour can more easily produce a fall in money wages, although of course this need not happen; but in any case, raw material costs fall sharply as well. Hence more room is provided for a fall in prices generally. Thus, over the course of boom and slump, prices fall more than they rise, and, in the longer run, the trend of prices is downward.

It is clear that, in this explanation, considerable emphasis is being placed on the behaviour of agricultural prices, which is regarded as being an important determinant of the behaviour of the general price level. The behaviour of agricultural prices depends on the magnitudes of the excess demands or supplies that appear in the course of industrial expansion and contraction; and these, in turn, depend on the expansions and contractions of industrial output relative to those of agricultural output. The larger is the expansion of industrial output relative to the expansion of agricultural output, the more will agricultural prices, and therefore prices in general, rise; and the less industrial output contracts relative to the contraction of agricultural output, the less will prices fall. But, as we said at the beginning of this discussion, the relative expansions and contractions of industrial and agricultural output in the course of boom and slump determine their relative growths over the longer run. A persistent tendency for industrial output to grow at faster rate than agricultural output in the booms may prove excessive, in the sense that agricultural output never, or only occasionally, matches the level of demand appropriate to the level of industrial output: hence although prices sometimes fall, there is in the longer run a constant upward pressure on them. Conversely, although lagging somewhat in the booms, agricultural output may reach a level in the slumps that is greatly in excess of the demand currently being produced by the level of industrial output; hence although prices may sometimes rise, they tend to fall in the longer run. In the former case, industrial output is growing over time at too fast a rate relative to the growth of agriculture, whereas in the latter case, the opposite is true.

It seems therefore that our explanation of the forces bearing on prices in the course of long run economic development is quite consistent with the fact that prices tend to rise and fall in the shorter run. On the other hand the analysis has been conducted in terms of a 'closed' economy; and it is doubtful whether any country can ever be so self-sufficient that it has no need to import

F

goods from overseas. A country may provide itself with the bulk of the raw materials and foodstuffs that it requires for economic growth, but even so, marginal requirements, arising for instance from a bad harvest or from a particularly violent industrial boom, may have to be met with purchases from abroad. But the fact that goods are sucked in from abroad during booms does not mean that prices do not rise: on the contrary, it is the tendency for prices to rise in the home market that induces importers to increase supplies from overseas. Similarly if the country is normally a net exporter of food and raw materials, an expansion of demand at home tends to raise prices and, in other ways also, to increase the attractiveness of selling in the home market, so that exports decline. Nonetheless, the fact that imports can rise and exports fall naturally limits the extent to which domestic prices do rise in the boom and fall in the slump: in other words, as far as any one country is concerned, it increases the elasticity of supply.

The world as a whole, however, is a 'closed' economy. Hence, it may be argued that the analysis developed in this chapter still largely applies, provided we now refer to the relative growths of *world* industrial output and *world* agricultural and primary product output. Within the world economy, of course, some countries specialise on the production and export of industrial goods, relying mainly on imports to meet their requirements for food and raw materials: others specialise on primary products, exporting most in exchange for manufactures: while others remain largely self-sufficient in the production of both industrial products and primary products. But the growth of demand for agricultural and primary products depends on the growth of *world* industrial capacity and output; and it would clearly be quite fortuitous if it consistently matched the potential growth of world supply of these products. Rates of growth of output in particular industrial and primary producing countries are subject to a number of independent forces that are likely to cause them to vary over time. Moreover, even if it were true that the rate of growth of industrial output in every industrial area remained constant over time, it still would not follow that the rate of growth of *world* industrial output would remain constant except in the unlikely circumstance of all industrial countries growing at the same rate. If some industrial countries are growing at a faster rate than others, then their 'weight' in total world industrial production will be increasing over time: accordingly, the average rate of growth of all countries together would tend to rise, as it came more and more to approximate to the rate of growth of the faster growing areas.[1] So too, therefore, would the rate of growth of demand for primary products. But this would suggest that unless the *maximum potential* rate of growth of output of primary products was at least as fast as the rate of growth of the fastest growing component of industrial demand, there must eventually come a point when primary product prices would begin to rise, no matter what had been happening to them beforehand: moreover, once they did start to rise they would do so without limit. Of course, if the actual rate of growth of primary product output was consistently higher than the growth rate of the fastest growing component of industrial demand, then prices would fall without limit,[2] although the speed at which they would fall would tend to diminish over time. If, therefore, the rates of growth of output of individual industrial countries, and of total primary output, remain constant over time, we would be faced with a situation in which product prices either fell without limit, or if they once began to rise, they would do so also without limit: there cannot, in other words, be a situation in which a rise is followed by a later fall. But this conclusion is clearly not realistic and certainly does not fit the facts. In the course of history, primary product prices have both risen and fallen; indeed in the nineteenth and twentieth centuries, quite a regular secular fluctuation can be observed. It follows that the rates of growth of industrial countries, and of world primary product output cannot have remained constant over time.

It would of course be surprising if they had. The growth of primary product output is subjected to a number of conflicting forces: it tends to be checked by the exhaustion of resources in older countries, and raised by technical progress in transport, cultivation and extraction; moreover, new areas of production may be discovered and exploited, bringing about quite radical changes in potential supply. Similarly, the growth of industrial areas is influenced by a variety of factors: it is, for instance, sometimes stimulated, sometimes retarded, by wars or political upheavals, and nations may experience sharp changes in their attitudes towards industrialisation and economic change. Many of these forces

---

[1] See Phelps Brown and Ozga, 'Economic Growth and the Price Level', *Economic Journal*, March 1955.

[2] This is clearly not likely since a persistent fall in primary product prices would eventually depress the growth of output. See later.

acting on primary product supply and demand operate quite independently of the contemporary balance between supply and demand. For instance, the opening up of new areas of production may take place as the by-product, rather than as the deliberate result, of the emigration of people from older countries; and wars and political upheavals are not generally produced by trends in primary product prices. Nonetheless, persistent trends in primary product prices do bring about corrective changes in supply and demand through the effects they have on industrial and primary product growth. A sustained rise in primary product prices, for example, makes the extension and intensification of raw material production worthwhile, while a sustained fall discourages such production; and even if the rate of growth of industrial countries is like to be more independent of the contemporary balance between demand and supply of primary products, sustained trends in the price level of primary products can have some effect on their growth, in a manner we shall describe later.

Meanwhile, we should note a possible outcome of the repercussions set up by any sustained imbalance between the demand and supply of primary products. It leads directly to the possibility of long term or secular fluctuations in the primary product price level. When demand is tending to grow at a faster rate than supply, prices tend to rise over time. Although the rise in price tends to produce a rise in the growth rate of supply and perhaps a fall in the growth rate of demand, the correction is not likely to be immediate: owing to difficulties in the way of quickly raising primary product output, the rise in prices is likely to go on for some time, and may be quite disproportionate compared with the initial discrepancy between demand and supply. Eventually however the fruits of investment and technical advance appear and an increase in the rate of flow of output takes place; but the danger now is that the flow will prove excessive. One cause of this danger is that the opening up of new areas of production or the extensive development of older ones normally requires large scale, indivisible investment outlays, which are typically associated with a long period of gestation. Consequently, no quick or short run checks on the profitability of investment expenditure are possible, and investment expenditure is therefore often continued beyond the point where demand in the immediate future is likely to prove it profitable. Thus over-investment and 'overshooting' of production may well take place, producing not just a check to the rise in primary product prices, but, instead, a fall. The latter now serves to check the further expansion of production, although once again the reaction is likely to be slow; and when it does take place it may prove equally excessive in the opposite direction. Thus if demand for primary products continues to grow over time, particularly if growth is accelerating, it may soon catch up with supply, and once again prices begin to rise, setting in train yet another burst of investment in primary producing areas. Thus a secular fluctuation in primary product prices may be generated, the nature and timing of which may be influenced by exogenous factors of the sort mentioned earlier, but whose existence essentially depends on the conditions of primary product supply.[1]

The most important point to be emphasised here, however, is that the price level of agricultural and other primary products entering into international trade can move quite independently of what is happening in any *one* importing country. It is possible of course that a major industrial country may be the importer of a significant fraction of the total supply of primary products entering into world markets, in which case expansion or contraction of its own demand alone may be sufficient to affect the prices it has to pay: but not many countries are in this position. The more usual case is that an importing country will find the prices of raw materials and foodstuffs rising or falling without reference to its own state of demand or its rate of growth. Nonetheless, its domestic price level will inevitably be affected and so, too, may its rate of growth.

There is no need to dwell further on the manner in which a rise in the price level of imported raw materials and foodstuffs affects the domestic price level of the importing country: the process will be largely the same as that described in relation to the closed, self-sufficient economy — except that the rise or fall in primary product prices may occur without there *necessarily* being a prior expansion or contraction in domestic demand. We can also take it that the growth of a 'specialised' industrial country takes place in a similar erratic fashion, with expansions of output and activity alternating with contractions — the latter being smaller than the former so that long term development is taking place. During the booms,

[1] See W. W. Rostow, *Process of Economic Growth* (Oxford) for the development of this argument.

prices will tend to rise more when import prices are rising than when they are stable or falling, since cost inflationary pressures, associated with the rise in raw materials and food prices, are added to the pressures of demand for goods and labour. On the other hand, when the boom comes to an end, it does not follow that import prices necessarily stop rising or begin to fall: hence although demand pressures disappear, cost pressures may remain, which even if they don't cause prices to rise in the slump, at least prevent them from falling as much as they otherwise would. Conversely, prices will tend to rise less in the booms and perhaps fall more in the slumps, when primary product prices are falling. In this way, secular price trends are produced.

Nonetheless we must not make too much of the point that the prices which a country has to pay for its imported raw materials and foodstuffs, etc., can move independently of the state of its domestic demand and activity. Booms and slumps seldom tend to be confined to one country alone, but transmit themselves throughout the international economy. Countries experience their booms and slumps roughly simultaneously, so that when they are all booming together, the price level of internationally traded primary products is forced up. Thus it is typical for an industrial country to find its import prices rising when its domestic economy is booming, despite the fact that its own demand for raw materials and foodstuffs, considered in isolation, would not have been large enough significantly to affect the world price level. Conversely, its import prices are likely to be falling when the domestic economy is slumping. It follows that the fluctuations in prices that do occur tend to be synchronised throughout the trading world.[1]

But if it is typically the case that countries tend to boom and slump together and to experience secular price raising or lowering forces together, then it may be asked why it was necessary to distinguish in our analysis between the relatively self-sufficient, or closed, economy and the more specialised one. The answer is that although the price level in the course of economic development is affected by the same forces in both types of country, their rates of

---

[1] This need not happen, of course. A country may successfully pursue policies which partly or wholly insulate its economy from the international economy so that it avoids the worst of the international booms and slumps. Thus, if it successfully pursues expansionist policies when the rest of the world is slumping, then it may derive substantial advantages from the fact that primary product prices are falling. Japan in the 1920's and '30's may provide a good example. See Chapter VIII.

growth need not be. There are, for instance, reasons for thinking that the rate of growth of a 'specialised' country will be affected by a change in the terms of exchange between primary products and industrial products more than will the rate of growth of a more closed economy; and we shall therefore conclude this chapter by considering just how the rate of growth might be affected. We first take the case of a specialised industrial country which imports the bulk of its raw materials and foodstuffs from overseas, and we contrast it with both the specialised primary producer and the more self-sufficient closed economy.

II

THE TERMS OF EXCHANGE OF PRIMARY PRODUCTS
AND THE RATE OF GROWTH

Consider first the results that might follow from a secular fall in primary product prices, produced, not by a check in the demand of the industrial countries,[1] but by the opening up of new areas of production, or the extension of old, which quickens the flow of output of raw materials and foodstuffs available to the industrial countries. Suppose, for instance, that both demand and supply of primary products have been growing at 5 per cent per annum for some time over the course of successive boom and slump, so that despite rise and fall in the short run, prices have remained stable over time. Suppose, now, the opening up of new areas of production raises the potential growth of primary production to 6 per cent per annum. What happens? A fall in primary product prices is immediately generated which, if continued long enough, may eventually produce its own corrective in checking the growth of supply. We are interested, however, in what happens in the industrial countries.

Producers in industrial countries may of course try to substitute cheaper raw materials for more expensive domestic resources used before: for instance manufacturers may bother less about wasting materials and economise on labour instead, whilst consumers may shift their demand towards goods with larger import content.[2] It is

[1] It is necessary to make this qualification since if primary product prices are falling *because* of a prolonged slump in or slowing down in the rate of growth of industrial countries then we cannot expect the former to have independent effects on the growth of the latter.

[2] We assume here that consumers have been 'notified' of the greater abundance of imports by being charged appropriately lower prices.

unlikely, however, that the demand for raw materials and food will be elastic, hence prices may have to fall very considerably before much substitution takes place. In any case such substitution is likely to have a 'once for all' character rather than be a continuing process; so that, in the long run, the growth of demand for primary products remains tied to the growth of industrial capacity and output: unless the latter is raised, the growth of demand remains below the growth of supply, and the downward pressure on prices continues. However, there are reasons for believing that the growth rate of industrial countries will be raised.

The fall in primary product prices will tend, normally, to be associated with an improvement in the terms of trade of the industrial country, since although the latter's export prices may well follow import prices down, they tend to do so only after a time lag and at a slower rate. In the case of an under-developed primary producer country it was seen[1] that an improvement in the terms of trade was an important stimulant to growth through the associated increase in the capacity to import which affected its rate of investment; but the stimulus is not likely to be so great in the case of the specialised industrial country. In the first place, the capacity to import cannot be expected to improve to the same extent as the terms of trade: falling, or at least more slowly growing incomes and foreign exchange earnings of primary producers check the growth of their demand for manufactures, that is, they check the growth of demand for the exports of manufacturing countries. Hence a fall in, or at least a slower rate of growth of export volume, offsets the favourable effect of a fall in the price of imports, and the balances of payments of the industrial countries do not improve by as much as the latter itself would warrant. It is of course true that if despite, or perhaps because of, the fall in primary product prices, a greater volume of primary products is being sold, then the capacity to import of the industrial countries must be rising to some extent, that is, these countries must have been able to buy the greater volume of primary products; but the question remains 'What is causing the industrial countries to increase their demand for primary products?' Aside from this, an improvement in the capacity to import is not as vital for the industrial countries as it is for the primary producers: the latter rely heavily on imports of capital goods and equipment for building up their productive capacity at

[1] Chapter III.

home. Industrial countries, on the other hand, are their own suppliers of capital goods; and whilst their ability to import food and raw materials must grow over time if development is to continue, their rate of growth depends largely on their own ability to save, as well as on technical progress.

The benefit to be obtained by a specialised industrial country from an improvement in the terms of trade stems not so much from favourable effects on the capacity to import, but from the effect on the capacity to save and the inducement to invest. The growth of real income is raised relatively to the growth of real output, and theoretically at least, the ability of the country to save and to invest is increased, without there being further adverse effects on the relative level of consumption at home. The gain takes the form of a relative fall in the volume of exports as against the volume of imports, so that other things being equal, resources may be diverted from export production to other uses, which may of course include (and must do so, if growth is to benefit) capital accumulation at home. Naturally, the potential advantage to be gained from an improvement in the terms of trade can be lost if resources are not very mobile, or if there is a lack of incentive to use them in other ways. In this case unemployment and stagnation may result which obviously will not be favourable for growth. But in the case of a long run improvement this is perhaps a danger we need not stress, and we shall therefore ignore it in what follows. Furthermore, there are reasons for believing that the incentive to use resources in the domestic sector of the economy will be raised when primary product and food prices are showing a long term fall.

Falling food prices may certainly stimulate some increase in food consumption in the industrial countries, but demand is likely to be quite inelastic so that the proportion of income spent on food declines. Purchasing power in the industrial economies is therefore diverted away from imported food to the products of domestic manufacturing industry, raising demand here. The employment of resources in the manufacturing sector becomes more profitable and investment in these industries may be stimulated. At the same time, investment overseas becomes less profitable: falling primary product prices reduce the profitability of production in the primary producer countries, making them less favourable areas for investment. Hence there may well occur a shift in the distribution of investment in favour of home industries so that even if the rate of investment (domestic and foreign) is unaffected, the rate of capital formation at home rises.[1]

But the rate of investment itself (i.e. investment expressed as a proportion of national product) may also rise. This may come about as a result of a fall in the money rate of interest. Suppose that falling primary product prices are producing a fall in the general price level in industrial countries, partly as the direct result of falling costs of production, partly as the result of more stable money wages which allow improvements in labour productivity to have maximum benefit on costs. If the total supply of money is inelastic, rates of interest tend to fall, and investment in manufacturing industry and elsewhere will be encouraged. It is of course possible that a falling price level will have adverse psychological effects on businessmen's incentive to invest offsetting any favourable effects that a fall in the rate of interest might have; but it is important to note that in the circumstances we have postulated, such effects may be somewhat irrational. The fact that prices are falling does not imply that profits are being squeezed: on the contrary, if material costs and labour costs are falling fast enough, a rise in profits, in monetary terms as well as real, can take place even though prices are falling. If monetary profits are rising, investment may benefit from important liquidity effects as well.

Summarising then, we can say that a fall in primary product prices can be expected to have favourable effects on the growth rates of industrial countries since it raises both the *capacity* to invest and the *inducement* to invest in these countries: moreover, investment in home industries becomes more profitable than investment overseas. But the advantages are potential and need not be realised: if they are not, development is likely to suffer rather than to gain. If, for instance, investors, finding it less profitable to invest their savings overseas, prefer to keep them idle rather than invest at home, or if domestic entrepreneurs choose not to use them at home, then savings go to waste and unemployment and stagnation may result. Furthermore, the connection between primary product prices and the rate of growth of industrial

[1] The thesis that investment overseas tends to fluctuate inversely with fluctuations in primary product prices was advanced by Professor Cairncross to explain the direction of British investment in the nineteenth and early twentieth centuries. Whilst it has come under considerable criticism and is not completely supported by the facts, nonetheless it clearly remains a logical possibility; and we return to the point in a later chapter.

countries depends crucially on the *cause* of the fall in the former. As we have said earlier we need to distinguish clearly between a downward trend of primary product prices produced by expansionary forces acting independently on the side of supply — for instance, the opening up of new areas of production or the application of technological progress in older areas — and one produced by prolonged slump in one or some of the major industrial countries. In the latter case, it is the decline in the demand of the industrial countries produced by a fall in their output which produces the fall in primary product prices, and the latter cannot be expected to reverse the fall in industrial output. It may of course improve the terms of trade of the slumping countries, so that part of the consequence of the slump is passed on to the primary producing countries: the real income of the industrial countries does not then decline by as much as their output. But obviously the improvement in the terms of trade cannot be expected to have significant effects on output, largely because in the circumstances we are considering, the incentive to invest is likely to be low. Only if the improvement in the terms of trade succeeds in raising the rate of investment does industrial output pick up and resume its rate of growth.

Primary producing countries, whether developed or underdeveloped lose heavily when the demand for their exports contract as a result of a slump in industrial countries; and for reasons outlined in Chapter III are likely to find that their rate of growth suffers. Even when the fall in primary product prices is caused by longer run supply forces, for instance, technological progress and the development of new areas of production, a large proportion of the gain is passed on to the industrial countries through an improvement in the latter's terms of trade. Obviously they gain most from a long-term improvement in their export prices caused by the extension of demand in the industrial world, which raises both their capacity to save and their capacity to import. As we have said, this need not stem from an acceleration in the rate of growth of existing industrial countries, considered separately: the fact that some industrial areas are growing faster than others automatically raises the growth rate of world industrial capacity and output over time: moreover, new countries are constantly entering into the stage of industrialisation, thereby extending the demand for primary products. But the fact that primary product prices are rising may have consequences for the growth rates of individual industrial countries, causing them to slow down, for reasons that are basically opposite to those we have just considered.

Thus, if the terms of trade of industrial countries are being worsened by a persistent rise in primary product prices, their capacity to save and invest are correspondingly reduced, since real income now rises less rapidly than real output. Moreover, if the rise in primary product prices contains within it a rise in food prices, purchasing power is shifted away from the products of domestic manufacturing industry towards imported food: the profitability of domestic industries is correspondingly reduced. Profitability of investment in raw material producing countries, on the other hand, tends to rise as prices of their exports rise and investment may therefore shift away from home industries to foreign sources of supply. Finally, the rate of investment as a whole may be checked by a rise in the money rate of interest, which will tend to take place in sympathy with the rise in the general price level. All these factors may result in a slowing down in the rate of growth of industrial countries.

III

CONCLUSIONS

The foregoing analysis gives rise to certain important conclusions. The first is that primary producing countries and industrial countries are unlikely to experience their fastest growth rates at the same time. When the former receive a stimulus to their growth, due to a secular rise in primary product prices and an improvement in their terms of trade, the latter suffer a check to growth: conversely, when the former's growth is slowed down by a fall in primary product prices, the latter's growth is stimulated. Furthermore, if it is true that conditions of primary product supply produce an inherent, secular fluctuation in primary product prices, then they tend to produce similar fluctuations in the growth rates of industrial and primary producer countries. Growth rates will be higher at some times than at others, and when industrial countries' growth rates are high, primary producer countries' growth rates will be low; and vice versa.

The second conclusion to be drawn bears on the general topic of inquiry with which this book is primarily concerned, namely, to what extent it can be said that faster economic growth goes hand-in-hand with inflation, and vice versa? We see now that the answer may well depend partly, although not of course wholly, on the type of country in question, for instance, whether it is a primary producer or whether it is a specialist manufacturing country. If it is true that a sustained rise in primary product prices causes inflation in both primary producers and industrial countries alike, and if it is further true that it quickens the overall economic growth of primary producers whilst retarding that of the industrial countries, then it follows that, ignoring all other factors affecting prices, inflation is likely to be associated with faster economic growth in primary producers and with slower economic growth in industrial countries. For opposite reasons, a falling or stable price level will go hand-in-hand with slower growth in primary producers and faster growth in the industrial countries. In the case of the industrial countries, however, the connection between falling or stable prices and faster economic growth is by no means as certain as is the connection between rising prices and slower growth. This is because of the reasons we have set out earlier, namely that a fall in primary product prices may itself be the direct result of a slump in, or at least a check to the growth of industrial countries, produced by forces quite independent of the balance between demand and supply of primary products; and even when the fall in primary product prices is caused by forces operating independently on the side of supply, the potential advantage to be gained by industrial countries may in fact be thrown away.

It by no means emerges so clearly that the rate of growth of a more self-sufficient, or closed, economy can be connected with the behaviour of its price level in the same way. We have argued earlier that a slowing down in the rate of growth of agriculture, produced autonomously by factors operating on the side of supply, will, in certain circumstances, produce a rise in the general price level. Moreover, since in a self-sufficient country, agriculture must remain an important sector of the economy, a slowing down in its growth rate must *directly* affect the growth rate of the economy as a whole, the extent to which it does being greater, the larger is agricultural output relatively to total national product.[1] But, in

---

[1] From this point of view, the specialised industrial country and the self-sufficient economy can be contrasted. In the former, variations in agricultural growth have negligible *direct* effects on the overall growth rate.

addition, other forces may be set up which operate to slow down growth in the rest of the economy. If, for instance, agricultural and primary product input is, for technical reasons, a fixed proportion of final output in the rest of the economy, then it would seem inevitable that the rate of growth of the latter should also slow down. But substitution of labour and other factors for raw materials can take place, and synthetic substitutes may be developed. Moreover, a change in the *composition* of non-agricultural, perhaps induced by relative price changes, can take place which reduces the growth of demand for raw materials without there being a fall in the rate of growth of final output.

In an exceptional case, a change in the terms of exchange between agricultural products and manufactures may involve a rise in the share of agriculture in national income at the expense of other sectors of the economy,[1] in which case some effect on the overall propensities of the economy to save and invest might be expected. For instance, it might be argued that because of the predominance of family type production units in agriculture and of employer/employee relationships in industry, a rise in agriculture's share increases the equality of income distribution and therefore lowers the propensity to save. On the other hand, it has been suggested that farmers are notorious hoarders and/or heavily in debt to the banking system, so that a rise in their share of national income leads to an increase in the propensity to hoard or to retire bank debt, with depressing effects on the overall propensity to invest. It is doubtful, however, whether anything useful can be said about this on purely *a priori* grounds. An important thing to note, however, is that in a closed economy changes in the terms of exchange between agriculture and industry do not involve losses of income, either absolute or relative, for the economy as a whole: industry's loss is the farm sector's gain, and *vice versa*. Hence any effect on saving and investment must stem from changes in the *propensities* to save and invest brought about by relative income shifts. In the case of the specialised industrial country or the specialised primary product exporter, however, changes in the terms of exchange between agriculture and industry necessarily involve relative shifts of income distribution which are *international* rather than national: the country *as a whole* can lose or

---

[1] This would be exceptional since in the long run the normal development would be for the share of agriculture to decline.

gain: so that saving and investment can suffer independently of what happens to the propensities. It is for this reason that the growth of specialised countries is more likely to be affected by such a change in the terms of exchange than is the growth of the more 'closed' economy.

There are, however, two possible ways in which the growth rate of the 'closed' economy may be affected by a slowing down in the agricultural growth rate — apart from the obvious *direct* effect associated with agricultural output being a component of national product. First, if the terms of exchange of agriculture are improving, agriculture becomes a more profitable sector in which to invest, and the distribution of capital formation may move in favour of agriculture. If agricultural investment typically has a longer gestation period than other sorts of investment[1] then, for a time at least, the growth rate of the economy as a whole may be further slowed down. In the second place, if an improvement in agriculture's terms of exchange takes place in the environment of a rising general price level — for which, for reasons given earlier,[2] there is a general presumption — then the money rate of interest may also be rising,[3] and investment may therefore be restricted generally. If this happens at the same time that industry is proving less attractive to investment than is agriculture, growth of the manufacturing sector may be significantly slowed down in sympathy with agriculture. For these reasons, therefore, we might expect to find that a slowing down in the overall rate of growth is accompanied by a general rise in the price level.

But it is not always the case that an improvement in agriculture's terms of exchange is caused by a slowing down in the agricultural growth rate: equally it may be produced by an acceleration of industrial growth. If this is the case, then clearly we cannot look for a slowing down in the growth rate of the self-sufficient economy as a whole. On the contrary, since we are not postulating a fall in agriculture's growth but an acceleration of industry's growth, then the economy as a whole will be growing at a faster rate than before. Admittedly, forces may gradually be produced that eventually tend to check industry's growth rate but these will take time to have

[1] See W. W. Rostow, *Process of Economic Growth* (Oxford).
[2] Pages 63–73.
[3] Although the quantity of money is unlikely to prevent prices from rising, increases in it may be lagging behind the rise in money incomes, causing interest rates to rise.

effect: in the meantime economic development is taking place at a faster rate, and at the same time, prices are likely to be rising.

Hence there is no general presumption that a rise in the general price level will necessarily be associated either with faster growth or with slower growth: it largely depends on what is causing the improvement in agriculture's terms of exchange, that is, whether it is a slowing down of agricultural growth relatively to industrial growth, or an acceleration of the latter relatively to the former, which is the underlying cause of the behaviour of the price level. Nonetheless, the most favourable factor for promoting faster economic development is a speeding up of agriculture's growth which both worsens agriculture's terms of exchange and is conducive to accelerated development in other sectors of the economy as well; and as we have seen, in these circumstances, there are good reasons for thinking that prices will fall, or at least remain stable. Hence, it is tempting to conclude that faster economic growth is more likely to be associated with a fall in the general price level than a rise in it. But this association would not, of course, exist if the worsening in agriculture's terms of exchange was produced by a slackening in industrial growth, itself caused by factors independent of agriculture.

It is obvious that in this chapter and the previous one we have laid great stress on the relative growths of agriculture and industry which, so it has been argued, play a large part in determining the behaviour of the price level in the longer run. But we must now recognise that this is not the only force that bears on prices: there are others that appear during the course of economic development that may reinforce or subtract from those we have just been considering. The most important of these are linked with changes in industrial organisation and market structure that tend to go hand in hand with economic development, as well as with the increasing influence and power of labour organisations, and the greater responsibility of government for general economic activity. In the next chapter therefore we shall go on to examine the nature of these forces; and, in later ones, we shall illustrate their workings in the post-war United States and United Kingdom economies.

Chapter V

ECONOMIC DEVELOPMENT AND THE PRICE LEVEL IN THE INSTITUTIONAL ECONOMY

Once a country has reached an advanced stage of industrial development and a high level of real income, new forces begin to bear on the price level and on the relationship between it and further economic growth. These forces stem partly from the nature of the output produced by the economy, partly from the nature of industrial organisation and of the markets in which products are sold, and partly from the greater responsibility of and intervention by government in economic and social affairs.

Traditional economic theory stresses that, in the absence of government interference, prices of goods and services are determined by the interplay of supply and demand: it teaches that prices tend to settle at the level at which supply and demand balance, clearing the market. Put in this way, theory suggests that producers do not directly fix the prices of the goods they sell but influence them indirectly by varying their outputs or supplies. Where there are many small producers, each producing a homogeneous product, the action of any one of them may not be significant enough to affect market price, so that unless there is collusion between them, each will have to accept price as determined by the market. This conclusion may hold broadly true in the case of many agricultural and other primary products sold in international, and even national, markets, but it clearly does not hold true for the great majority of industrial goods and services, over which producers do hold some price control. Of course, economic theory recognises that producers do fix their prices directly in uncompetitive markets, whether as the result of being able to control a substantial proportion of total supply or whether as the result of being able to differentiate their products. Nonetheless, theory emphasises that prices are not set arbitrarily since producers generally aim at maximising profits. In fixing their prices, in other words, they have to take account of demand and cost of supply; and the

G

notion of the *equilibrium* price (that is, the price that clears the market) therefore remains valid. In these circumstances, when price is directly fixed by the producer, output and sales have to be adjusted to demand: the producer cannot choose freely both his price and his output. Theory teaches further that when output can be expanded without a significant rise in marginal costs, an increase in demand will cause no rise in price;[1] but if it cannot be expanded at all or only at the expense of a significant rise in marginal costs, then price will tend to rise as producers carry out the necessary price adjustment to maximise profits. Conversely, a fall in demand tends to result, at some point, in a fall in price.

Whilst it is obvious that the great majority of goods and services sold in an advanced industrial economy have prices that are formally fixed by producers, it is not clear that these prices are always or even generally fixed at the level that just clears the market and maximises the short run profits of the producers. If they were fixed in this fashion, we should expect them to move much more frequently than they do in practice, particularly when the economy is working at or close to the point of full employment of labour and capacity. It is well recognised that the prices of many services in a modern economy are typically very inflexible: for example, lawyers' and doctors' fees, and prices charged by hairdressers change very infrequently, and then usually when there has been some significant change in the value of money. Of course, the supply of many personal services is highly elastic even in the short run, but it is doubtful whether this fact alone explains price rigidity. Custom no doubt plays at least as large a part. In many cases, too, the rigidity of price in the face of short run fluctuations in demand has a great deal to do with the nature of the product itself: it is not possible, for instance, for the price of a newspaper to fluctuate during the course of the day to ensure the sale of the editions, nor is it likely that it will fluctuate from week to week in response to changes in its popularity. Many goods, particularly those of a capital nature, are made to order and according to particular specifications; and the idea of a market clearing price has therefore very little meaning. Prices of other goods are either fixed or regulated by government, or are subject to legal agreements. For instance, public utilities, whether they are nationalised or not, are not usually allowed to set prices that would maximise profits;

---

[1] Assuming no change in the elasticity of demand at the same price.

instead price increases have usually to be justified to government and public on grounds of higher costs. And rents of houses and property are often controlled by governments or are subject to long leases, and change very slowly over time, without much reference to the current state of demand and supply. Apart from these somewhat special cases, however, short run price inflexibility is characteristic of a wide range of manufactured goods as well.

The elasticity of supply of manufactured goods tends to be quite high, even in the short run, but this fact alone cannot explain why prices fail to respond readily to demand. Even when firms, because they are working close to full capacity, are unable to satisfy current demand from current output, they do not always try to choke off this demand by raising prices. Recent experience in both the United Kingdom and the United States — for example in the automobile industry — suggests that firms often prefer to allow orders to accumulate, to quote longer delivery dates and to ration their wholesale and retail outlets, whenever this is possible. Nor do they readily lower their prices with a view to increasing their sales, or preventing them from falling, at the expense of their competitors: instead, they prefer to employ various forms of non-price competition, such as advertising and product differentiation, etc. There are good reasons why established firms should behave in this way. Their position in the market depends not only on the prices they charge for their products but on a variety of other factors as well, for instance, on the extent to which they advertise, and offer complementary services, and on their reputation as to quality and fair dealing. As a result of these factors, they will have built up a network of relationships with suppliers and customers which they will not wish to destroy by taking advantage of what may prove to be a temporary boom in the demand for their products.[1] They realise, too, that other firms are in a similar position, and they therefore expect that any attempt on their part to attract customers by cutting prices will be met with retaliation by their competitors. Moreover, in many industries competition by price cutting may prove highly dangerous. Thus, where an industry is dominated by a few large concerns, prices tend to be set with a view to the reactions of the main competitors rather than with a

---

[1] See R. Heflebower, 'Towards a theory of Industrial Markets and Prices', *American Economic Review*, May 1954; and 'Full Costs, Cost Changes and Prices', 'Business Concentration and Price Policy', *National Bureau of Economic Research*, 1955.

view to the reactions of consumers. Where no agreement between
the firms exists, a price reduction made by one producer is likely
to be met by a similar reduction by his competitors. The first must
lower his price again to retain his competitive advantage, and the
process may continue. In industries where capital costs relatively
to other costs are high, the limit to price cutting will be average
prime or direct costs which will be much below average total costs.
All firms may therefore end up by failing to cover their full costs,
and they would remain in this unprofitable state until agreement
between them is reached or some have been forced out. There is
good reason, therefore, for agreement on prices to be reached at
the outset; and once prices have been set little change in them will
take place, except in response to a change in costs that affects all.
Even then prices are more likely to rise when costs rise, than fall
when costs fall; for whereas a rise in price may be necessary to
maintain the customary, satisfactory profit, a fall cannot be relied
on to increase total sales and revenue if consumers' demand is
inelastic; profits are therefore best allowed to rise. Similarly, a fall
in total demand for the output of the industry will not lead to a
fall in price: producers have an interest in avoiding a price war and
probably assume that consumers' demand is inelastic in the face of
a generally agreed cut in prices. Whilst such price behaviour is no
doubt more obviously found in oligopolistic and capital intensive
industries, there seems reason to believe it typical of smaller
producers and more competitive industries as well. Quite apart
from the risk that customers will be annoyed by repeated adjustments to prices a policy of meeting short run fluctuations in demand with price variations may introduce an element of speculation into consumers' demand. Consumers may refrain from buying
if they expect prices to fall, and accelerate their purchases when
they expect them to rise. At times, such behaviour on customers'
part would be an advantage; at other times, however, it might
militate against a smooth flow of output and deliveries, and, in the
end, possibly raise costs. Producers might find that they lost more
than they gained. In many cases, it is often quite impracticable for
producers to change their prices at frequent intervals: prices have
to be set for the season or the year, they must be advertised, and
there must be time for them to become known by consumers so
that comparison between competing products can be made. In
consequence, competition between firms in a modern industrial

society tends to be carried on more by means of advertising, product differentiation, and the provision of complementary services; and where price competition does take place, it tends to be concealed, for example through the offering of rebates, discounts, special offers, trade-in prices and so on, rather than be overt.

The implication of such a pricing policy is that prices are fixed in some relation to costs. The relevant costs may be average *direct* costs (i.e., the cost of materials and wage labour per unit of output) or average *full* costs, including overheads, at some standard level of output, which is likely to be somewhat below full capacity output. In either case, a margin will be added which, provided the standard output is successfully sold, will be sufficient to produce at least a prescribed return on invested capital.[1] In fact, of course, in fixing his price initially, the producer must relate his expectations concerning sales at various prices (derived from his appreciation of the existing market situation) to his expectations concerning costs at various outputs: he chooses those levels of price and output that are likely to yield the maximum return on capital that he thinks can be sustained over a longish period. Hence demand obviously enters into the pricing decision. But the important thing is that, provided *satisfactory* profits are being earned, the producer will not experiment with prices, once they have been set, in the hope of maximising his profits in the short run: in conditions of long run uncertainty, probably the best way of maximising profits in the long run is to ensure that satisfactory profits are constantly being earned in the short run.[2] Naturally, producers will not leave prices unchanged for long if experience shows that they have been set at a level that fails to cover costs and give a satisfactory profit, or if costs show a subsequent and significant rise. Moreover producers may also take advantage of periodic reviews of their price, sales and costs position to raise or lower their profit margins when it is obvious that their estimates of demand have been far out of line. But granted this, it remains true to say that prices are relatively inflexible in the short run; and, when they do change, respond more easily to changes in costs than they do to changes in demand. In

[1] Prescribed, in the sense that at least this return is required if the entrepreneur is to go into production at all.
[2] See R. A. Gordon, 'Short Period Price Determination in Theory and Practice', *American Economic Review*, June 1948; and Fellner 'Average Cost Pricing and the Theory of Uncertainty', *Journal of Political Economy*, June 1948.

practice, this implies that they are more likely to rise when there is excess demand than fall when demand is deficient.

Typically, then, prices of goods and services in a modern industrial community are not determined on a market clearing basis. The same is largely true of the remuneration of factors of production, particularly of labour. The existence of strong labour unions and of employers' federations precludes a highly competitive labour market, and wage rates, at least, tend to be settled by bargaining between the two sides of industry. This is not to deny that wage earnings tend to rise when labour is scarce in relation to demand: whatever the actions of the trade unions, which, since union solidarity is high and employers are vulnerable to strike action, are likely to be both militant and successful in such conditions, wage earnings are likely to be bid up as employers pay overtime rates, and attempt to attract labour from each other by paying over the negotiated rates. Full employment of labour is likely to be associated with high profits in industry and a sellers' market for goods; hence employers are not reluctant to grant wage increases, even in excess of productivity changes, most or all of which they can pass on in higher prices. The important thing is, however, that wages do not necessarily cease to rise when there is no excess demand or even when the level of employment is not excessively high. In modern societies, trade unions have achieved an independent wage determining role which enables them, through threat of strikes, non-co-operation, etc., to force through wage awards despite current demand. Moreover, the climate of public opinion is often favourable to wage increases which take place, not on grounds that labour is short, but on grounds, for instance, that certain classes of labour are badly paid relatively to others: the social conscience is a potent factor in determining the rewards of many types of labour. Also, employers and public are often sympathetic to wage demands made on the basis of earlier rises in the cost of living even when labour is not in a strong bargaining position. The right of labour to share in productivity increase is also widely accepted; and although this might be achieved by falling prices, unions feel, probably rightly, that money wage awards are quicker and more certain. Indeed, in some industries, in which stable labour relations are highly important, wage agreements are made to cover a number of years, and include agreed adjustments for changes in the cost of living and agreed periodic wage increases to cover anticipated rises in productivity. The implication of such agreements and of the other factors mentioned earlier is that wage changes take place which are largely independent of the current state of demand and supply. Moreover, the fact that wage earnings tend to rise automatically with productivity is a further factor reducing the downward flexibility of prices.

The bargaining power of unions is not the same in all industries. It is probably strongest in those whose production processes involve much capital relatively to labour. Changes in wage rates then affect total costs less; moreover, in such industries annual increases in productivity tend to be substantial. The cost to employers of a prolonged strike is also great since, in the event of one, expensive capital equipment has to be left idle. In consequence, employers are keen on ensuring stable and peaceful relations with their employees, and are often therefore prepared to enter into long term wage contracts which give guaranteed annual wage rate increases plus appropriate adjustments for changes in the cost of living. Also, the output of many capital intensive industries, for instance, steel, provides the basic industrial materials for other industries, and the demand for it is likely to be quite inelastic: hence producers have little fear that they cannot pass on the increase in their costs. These industries, therefore, occupy a key role in the wage struggle. Once wage increases are granted here — and it is easier to get them than in other industries even when demand for labour is not excessive — wage demands, on grounds of parity, begin to spread elsewhere. Employers feel forced to grant them in order to retain their labour force or to ensure peaceful labour relations, and to the extent that they cannot meet them with increased labour productivity, pay for them by charging higher prices. Thus wage increases begin to spread throughout the economy, and prices of many goods and services begin to rise. Further pressure, on grounds of rising cost of living, is then put behind the wage-price spiral.

Even if it be accepted that trade unions can and do exert an independent wage determining role, is it legitimate to ignore aggregate monetary demand? Theory does not deny that money wages and perhaps the prices of goods, can be raised by trade union pressure, but it maintains that employment will consequently fall, if demand for the product does not rise. But this is a partial view. Employment would tend to fall if the rise in money wages was concentrated in one industry only. If the rise in money wages is general or at least widespread throughout industry, then to some extent it is self-supporting. The rise in money wages will not be immediately countered by a rise in unemployment, and if it is not, then the total wage bill in the economy rises and so does the purchasing power in the hands of a large section of the community. In other words, wages are not only costs, they are also incomes. Hence at the same time that costs are rising so are money incomes and demand.[1] In this sense, the wage-price spiral is self-supporting, and once again it is difficult to disentangle cause and effect: both demand and cost pressure are at work simultaneously.

But the spiral *is only to some extent* self-supporting. A substantial part of aggregate monetary demand for goods and services is not directly related to consumers' purchasing power and therefore is not directly increased by any growth in the latter. Even if we put aside export demand, there remain the substantial components government expenditure and investment. The former, however, is likely to rise automatically with the cost of satisfying it, since most government expenditure is of an essential nature and normally governments will not be prepared to see it cut back in real terms when prices and wages rise. To some extent, too, increased *money* expenditure by government is automatically self financing: rising wage and other incomes increase the tax yield of a given tax rate structure, more than proportionately to the rise in incomes when the system is progressive. In other words, the government may find itself in no financial difficulty in raising its expenditure to keep pace with prices. With private investment expenditure it is a different story. On the one hand, of course, rising prices may increase the inducement to invest: on the other hand, if the government is pursuing an inflexible monetary policy, credit may become tight and interest rates rise. In a modern economy with a well developed financial system, there exists a large fund of liquidity that can be drawn on for a time, so that in the early stages of the inflation, a shortage of finance may not inhibit investment. But there is a limit to this, and if the money supply is not allowed to expand, eventually investment and perhaps consumption (where this is geared to credit, for instance, through instalment buying)

[1] Monetary demand does not rise proportionately to money incomes since with a progressive tax system, an increasing proportion of incomes is taken in taxation.

will tend to fall, or at least not rise with prices. If export demand is also cut back, then the spiral of wages and prices eventually produces a rise in unemployment.

But the recession in employment and output may have to go a long way before the spiral is brought to an end. Rising unemployment gradually reduces the power of trade unions to play an independent wage determining role, but the experience of many countries shows that unemployment may have to rise to quite high levels before union policy is significantly affected. It is in this respect that government aims and policies become crucial. In most advanced industrial societies, governments have come to accept the responsibility of maintaining a high level of employment and of ironing out booms and slumps. They are often therefore presented with a dilemma — should they let monetary demand rise sufficiently to permit wage and price increases without causing further unemployment, or allow the unemployment to take its course in the interests of stabilising wages and prices? Unemployment is the more obvious evil, and political pressure to avoid serious unemployment soon becomes intense. Moreover, as will be stressed later, firm action to prevent the average price level from rising at all may involve policies checking growth, which again is undesirable. Faced with such a dilemma, it is not surprising that governments often choose to let prices rise rather than to let output and employment fall. In effect government economic and social aims tend to underwrite the cumulative rise in wages and prices.

To summarise these brief introductory remarks so far: in a modern industrial society prices are not typically set at a level that maximises the profits of producers, certainly not in the short run and probably not in the long run either; nor do they respond quickly and freely to the changing balance between supply and demand. Instead, they tend to be set in some relation to costs, probably average prime costs, changing when these change: and the gross profit mark up is probably a matter of custom or practice, in the particular trade or industry concerned, but it will be large enough to cover average fixed costs at some planned or expected level of output (which is not likely to be the maximum that the plant is capable of) and at the same time produce a satisfactory return on capital. Similarly, trade unions, public opinion and government policy play an important, independent role in the determination of both the level of wages and wage differentials, whilst the consequences for employment of such independent wage fixing tend to be looked after by government objectives and policies. Thus, although such an economy may well remain free enterprise, in the sense that the means of production are privately owned and production is carried on for private profit, it is not characterised by free competitive markets; and money wages and prices cannot be said to be determined solely, or even mainly, by purely economic forces. An appropriate name to give to such an economy is the *institutional* economy, and in the remainder of this chapter we shall refer to it in these terms.

With these considerations in mind, we shall now go on to examine their consequences for the behaviour of the price level in the course of economic growth.

Economic growth implies that both aggregate demand for goods and services and the capacity to supply them are growing over time. On the supply side, there will be a potential maximum rate of growth which is determined partly by the rate of increase of available factors of production, land, labour and capital, and partly by the rate at which their efficiency in use rises. If the rate of growth of aggregate demand falls short of this maximum rate of growth of output, then the latter will remain potential and unrealised and development will be slower than it might otherwise be; on the other hand if demand is growing at a faster rate, then excess demand pressures will appear. Hence, the task of policy appears to be to keep a balance between the growth of demand and the growth of potential supply.

If demand is growing at a faster rate than supply then the excess demand pressures that are set up will tend to cause prices to rise. This is so despite what we have said about the relative inflexibility of prices to demand. Most producers in pricing their products have in mind some normal or standard level of output which their plant and equipment is best able to produce; but if demand warrants it, actual output can usually be taken beyond this point, with, at first, little effect on direct costs per unit of output. There is then no immediate pressure to raise prices, since fixed costs per unit of output will still be falling, and profits may therefore be rising. Once average direct costs rise significantly, however, more than offsetting the fall in average fixed costs, then prices will soon be adjusted upwards: but producers will see this adjustment as one necessitated by a rise in their costs, not as one that is taking advantage of demand to raise profits. Furthermore, the producer may be involved in hiring more labour to satisfy the demand for his product, and if this can only be obtained at the expense of rising wage rates or earnings generally, then again prices are likely to rise. Although rising costs seem to provide the immediate justification for a rise in price, nonetheless it is clearly the expansion of demand for the product that lies at the bottom of inflation. This remains true even when a particular producer has not experienced a rise in demand for his particular output — or at least has not experienced a rise in demand greater than he can easily satisfy on the basis of his existing plant and labour — but still has to raise his price because of the generally higher cost of labour and raw materials: for him the rise in price has been produced by a rise in cost but the latter has been caused by generally excessive demand elsewhere in the economy. In such circumstances a debate about whether the resulting price inflation is demand induced or cost pushed, is rather sterile. To the producer, a rise in his price is a defensive reaction against a rise in his costs, but the economist has to point out that the producers' costs are in the last resort the prices of factors of production, and the latter are rising because of a deficiency of supply relatively to demand. From the view point of one aspect of policy, however, two things are important. First, in the case where factor of production prices are rising because of excess demand for them, employment is also likely to be rising — at least, it is not likely to be falling. Hence, the government objective of full employment of labour is not being jeopardised by the rise in money wages and prices. Second, where the rise in prices and wages is being produced by aggregate excess demand for both goods and labour, inflation can be checked by removing the excess demand without unfavourable effects on employment. Thus from this point of view no dilemma confronts government policy: it can aim at price stability without worrying about adverse effects on employment.

Even so, governments may be faced with another dilemma. There is advantage to be gained from pressing an economy to produce at near its maximum capacity output. As we indicated earlier, profits are likely to be rising substantially when the 'planned' capacity output is being exceeded. Hence producers do not lack financial resources for further investment. At the same time, when existing plant and machinery are being worked to the limit, the inducement to invest in further capital equipment is so much the greater. The prospects of further economic growth are therefore enhanced, and the government may be reluctant to spoil these prospects by keeping the economy on too tight a rein. Thus there may be some incompatibility between faster economic growth and price stability even when the latter is being menaced by forces on the side of demand; but this is by no means the most serious form which this incompatibility takes, as we shall now go on to demonstrate.

To argue that excess demand for goods and services *in aggregate* eventually causes prices to rise is not to deny that prices can rise in its absence. In an open economy, for example, a rise in imported raw material costs may put pressure on producers' costs and prices even when no excess demand exists. If prices rise as a consequence, trade unions will not be slow to ask for compensating wage adjustments, and a spiral is soon under way. Moreover, as we have implied earlier, trade unions may exert an *independent* autonomous pressure on prices by demanding periodic increases in wage rates, in excess of the corresponding increases in productivity. But in addition to these pressures, there is yet another inherent in the process of growth, which taken in conjunction with the prevalent mode of price fixing discussed earlier, ensures that prices will tend to rise over time.

We have said that economic growth implies an increase in aggregate demand for goods and services over time. But it does not follow that demand for the products of every industry is growing at the same rate over time. Some demands will be growing at a faster rate than others, some may not be growing at all, and some may even be declining. Thus even if *aggregate* demand is kept in line with *aggregate* supply, it is possible that excessive demand will appear in some sectors of the economy, matched by deficiency of demand elsewhere. It is of course the function of relative price changes to induce redistribution of resources so as to bring accord between the composition of output and the composition of demand; but prices are not so flexible nor resources typically so mobile that imbalances do not occur. Hence we can be sure that the most effective control over *aggregate* demand will not prevent excess demand from appearing in some sectors at least; and for the reasons we have just indicated, some prices are likely to rise. Even so, the *general price* level might still remain stable, if prices fall in other sectors where demand is deficient in relation to supply. However, we have argued earlier that prices are not typically very responsive to the pressure of demand except where cost changes are also involved: furthermore, prices of industrial goods tend to rise more easily than they fall.[1] Thus the relative price changes that must take place when the compositions of aggregate demand and supply do not match, tend to occur in the context of a rise in the general price level, since rising prices tend to predominate over falling ones.

But this rise in the general price level is not just a statistical phenomenon associated with a particular form of relative price change: it is also the direct result of the spread of cost inflation throughout the economy as a whole. Excess demand for the products of some industries induces producers in these industries to take steps to increase their output. The demand for particular types of raw materials and for specialised intermediate materials will therefore increase, causing their prices to rise. More labour will be demanded, which will generally involve producers in paying higher money wages to draw labour from elsewhere. This will not greatly disturb producers in expanding industries since it is typical for labour productivity to be rising fast when output rises fast. In any case, unions are likely to put pressure on employers once they see profits rising with output. Thus a wave of rising material prices and of wage rates begins to spread out from the expanding sector of the economy; and industries for whose products demand is not excessive and may even be deficient cannot fail to be affected. Even if their own demand for materials and labour declines, it by no means follows that the prices and wages they have to pay will fall. Many intermediate materials, for instance, steel, are produced by highly capital intensive industries which are reluctant to lower their prices in the face of a decline in demand; and although the relatively contracting industries might be quite prepared to see their labour force decline, they still have to pay out higher money wages to what remains. They will be faced with pressure from trade unions who will demand that they give wage increases comparable to those obtained in the more successful parts of the economy; and in any case, it may be to the advantage of even the stagnating industries to raise money wages when they are rising elsewhere, for although sufficient labour can be obtained at lower money wages, the result might be a disgruntled and less efficient labour force.

[1] We really mean by this that a given amount of excess demand will tend to produce a larger *rise* in price than the same amount of excess supply will produce a fall.

But the rise in money wage rates will seldom be matched by a comparable increase in productivity: indeed the stagnating industries may find their labour costs rising even more than they are rising in the expanding industries, since it is typically the case that productivity increases faster when demand and output are rising. Moreover, the contracting industries will find their overhead costs per unit of output also rising if output has to be contracted. For all these reasons, therefore, some sectors of the economy in which there is no excess demand and in which it may even be deficient, will find their costs of production rising at least as fast as in the more rapidly expanding ones. Unlike the latter, however, the former will not be in a position to pass on fully their higher costs to their customers, and in consequence their profits will suffer. Even so, it is unlikely that they can lower their prices; and declining demand will normally be met by a decline in output.

Thus it follows from this discussion that a contrived balance between the growth of aggregate demand and the growth of aggregate supply cannot be relied on to keep prices stable; and a policy recommendation framed with purely aggregate demand in mind is therefore not sufficient. In the same way and for largely the same sort of reason, a policy recommendation which emphasizes the regulation of wages also falls down. It is often argued, for instance, by those who put emphasis on the role of costs as the prime mover of prices, that inflation can be avoided if wage increases are kept in line with productivity increases. But it is clear that this argument comes up against the same snags as that which emphasises control over aggregate demand.

The reason for this is the fact that productivity increases do not take place uniformly throughout the economy. Some industries, by virtue of the nature of their product and of the production processes involved, are able to increase productivity at a rapid rate, whilst others, through no fault on the part of management or labour, can increase productivity only slowly, if at all. The question then arises: what productivity growth is to be taken as the measure for money wage increases? There seem to be two possibilities, both of which clearly give rise to considerable difficulties.

First, it might be argued that money wages paid in each industry should rise with productivity in each industry: this would ensure that labour costs remained constant in each industry. Prices would also remain constant *provided the government is able to regulate demand for each industry's product* so that it does not outstrip the growth of supply. But a number of objections must be considered. In the first place, considerable and growing inequalities between workers in different industries would arise: some workers would find their pay packets increasing rapidly from one year to the next, whilst others would benefit only slowly. Such unequal treatment could not always be defended on grounds of harder work, greater skill and efficiency, etc.: for as we have said, it is not necessarily the fault of workers or managers that a particular industry increases its productivity only slowly compared with some other. Trade unions would not easily accept wide and growing differentials not justified by skill or effort: indeed as we have argued earlier they are likely to use the large wage increases granted by the faster growing productivity industries as the basis for wage claims elsewhere. Equally important is the fact that society itself would not be prepared to accept large and growing inequalities over time: the general view in modern communities is that all sections of the community should benefit fairly equally in the fruits of economic growth; and although many weapons, such as fiscal policy, may be deployed towards this end, the determination of relative incomes and rewards also plays a part. Hence pressure to even out money wage increases would soon build up, and the policy could hardly survive for long. Quite apart from the ethical considerations involved, lagging money wages in the more backward industries would make labour recruitment difficult. It does not follow that because productivity can only grow slowly in a particular industry, demand for its output also grows slowly as economic growth takes place. In the absence of selective control over demand by the government it might be that demand for the product of a particular industry is increasing at a faster rate than increases in productivity alone would satisfy; hence the labour force may have to be added to over time, and this will be difficult if money wage increases are lagging far behind those paid by other industries. Conversely, whilst demand for the product of the faster productivity growth industries will be rising over time, it may not grow fast enough to absorb all the extra output that productivity increases would permit; over time the labour force would have to be contracted relatively to other industries, and this might involve a check to money wages. Hence an evening up of money wages may take place quite apart from pressures exerted by unions and society.

This suggests that the alternative policy should be followed, namely that money wages generally should rise at the same rate as *average* productivity in the economy.[1] Theoretically, some prices would then rise, some would fall, but the average price level would remain unchanged. All sections of the community would then benefit from the rise in their money incomes.[2] In practice, however, this policy comes up against the reluctance (which we have been stressing so much) of producers in a modern industrial economy to compete by reducing their prices, even when their costs enable them to do so. Certainly some prices would have to rise, as money wages increased at a greater rate than productivity; others, however, would not fall so readily, even though money wages rose less fast than productivity. Hence, the general price level would tend to rise, and statistically we should once again have inflation. Moreover, in industries where prices did not fall with labour costs, profits would rise, and this again would make it difficult to confine wage increase in these industries to the average rise elsewhere. The policy in fact would soon break down.

We must conclude that neither a policy which turns solely on the control of *aggregate* demand nor one that turns on the regulation of money wages can be regarded as the complete answer to the problem of achieving growth with price stability. Both tend to fall down, partly because changes in the *pattern* of aggregate demand and differing rates of productivity growth are inherent in the process in growth, and partly because institutional factors produce an inflexibility of prices, particularly in the downward direction. It could be argued that neither changes in the pattern of demand nor differing rates of productivity growth are new phenomena in developing economies yet prices have not risen constantly over time: in fact we can point to the experience of the United Kingdom, the United States and other countries to demonstrate that economic growth is compatible with a long period of falling prices.[3] Of course this is true, but there are at least two important factors that must be taken into account.

In the first place, it is probably true that prices tend to be more

---

[1] Except perhaps for differentials required to redistribute the labour force according to the pattern of demand.

[2] This ignores the problems of those such as pensioners, who are unable to bring about an increase in their money incomes by their own efforts, since they do not sell anything and do not have bargaining power.

[3] For instance, in the last quarter of the nineteenth century.

flexible in the less developed economy. This is partly a matter of industrial organisation and markets: firms tend to be smaller, less capital intensive and less monopolistic, but mainly it is the result of agricultural output being a larger part of total output, and, as we have admitted, agricultural prices tend to be much more flexible both upwards and downwards than industrial prices. The second factor is more important, particularly with respect to policy recommendations. The fact is — we have emphasised it in an earlier chapter — the economic growth of the present day developed countries did not typically pursue a smooth path of constantly rising output and income. Periods of rapidly rising output were followed by periods of falling output, the former, of course, predominating in amplitude, so that output rose over time. Prices tended to rise in the course of the boom, but were checked in the subsequent slump. If the latter was severe enough prices of industrial as well as agricultural products could even be forced down. Taking boom and slump together prices could therefore remain stable or even fall.[1] During severe slumps, however, unemployment and bankruptcies were quite severe and led to considerable social distress. Hence governments became increasingly determined to avoid severe declines in economic activity; moreover their ability to do so has increased over time. Thus the onset of a slump is likely to lead to rapid and effective measures on the part of government to maintain demand and output, and to prevent employment from falling. All of which, of course, is highly desirable but which clearly has implications for the price level.

If governments are not prepared to allow severe depressions to occur then there is obviously less likelihood that prices will tend to fall: indeed, the mere recognition by businessmen and trade unions that governments will take action to prevent business contractions and unemployment, will increase their determination not to lower wages or prices when demand temporarily falls off. But if prices are never to be allowed to fall, then a stable price level over time requires that they never rise: the 'ratchet' must not be allowed to operate. This, of course, is easier said than done. It must be emphasized again that it is not just a matter of controlling aggregate demand for goods and services, although this in itself is no easy matter. As we have tried to emphasize in this chapter, changes

---

[1] But see the previous chapter for a discussion of the factors likely to determine the outcome.

H

in the composition of demand also tend to affect the general price level. It seems unlikely, and perhaps not even desirable, that governments will be able to regulate closely the *pattern* of demand, as well as its level. Relative price changes must occur, and if many prices are rather rigid in the downward direction then a rise in the general price level is almost bound to follow.

We are left therefore with the conclusion that the continued economic growth of an advanced industrial economy — what we have described as an *institutional* economy — is likely to be accompanied by a rise in the general price level. This is not the fault of the trade unions alone, nor of government economic and social policy. We cannot avoid differing rates of productivity growth nor changes in the composition of demand: nor can we (or should we) allow large income inequalities to appear, particularly when they cannot be justified on grounds of skill or effort. But this implies that in the absence of price competition and of a willingness of producers to reduce prices when their costs fall (rather than spend more on advertising) inflation is inevitable. It can, of course, be checked if the government operates the economy at a level at which productivity increases cannot in fact take place nor excess demand appear in any sector: the problem then certainly disappears but at the same time it is likely that economic growth disappears as well.[1] Hence the government is caught between the horns of a dilemma—a choice between growth with inflation and no inflation but no growth: and whilst this dilemma is probably best escaped in the long run by measures aimed at increasing the extent of price competition in industry (or, if these fail, by the more effective regulation of both wages *and* prices in industry), in the short run the worst solution is to check growth. In the last resort, the standard of living depends on rising productivity, no matter what happens to prices; and the sort of inflation with which we have been concerned here is not likely to be rapid or to lead to a lack of confidence in money; it is not likely, in other words, to accelerate. Moreover, the more rapidly average productivity grows over time, the faster can average money wages rise without effect on costs, and the less need there is, therefore, to maintain a level of unemployment that will restrict money wage demands. Promoting economic

[1] If the government operates the economy at a level at which productivity increases cannot take place, then unless it stops wages from rising as well, it increases the danger of inflation.

growth, in other words, may be the best way in the long run of preventing inflation.

In the next part of this book we go on to examine the growth and price experience of a number of countries with a view to illustrating the arguments we have set out in this and the preceding chapters: hence it may be desirable to summarise these arguments at this point. In Chapter II it was argued that a government of an under-developed country could take deliberate steps, for instance, liberal credit creation, to cause inflation with a view to promoting faster economic growth. Sometimes, of course, inflation might occur without such deliberate action on the part of the government: for example, if the government did not have firm control over the money supply or fiscal system when the incentive to invest in a private enterprise system was high. In either case, however, whether inflation proves favourable to growth depends largely on its effects on saving and investment. Saving may be increased if the distribution of income changes appropriately, and investment in productive capital may be encouraged if entrepreneurs are thereby made more optimistic. But inflation must not get out of hand, for, if it does, then speculation may take the place of productive activity and confidence will be lost in money and other financial assets which reduces the willingness to save. Economic development cannot then benefit. The important factor which, in under-developed countries, may well determine whether inflation does get out of hand and whether saving can be forced, is the price of food. If food prices start to rise very early on in the inflation then money wages in industry can hardly be kept stable. Once they begin to rise then inflation of industrial prices takes more the form of a *cost* inflation than a *demand* inflation, and profits and saving do not necessarily benefit. This led us to the conclusion that in the early stages of growth, the development of manufacturing and of other non-agricultural industries must not take too great a precedence over agriculture, for if the latter lags well behind it will be difficult to prevent food prices from rising. The income elasticity of demand for food is the crucial factor which determines the appropriate growth rates of agriculture and industry.[1] There is little doubt that food prices have played a key role in the severe inflations experienced by many under-developed countries; and in

---

[1] Also, of course, the possibility of developing an export trade in manufactures.

a later chapter we show what part they played in the inflations of Latin America. Many under-developed countries also experience inflationary pressure as a result of external forces affecting their international terms of trade. These, too, have been an important source of monetary instability and again we illustrate their operation by referring to Latin American experience.

We then turned to the problem of the more developed economies. As a result of their greater elasticity of supply of output in general, these countries are not prone to runaway inflation which often plagues the poorer under-developed countries — except in times of war and its aftermath. Nonetheless, they do experience longer term pressures on their price levels which often present them with a policy dilemma. In Chapter IV we emphasised the importance of changes in the relative growth rates of agricultural (including primary) output and non-agricultural output, arguing that if, because of unfavourable supply factors, the growth of the former began to lag behind the growth of the latter by more than could be expected given the income elasticity of demand for food, then prices would tend to rise: conversely, if the relative growth rate of agriculture rose, then prices would fall. Reasons were also suggested for believing that changes in the terms on which agricultural products exchanged for other products would affect the growth of the non-agricultural sector of the economy, as well as affect prices; and it was concluded that, *other things being equal*, predominantly industrial countries would experience their faster rates of economic growth when prices were falling and slower rates when prices were rising. Conversely, specialist primary producers would grow faster when prices were rising.

Finally in this chapter we turned to pressures of an institutional nature which tend to bear on prices the more developed an economy becomes and the larger and more complex its industry grows. Administrative pricing becomes more prevalent throughout industry with the result that competition between firms takes more the form of advertising and product differentiation than price cutting. Price rigidity is therefore introduced. Moreover, labour organisations assume greater influence and power, and governments become increasingly responsible for economic and social affairs. As a result prices are more likely to rise than to fall. It does not follow that prices must inevitably and persistently rise over time. If the trend of agricultural and primary product prices is downward this will offset to some extent the institutional forces mentioned above; in which case it will be easier to obtain faster economic growth with reasonable price stability. But if the trend of primary product prices is upward then growth will almost certainly be accompanied by some rise in prices and it may be slower. These pressures are long run and slow in operation, and it is hardly likely that they will lead to hyper-inflation and the breakdown of the monetary and financial system. Nonetheless they do give rise to economic, political and social difficulties and force governments to choose between allowing inflation and further slowing down growth. In the concluding chapter of this book we go on to examine the nature of this policy dilemma in more detail.

We now turn to the analysis and interpretation of the actual price and growth experience of one or two countries with a view to discovering whether the preceding arguments are both valid and useful.

PART II

SOME HISTORICAL EVIDENCE

Chapter VI

THE UNITED STATES

Quantitative information concerning the growth of the United States before 1870 is not very reliable. Estimates of national income back to 1800 are available,[1] but these cannot be accepted with a great deal of confidence.[2] For what they are worth they suggest that national income more than trebled from 1800 to 1840, and about trebled again from 1840 to 1880. Population increased at a somewhat faster rate than national income in the earlier period and at a slower rate in the later period. Hence, it seems that, despite the widespread destruction and dislocation of the Civil War, living standards in the United States rose after 1840, whilst in the more peaceful era before 1840 they fell — a somewhat surprising implication that may cast doubt on the reliability of the estimates. As far as price behaviour is concerned, it appears that prices were falling up to the mid 1840's, no doubt reflecting the behaviour of the world price level after the cessation of the Napoleonic Wars. Between the mid 1840's and 1860's, however, they rose, which is not surprising in view of the inflationary methods of financing the Civil War. Given the probable unreliability of these early statistics it seems unwise to look for a connection between growth and prices, and we therefore turn to the period after 1870.

I

CYCLICAL AND SECULAR PRICE MOVEMENTS, 1870–1948

Much more is known about the growth behaviour of the United States economy in this period. In particular, we have Professor Kuznets's essay on *Long Term Changes in the National Income of the*

[1] R. F. Martin, *National Income in the United States, 1799–1938* (National Industrial Conference Board, New York 1939).
[2] For a discussion of them, see S. Kuznets, *Long Term Changes in the National Income of the United States Since 1870*, Appendix, which appears in *Income and Wealth*, Series II (Bowes and Bowes, 1952).

United States of America since 1870, which provides the most complete statistical account.[1] Professor Kuznets draws two main conclusions from his estimates: first, that rates of growth of national product, even when computed in a way that would largely eliminate the influence of short run fluctuations associated with the business cycle, show marked longer term variations; and second, that over the whole period (namely, the 1870's to the 1940's) the rate of growth seems to have slowed down. The evidence for the latter conclusion lies in the fact that whereas in the early decades national product grew on average at about 50 per cent per decade, towards the end it was growing at nearer 25 per cent per decade. If national income *per capita* is taken as the measure, the evidence for retardation is less but still seems clear, growth rates averaging about 25 per cent per decade in the early years, and only 15 per cent towards the end.[2] But the long term picture is somewhat clouded by the very unsettled nature of the latter half of the period. There were, for instance, the two wars and their aftermaths, and, in between, the severe slump of the early thirties; and the magnitude of the fluctuations in the absolute values of the variables makes it difficult to arrive at a significant long term trend. Moreover, the average rate of growth of the early decades bears the marked influence of the high growth rate of the first decade. From the mid '70's to the mid '80's United States growth was very fast indeed: national product almost doubled whilst national product *per capita* rose by as much as 50 per cent. But growth during the remainder of the nineteenth century and early years of the twentieth was less fast than this and not much greater, if national income *per capita* is used as the measure, than during the decades following the First World War. It seems safer therefore to concentrate attention on the unmistakeable variations that have occurred in rates of growth over the period, particularly

---

[1] *Income and Wealth*, Series II (Bowes and Bowes). See also S. Kuznets, 'Quantitative Variations in the Growth of Nations', in *Economic Development and Cultural Change*, Vol. V, No. 1, October 1956; and Handfield-Jones and Weber, 'Variations in the Rate of Economic Growth in the U.S.A. 1869–1939', *Oxford Economic Papers*, June 1954.

[2] S. Kuznets, *Income and Wealth*, Series II, Tables 3 and 4. These averages are derived from geometric means of five overlapping decadal rates of growth at the beginning and end of the period. Professor Kuznets has since revised his calculations, but the later results do not differ very much from these earlier ones. See R. W. Goldsmith, *National Product and Income: Long Term Trends*. Statement before the Joint Economic Committee, Congress of the United States, April 1959. *Employment, Growth and Price Levels*.

since we are mainly concerned with a possible connection between the rate of growth and the behaviour of the price level.

CHART I. *United States National Product per Head, 1869–1959*
(In 1929 prices)

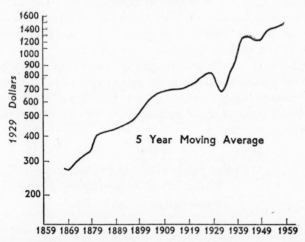

In Table I we give Professor Kuznets's estimates of the percentage changes in United States national product for overlapping decades; and in Chart I we show on a logarithmic scale the behaviour of United States national product *per capita* since 1870, so as to bring out variations in the rate of growth over time. In the Chart, a five year moving average is used so as to eliminate as far as possible short run fluctuations in the absolute values of the variables. It appears that periods of relatively high rates of growth alternated with periods of lower rates. As we have said, the late 1870's and early 1880's was a period of exceptionally fast growth, but growth in the late 1890's and early 1900's, as well as in the 1920's and late 1930's, was also above the average for the whole period. On the other hand, the late 1880's and early 1890's, the 1910's and the early 1930's, were all periods when growth rates were lower than average.[1] The same variations, although to a lesser degree, are also shown in the growth rate of United States manufacturing production, the behaviour of which is plotted on a log scale in

[1] On the average, national product *per capita* in real terms increased by about 10 per cent per decade. See Kuznets, ibid., Table 4.

Chart II. It is interesting to note, however, the absence of any marked long term retardation in the rate of growth of manufacturing production: despite the serious slumps of 1918–20 and 1929–32, manufacturing production seems to have reached a level in 1944[1] that was consistent with a steady rate of growth at the pre-1900 rate. The rate of growth of agricultural production, however, certainly has slowed down, the most severe check seeming to occur in the late 1880's.[2] The growth of agricultural production was very fast in the 1870's and no doubt was an important factor behind the very high growth rate of the economy at this time. After the 1880's, variations in the rate of growth of manufacturing production probably account for the variations in the rate of growth of national product, since variations in agricultural growth seem much less significant.

Table I

United States National Product and
National Product *per capita*

(Percentage change per decade)

Decade	Net National Product	Net National Product per capita
1869/78 to 1874/83	45·7	30·1
1874/83 to 1879/88	30·7	16·0
1879/88 to 1884/93	17·3	5·2
1884/93 to 1889/98	15·2	4·4
1889/98 to 1894/03	24·4	13·4
1894/03 to 1899/08	24·6	13·5
1899/08 to 1904/13	19·5	8·5
1904/13 to 1909/18	12·3	3·0
1909/18 to 1914/23	13·7	5·8
1914/23 to 1919/28	20·6	12·3
1919/28 to 1924/33	6·2	− 0·8
1924/33 to 1929/38	− 1·8	− 5·8
1929/38 to 1934/43	22·1	17·5
1934/43 to 1939/48	23·9	17·6

SOURCE: Kuznets, 'Long Term Changes in the National Income of the United States of America since 1870', *Income and Wealth*, Series II (Bowes & Bowes), 1952. Tables 3 and 4.

Can we relate in any significant way the behaviour of the price level with these variations in the rate of growth of national output?

[1] It later fell from this wartime high.
[2] The rate of growth of construction also seems to have declined markedly at this time.

It can be seen from Chart II, in which we show the behaviour of
the United States price level as well as that of manufacturing
production, that there is no apparent one way connection between
the secular variations in rates of growth of national product
indicated in Table I and the movement of prices. The very high
rates of growth that characterised the 1870's and early 1880's were
associated both with rising prices and with falling prices; and
although prices were rising in the late '90's and early 1900's when
again rates of growth were above average, they were also rising in
the decade before the first world war when rates of growth were
well below average.

The problem is of course complicated by the fact that we have
shorter term fluctuations in prices imposed on longer term trends.
These short run price fluctuations are associated with short run
fluctuations in national product, and, more particularly, with short
run fluctuations in manufacturing production. That the growth of
the United States, in common with the growth of many other
major industrial countries, was accompanied by these fluctuations
in production is, of course, well known. Indeed there has been
some attempt to discern a regular periodicity in them, giving rise
to the idea of the trade or business cycle. The existence of a 3 to
4 year regular cycle in general business activity[1] is in fact reasonably well established, but there is some doubt whether a 7 to 10
cycle, which has been stressed so much in economic literature, can
be found.[2] However, we are not so much interested in the periodicity of the short run fluctuations: rather we are concerned with
what happened to prices when production rose and fell, and also
what happened to them in the longer run. Hence, in Table II we set
out the proportionate changes in production and prices in the
course of boom and slump.[3]

[1] 'General business activity' is the term used by the National Bureau of
Economic Research, which dates the *lower* turning points of such activity as
follows:

1867 December	1894 June	1914 December	1938 June
1870 December	1897 June	1919 April	1945 October
1879 March	1900 December	1921 July	1949 October
1885 May	1904 August	1924 July	1954 August
1888 April	1908 June	1927 November	
1891 May	1912 January	1933 March	

[2] See R.C.O. Matthews, *The Trade Cycle* (Oxford 1959).
[3] It will be noted that the turning points of manufacturing production are not
identical with those listed in footnote 1, but, it should be remembered that the
latter applied to 'general business activity' which is more inclusive than manufacturing production.

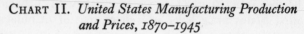

CHART II. *United States Manufacturing Production and Prices, 1870–1945*

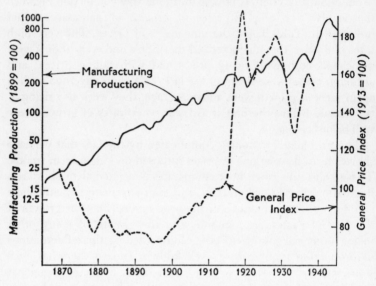

In Chart II as well as in Table II there is clear evidence of a short run, one way relationship between prices and manufacturing production: generally, when the latter rose so did the former, and vice versa. The facts are summarised in the table. Excluding the two wars and their immediate aftermaths,[1] there are 13 distinct periods of rising production and 12 of falling production. In 10 of the periods of rising production, prices also rose, whilst they fell in 8 of the periods of falling production. Moreover, it seems reasonably clear that when production was rising fastest, prices also rose more, for instance, during the strong booms of 1879–83, 1896–1902 and 1932–7,[2] booms which were clearly the important elements underlying the secular variations in the rate of growth of United States national product shown in Chart I. Hence, whatever the reasons: whether it was the need for saving to be forced to match investment, or whether other pressures began to bear on costs of

[1] The war years saw, of course, a very large rise in both production and prices; but given the tremendous and rapid redistribution of resources required at these times, the rise in prices is not surprising. The war years cannot throw much light on the longer term connection between prices and growth.

[2] The 1885–90 boom seems to have been an exception.

production: there seems no doubt that in the short run at least rising prices and rising production tended to go together.[1]

But this, of course, is not the end of the matter. The year to year movements in prices may produce a trend in the longer run; and indeed perhaps the most interesting thing to emerge from Chart II is that the direction of the longer term trend has not remained the same throughout the course of United States development. A very clear cut reversal of direction, for instance, clearly took place about the middle of the 1890's.[2] From the 1870's to the 1890's United States prices tended to fall, so that by 1895 the level of wholesale prices was about 48 per cent below what it was in 1870. The fall in the cost of living was less than this, but at 20 per cent, was still substantial. Admittedly, the largest part of the fall, about two thirds of it, occurred during the slump years of the early 1870's; it was no doubt part of the reaction from the inflation of the Civil War: but prices continued to fall in the 1880's and 1890's as well, although at a slower rate. But from 1896 to 1914 (that is, even ignoring the First World War) the trend of prices was clearly upwards, both the index of wholesale prices and the index of the cost of living rising by about 40 per cent. Indeed by 1914 prices had almost regained their earlier (1870) level.

It is more difficult to pick out such longer term trends from 1914 to 1939. The First World War produced very severe inflation but it was followed by an almost equally severe collapse. In the immediate post-war years, prices and production fluctuated; and although the later 1920's saw greater stability, it did not last long. There followed the massive slump of the early 1930's in which both production and prices declined substantially. Recovery was associated with a rise in prices, and although there was some recession in 1938, the onset of the war produced further inflation. But it is significant that even when this came to an end, there has been little tendency for prices to fall. From the mid 1930's to the mid 1950's it is evident that the course of prices has been upwards, wholesale prices having risen by about 100 per cent in the course of 20 years.

As we have just implied, the movement of prices in the longer

[1] Since booms in production were normally associated with additions to real capital, it could be argued that, in the short run at least, inflation was acting as a mechanism for forcing saving. On the other hand, it should be noted that real wages did not fall at all in the booms prior to 1895, and fell only slightly in those after 1895.

[2] Other such reversals of secular price movements had taken place, but usually as the result of the outbreak of war.

run is the accumulation of movements in the shorter runs. Hence in terms of actual price movements, the difference between, say,

Table II

Prices and Production: United States, 1870–1948

	(1)	(2)	(3)	(4)	(5)	(6)
		Prices (Percentage Change)		Price Flexibility (% change in prices ÷ % change in production)		
Period	Manufacturing Production (Percentage change)	General Index	Cost of Living Index	General	Cost of Living	Farm Prices (Percentage Change)
1872–76	− 10	−15	− 9	1·5	1·0	−18
1876–79	+ 28	−11	−15	P	P	−19
1879–83	+ 40	+13	+ 9	0·32	0·2	+39
1883–85	− 6	−12	−10	2·0	1·66	−27
1885–90	+ 50	+ 1	+ 4	0·08	0·08	− 1
1890–92	+ 12	− 3	− 2	P	P	− 3
1892–94	− 14	− 7	− 5	0·46	0·36	− 8
1894–95	+ 20	+ 1	− 1	0·05	0·05	− 1
1895–96	− 9	− 2	− 1	0·16	0·1	−10
1896–02	+ 72	+15	+12	0·2	0·15	+46
1902–04	− 5	+ 3	+ 4	P	P	0
1904–07	+ 28	+ 8	+10	0·28	0·32	+ 6
1907–08	− 19	− 2	− 4	0·1	0·21	0
1908–10	+ 36	+ 7	+ 8	0·2	0·22	+20
1910–11	− 4	− 1	0	0·25	0	−10
1911–13	+ 23	+ 5	+ 4	0·17	0·17	+ 6
1913–14	− 6	0	+ 2	0	P	0
1914–17	+ 38	+39	+30	1·0	0·8	+81
1917–19	− 14	+26	+35	P	P	+22
1919–20	+ 10	+11	+15	1·1	1·6	− 5
1920–21	− 20	−15	−14	0·75	0·7	−42
1921–22	+ 50	− 3	− 6	P	P	+ 7
1922–24	− 10	+ 5	+ 3	P	P	+ 6
1924–26	+ 20	+ 3	+ 4	0·15	0·17	0
1926–29	+ 5	+ 4	− 4	0·8	P	+ 4
1929–32	− 45	−26	−20	0·57	0·44	−55
1932–37	+ 90	+25	+ 5	0·28	0·05	+33
1937–38	− 22	− 4	− 2	0·19	0·07	− 9
1938–43	+200	+32	+22	0·16	0·11	+30
1943–46	− 33	+16	+12	P	P	
1946–48	+ 12	+32	+23	3·0	2·0	

SOURCES: Column (1): Calculated from an index of manufacturing production in Ames, 'Trends, Cycles and Stagnation in United States Manufacturing since 1860', *Oxford Economic Papers*, Oct. 1959.

Columns (2), (3) and (6): *Historical Statistics of the United States, 1789–1945* (U.S. Dept. of Commerce).

the last quarter of the nineteenth century and first decade and a half of the twentieth, must lie in the fact that, in the earlier period, prices must have fallen more in the slumps than they rose in the booms, whilst for the later period the reverse must have been true. Columns 1, 2, and 3 of Table II show this to be the case. During the booms of the period 1870 to 1896, the *average* rise in wholesale prices was about 1½ per cent, whilst the cost of living usually fell:

in the slumps, wholesale and retail prices fell about 9 and 5½ per cent respectively. After 1895, the average increases in wholesale prices and the cost of living in booms were 9 and 7½ per cent respectively, whilst in the slumps the average falls were in both cases less than 1 per cent. Moreover, it should be noted that in each period there were two cases in which production and prices moved in opposite directions: in the former period, however, prices fell when production rose; in the later period they rose when production fell.

The fact that prices rose more in the booms of the post 1895 period and fell less in the slumps, as against the earlier period, cannot be accounted for by the fact that production rose more and fell less. This could not have happened since the longer term rate of growth of manufacturing production after 1895 was somewhat lower than earlier; but we also demonstrate it in columns 4 and 5 of Table II. We head these two columns *price flexibility* which is measured by dividing the percentage change in prices by the percentage change in production. Larger values of the quotient indicate greater flexibility. In cases where production and prices move in opposite directions, that is 'perversely', we do not derive a quotient, but indicate it merely by writing the letter P. Omitting the 'perverse' cases, it seems that the most significant difference between the two periods lies in the fact that in the earlier period prices were much more flexible in the downward direction during the slumps. There are indeed two cases prior to 1895 in which prices fell in at least the same proportion as production. There are no such cases after 1895, the larger values of price flexibility occurring when production and prices were rising. Of course, the perverse cases are important, too, for they indicate clearly that expansions of output could be obtained with substantial falls in prices in the period 1870 to 1895 whereas they couldn't in the following twenty years: in fact, in this period prices sometimes rose when production fell. These facts point, therefore, to the possibility of different underlying forces operating in the two periods.

Prices were, of course, very flexible during the First World War years and immediately afterwards: prices and production both rose and fell sharply together. They were probably most flexible in the upward direction, and in two of the three cases of perversity, prices rose when production fell. From 1924 to 1939 flexibility seems to have been greater in the downward direction, although

I

we must make due allowance for the severely depressing effects of the 1930 slump. Prices also rose considerably in the Second World War when the expansion of production was massive. But, as we have said, perhaps the most significant feature is the decline in the price flexibility in the post second war years, as compared with previous periods. The fact that prices hardly ever fell may be due to the relative smallness of the declines in production which in fact took place: it may also be due to the institutional factors that were outlined in an earlier chapter.[1] We therefore consider this period in more detail later on.

II

THE UPTURN IN THE SECULAR PRICE LEVEL
IN 1895

The problem of explaining historical long term price trends, is, then, the problem of explaining why in some periods prices rise more in booms than they fall in slumps, whilst at other times they do the reverse. One explanation that has been advanced to account for the reversal of the price trend in the mid 1890's has been alluded to in the introductory chapter of this book. The explanation is a purely monetary one and emphasises the importance of gold discoveries around the turn of the century, which enabled the world's stock of money to increase at a faster rate than before, so putting a persistent upward pressure on prices. Prices sometimes rose, sometimes fell, but because of the increasing abundance of money relative to the flow of goods and services being produced, they fell less than they rose. In the introductory chapter doubts were cast both on the closeness of the connection between changes in the world's stock of gold and changes in the money supply, and on the nature of the casual process through which money supply and prices are presumed to be connected. In Chapters IV and V an alternative explanation of secular price behaviour in the course of economic growth was therefore presented, and in this chapter we examine the evidence from United States experience that might serve to support it. This explanation stressed the crucial nature of the balance between the rate of growth of agricultural output and the rate of growth of non-agricultural output for the longer run behaviour of prices. It was agreed that in the course of economic

[1] Chapter V.

development the rate of growth of agriculture was bound to decline relative to the growth of output in other sectors of the economy, particularly manufacturing output, purely because of the relatively slower growth of demand for agricultural products; but it was argued that if, perhaps because of an unfavourable supply factor, this relative decline occurred at too fast a rate, or if the rate of growth of non-agricultural output quickened too much relative to the growth of agricultural output, then the terms of exchange between agriculture and 'industry' would turn in favour of the former. The shift in the terms of exchange could take place in an environment of falling or stable prices, but reasons were advanced for believing that it would be more likely to take place in the context of a rise in the general price level. This would be particularly the case if the significant factor was an autonomous decline in the growth rate of agriculture. Conversely, an acceleration in agricultural growth would tend to cause the general price level to fall.

This explanation was shown to be quite consistent with the fact that economic growth typically pursues a rather fluctuating path, output rising and falling alternately. Indeed, it was pointed out that the relative growths of agricultural output and non-agricultural output in the long run depended on their relative rise and fall in the course of short run boom and slump. It was further argued that the more agricultural output tends to lag behind the rise in non-agricultural output (in particular, manufacturing production) during the boom, the more will agricultural, and therefore other, prices tend to rise: and the less readily will they tend to fall in the subsequent slump. In consequence, prices are likely to fall less in the slumps than they rose in the boom; and in the longer run the price level will tend to rise. Conversely, the less agricultural output lags behind non-agricultural output in the booms, the less will prices rise and the more easily will they fall in the subsequent slumps. In the longer run, therefore, the price level tends to fall.

In fact, the elasticity of supply of agricultural output, particularly of foodstuffs, tends to be very low in both boom and slump since farmers do not readily adjust their production plans in response to short run fluctuations in prices.[1] Hence changes in the

---

[1] See T. W. Schultz, *The Economic Organisation of Agriculture* (McGraw-Hill, 1953), Chapter 13. Fluctuations in agricultural output do occur, of course, but these are usually the result of harvest conditions.

relation between agricultural output and industrial output in the course of boom and slump depend largely on fluctuations in the latter. In the long run, of course, agricultural output does rise, but we can view this as being the result of many small shifts in the short run agricultural supply schedule; that is, we can think in terms of a *steady* growth of agricultural output over time, in contrast to the rise and fall of industrial output. Nonetheless, of course, the *rate of growth* of agricultural output can, and does, vary over the long run, depending on long run developments in the supply of inputs and their efficiency in use.

With this in mind, we can imagine a situation in which agricultural output has been rising at a rate adequate to meet the long run growth of demand stemming from the growth of industrial output and real income, without a change in its terms of exchange being necessary. During the industrial booms, of course, there will appear excess demand for agricultural products, and prices will rise; but in the following slumps, excess supply will cause prices to fall. If all prices in the economy are reasonably flexible, then they will probably fall as much in the slump as they rose in the preceding boom; and in the long run prices will remain stable. Suppose now that the growth rate of agricultural output begins to fall off, too quickly in comparison with the normal expected decline in the growth of demand. Excess demand for agricultural products will now be greater in the booms than it was before, whilst excess supply in the slumps will be less. Hence agricultural prices will tend to rise more in the booms than they did before and fall less in the slumps. Hence, the long run price level will now begin to rise.

If this explanation is a correct account of the secular fall in the United States price level in the quarter century prior to 1895, and the secular rise afterwards, then we should expect to find a greater disparity between the relative changes in agricultural and non-agricultural output in the booms and slumps of the period after 1895 than in the booms and slumps prior to it: furthermore, we should expect to find that agricultural prices rose more in the booms of the later period than in those of the earlier one, and/or fell less in the slumps. Table III shows that these expectations are largely borne out by the facts.

It emerges quite clearly from the table that the increase in agricultural production *relative* to the increase in manufacturing production was much greater in the booms prior to 1896 than in

Table III

Percentage Changes in Prices and Production, United States 1870–1914

Period	Manufacturing Production	Agricultural Production	Farm Prices		Manufactured Good Prices		General Price Index
			Farm Products	Foods	Textiles	Metals and Metal Products	
1872–76	−10	+13	−17	− 7	−22	−40	−15
1876–79	+28	+18	−19	−20	−17	−14	−11
1879–82	+40	+ 9	+38	+26	+ 4	+17	+13
1876–82	+80	+30	+11	0	−14	0	0
1882–85	− 6	+ 7	−27	−26	−12	−30	−11
1885–90	+50	+10	− 1	+ 2	− 2	+13	+ 1
1890–92	+12	+ 5	− 3	− 8	− 5	−20	− 3
1885–92	+68	+15	− 4	− 6	− 6	−10	− 1
1892–94	−14	0	− 8	− 5	−16	−21	− 6
1894–95	+20	+ 5	− 1	− 2	− 4	+ 8	+ 1
1895–96	− 9	+ 5	−10	− 7	− 2	0	− 1
1896–98	+23	+13	+12	+ 9	+ 4	− 7	+ 3
1898–02	+40	+ 1	+33	+12	+10	+40	+15
1896–02	+72	+14	+50	+22	+14	+30	+18
1902–04	− 5	+ 7	0	+ 1	+ 7	−12	+ 2
1904–07	+28	+ 3	+ 6	+ 5	+20	+37	+ 8
1907–08	−19	+ 3	0	+ 3	−14	−21	− 2
1908–10	+36	− 2	+20	+11	+ 7	− 1	+ 6
1910–11	− 4	+ 5	−10	− 5	− 5	− 5	− 1
1911–13	+23	+ 1	+ 7	+ 4	+ 3	+11	+ 4
1913–14	− 6	0	0	0	− 5	−11	0

SOURCES: *Manufacturing Production*: Calculated from an index in Ames, 'Trends, Cycles and Stagnation in U.S. Manufacturing', *Oxford Econ. Papers*, Oct. 1959. *Agricultural Production*: U.S. Dept. of Agriculture, *Gross Farm Income and Indices of Farm Production, 1869–1937* (Technical Bulletin No. 703). Prices: *Historical Statistics of the United States, 1789–1945*, Series L. 1–14.

those afterwards. The ratio of the latter to the former averaged about 3½ to 1 in the earlier period as against 10 to 1 in the later period and it was particularly high in the booms of the first decade of the twentieth century. Prior to 1896, agricultural prices even tended to fall somewhat in the course of manufacturing booms, the only exception being the boom of 1876 to 1882 when they rose rather strongly: even in this boom, the rise took place solely in the later stages when the rate of increase of manufacturing production had accelerated and the rate of increase of agricultural production had sharply fallen off. But they rose substantially in all the booms after 1896, the average rise being something like 20 per cent. Perhaps the most important feature, however, is the fact that agricultural prices fell far more strongly in the slumps of manufacturing activity prior to 1896 than in those afterwards. In all slumps, pre *and* post 1896, agricultural output tended to rise, but more so in the earlier period than in the later one. The average rise in farm output during slumps was about 6 per cent prior to 1896 and less than 4 per cent afterwards. Moreover, manufacturing production itself tended to fall more in the slumps of the early period than in those of the later one (10 per cent as against 8 per cent), so that it is perhaps not surprising that farm prices fell by about 15 per cent in the slumps of the early period as against only 3 per cent in those of the later ones.

The slower rate of growth of agricultural output in the two decades prior to World War I, as compared with the previous quarter century, is well brought out in Table IV in which we show the growth of output in various product producing sectors of the United States economy in the 20 years prior to 1895 and the 20 years following. In order to eliminate as far as possible the influence of short run fluctuations in output, averages of decades are compared. Thus we compare the annual average output of the decade 1869–78 with that of 1889–98 and 1909–18, putting the first equal to 100 as the base for the comparison. In the second half of the table we compute the rates of growth of output in each sector for both periods.

We see that whereas from the 1870's to the 1890's agricultural output rose by about 75 per cent, in the following 20 years it rose by less than 50 per cent. In *per capita* terms the increase in the first period was about 12 per cent whereas in the later period there was hardly an increase at all. The important point to note is that the decline in the growth of agriculture was not only great in absolute terms, it was also substantial relatively to the growth of manufacturing production and to the growth of output in other sectors of the economy. Manufacturing output *per capita* of the population, whose rate of growth seems to have been only slightly less after 1895 than it had been before, grew at about five times the rate of agricultural output *per capita* before 1895 but twenty-eight times as fast after 1895. Correspondingly, whereas net national product *per capita* (i.e. roughly real income per head) had risen about four times as fast as agricultural output per head in the early period, in the later period it rose at eighteen times the rate of increase of the latter.[1]

[1] The rate of growth of construction output declined even more than the growth of agriculture; but this was to be expected since by the 1890's much of the construction for the extensive development of the continent had been completed.

Table IV

United States Growth: 1870 to 1914

Average Annual Output of Decade	Population	Net National Product per capita	Agricultural Output		Manufacturing Output		Mining		Construction	
			Total	Per Capita	Total	Per Capita	Total	Per Capita	Total	Per Capita
1869–1878	100	100	100	100	100	100	100	100	100	100
1889–1898	155	165	174	112	276	178	335	216	310	200
1909–1918	222	239	257	115	688	310	1000	450	444	200
Percentage Rate of Growth per Annum										
1869/78–1889/98	2·3	2·5	2·8	0·6	5·2	2·9	6·2	4·0	5·8	3·5
1889/98–1909/18	1·9	1·8	2·0	0·1	4·7	2·8	5·6	3·8	1·8	0

SOURCE: Calculated from S. Kuznets, *Income and Wealth, Series II*, Tables 4 and 16.

The statistics as they stand suggest an almost zero income elasticity of demand for agricultural products after 1900 which, of course, seems unlikely. But in the early 1900's, United States exports of foodstuffs began to decline quite sharply and imports rose; and from 1905 on the country became a substantial net importer of food.[1] Unfortunately it is not easy to estimate the extent to which declining exports and rising imports maintained the growth of supplies to the domestic market. In the case of some commodities, for instance wheat, it probably was so. Towards the end of the nineteenth century, about 40 per cent (by value) of United States wheat production was exported: by the outbreak of World War I this proportion had fallen to about 20 per cent, whilst the *volume* of wheat exports had probably risen not at all. Since domestic wheat production rose by about 35 per cent in the same period, the implication is that the supply of wheat to domestic consumers rose by about two-thirds. In *per capita* terms, therefore, available wheat supply rose by about 10 per cent, a rate of growth over two decades of about one-half per cent. Thus it appears that the falling share of wheat exports did in fact protect domestic consumers. It is doubtful whether this is true in the case of meat products. Domestic production of these increased by about 15 per cent during the two pre-First World War decades. The share of exports fell from about a quarter to somewhat less than 10 per cent: hence we can deduce that the domestic supply of meat products to domestic consumers increased by between 35 and 40 per cent, that is, by less than the increase in population. On the other hand imports of meat products rose in the course of these two decades, but whether sufficiently so to keep the growth of domestic meat supply abreast of population is not very clear. In any case it must be remembered that the income elasticity of demand for meat was probably high at this time: hence imports would have had to have risen very considerably to avoid a relative rise in meat prices. In fact, whereas wheat prices rose by less than the average rise in food and farm prices, meat prices rose by much more.

[1] Between 1893/7 and 1909/13 the volume of United States exports of food fell by over 25 per cent., whilst the volume of food imports rose by over 50 per cent. These figures, and those that immediately follow in the text, are calculated from statistics of agricultural production, and exports of merchandise, contained in U.S. Dept. of Commerce, *Historical Statistics of the United States, Colonial Times to 1957,* Series K 316–328, U 73–93. Wide annual fluctuations in export value make it difficult to assess long period changes.

In the case of the two other most important export products, cotton and tobacco, cotton prices were probably affected much more by the expansion of world demand than by a check to the growth of United States production. In the two decades prior to World War I, cotton production rose very substantially (by 80 per cent) whilst *the volume* of cotton exports probably doubled. The share of exports therefore rose from about 55 per cent to about 70 per cent. Even so, supplies to domestic consumers must have increased by more than the growth of population. Tobacco production, on the other hand, no more than kept pace with the growth of population. The share of exports seems to have remained constant, so that available supplies of tobacco per head of the population also remained roughly constant.

It cannot be said conclusively that the *per capita* supplies of food and other agricultural products lagged seriously behind the growth of United States real income *per capita*. But if they did not, it was because of a relative fall in exports and a relative rise in imports. Moreover, it is doubtful whether this development could protect the United States price level. In the last quarter of the nineteenth-century the United States was the major contributor to the total supply of these commodities entering into international trade[1]: hence a check to the growth rate of her production would be bound to affect the world price level of them, and the United States price level could hardly remain unaffected. At any rate it is quite clear that demand had to be shifted away from agricultural products towards manufactures, since a large relative price change in favour of agricultural products took place: from 1896 to 1914, United States farm prices rose by about 60 per cent whilst manufactured good prices rose by only 22 per cent, thus improving the terms of exchange of agriculture by about 30 per cent. The rise in food prices was substantial, although not as great as the rise in farm prices in general; and it must have played some part in the rise in money wages after 1895. In conjunction with the rise in raw

[1] In the last decade of the nineteenth century, United States exports of wheat and wheat flour were between 40 and 50 per cent of the total exports of the four main wheat exporters, United States, Canada, Russia and Argentina. Exports of animal food products were between 75 and 80 per cent of the total exports of these products of the United States, Argentina, Australia, New Zealand and Russia. See Freund, 'Strukturwandlungen der Internazionalen Weizenwirt-schaft', *Weltwirtschaftliches Archiv*, Vol. 25, 1927 (1), Chart opposite page 12*; and the same author, 'Internazionale Tendenzen der Viehwirtschaft', Part II, *Weltwirtschaftliches Archiv*, Vol. 27, 1928 (1), Chart opposite page 5*.

material prices, it must therefore have contributed to the rise in manufactured good prices.[1]

But if an improvement in agriculture's terms of exchange *after* 1896 forced up the general price level, why did it not do so *before* 1896? From 1870 to the mid '90's farm prices fell by about 40 per cent whereas manufactured good prices fell by about 55 per cent. In this secular period, therefore, a 20 per cent improvement in agriculture's terms of exchange took place in the context of a fall in the general price level.

It is possible to argue that the reason for the difference between the two periods lies in the increasing monopolisation of industry and the growing power of labour organisations at the end of the century: institutional pressures against falling prices and in favour of rising prices were greater in the decades after 1895 than in the decades before. It seems unlikely, however, that these should have come to a head in the 1890's thereby producing a sudden reversal in the direction of price movements in 1895. The growth of monopoly and of trade unions was a gradual process which certainly affected price and wage determination, but surely not in so sudden a fashion as the statistics require. On the other hand, it seems clear from Table IV that, prior to 1895, the secular relationship between the growth of agricultural output and the growth of real income per head was a more satisfactory one (that is, more in accord with

---

[1] The argument that United States exports of foodstuffs declined after 1900 *as a result of* a check to the growth of domestic production runs counter to the opinion of some other writers on the subject. Professor W. Lewis and Mr. O'Leary, in an article in the *Manchester School* of May 1955, maintain that the causal connection ran the other way, that is, the growth of domestic production was checked by the check to the growth of exports. Their view is that in the first decade after 1900, United States exports of food, which were mainly to the United Kingdom, fell below the trend for the whole period, 1870 to 1913, because of a downswing in building activity in the United Kingdom. Although they admit that worsening terms of trade of the United Kingdom might have contributed something to the relative decline in British imports, they deny that it was the main factor, on grounds that the import of manufactures also fell below the trend line of the period at this time. But the fact that imports of both food and manufactures declined below the trend is not inconsistent with a rise in food import prices brought about by a check to supply in the United States. Given an inelastic demand for food in Britain, (and also a fall in the share of wages in national income which occurred at the same time), then it is to be expected that demand for both food and manufactures would be reduced (relatively) by a rise in the price of food. It is true that, *if we exclude building activity*, Britain's own industrial production did not fall below the 1870–1913 trend; but this could be explained by the great upsurge in British investment overseas which kept up the demand for British manufactures. Moreover, it is possible, as Professor Cairncross has argued, that the rise in the price of food and primary products was itself an important factor in causing a large proportion of Britain's investment resources to go overseas.

what one might expect the income elasticity of demand for agricultural products to be at this time) than it was after 1895: the rate of growth of real income per head was only about 4 times the rate of growth of agricultural output per head prior to 1895, as against 18 times after 1895; and it does not seem likely that this large difference purely reflected the difference in real income per head between the two periods. In consequence, it is possible to argue that there was no upward pressure on farm prices prior to 1895, in fact, quite the reverse. But manufacturing output was growing very fast, particularly in the late '70's and '80's, so that demand had to be drawn towards it by a relative fall in manufactured good prices: agriculture's terms of exchange had to improve, not to induce consumers to buy less agricultural goods in relation to their real incomes as was the case after the mid 1890's, but rather to induce them to buy more manufactured ones. Since there was no upward pressure on farm prices but a strong downward one on manufactured good prices, the general price level tended to fall. There was therefore less pressure on money wages, so that gains in productivity in manufacturing were more easily reflected in falling costs; and a cumulative fall in prices thus emerged. In fact, most of the fall in the general price level occurred in the 1870's and first half of the '80's[1] when agricultural output was rising very fast; and indeed, agriculture's terms of exchange improved only slightly at this time. A check to agricultural growth in the late '80's and early '90's however, checked the rapid fall in agricultural prices; but since productivity in manufacturing industry was still rising rapidly, manufactured good prices continued to decline; and so did the general price level, although at a much slower rate than before. Once agricultural output *per capita* ceased to rise significantly, as it did around the turn of the century, the secular price level began to rise.

The substantial decline in the rate of growth of agricultural output after the 1890's does not seem to have been caused by a decline in the rate at which labour productivity in agriculture rose: rather, it was produced by a relative shift of labour from agriculture towards the rest of the economy, particularly manufacturing. This is shown in Table V in which we indicate growth rates of population, labour force and productivity. It will be seen that the rate of

---

[1] Between 1870 and the 1880's farm prices fell by about 33 per cent and manufactured good prices by between 35 and 40 per cent.

growth of labour productivity in agriculture was 1·4 per cent per annum after 1895 as against 1·1 per cent before. On the other hand,

Table V

Rates of Growth of Labour Force and Productivity in Agriculture and Manufacturing: U.S. 1870–1915

Per cent per annum

	Popula-tion	Total Labour Force	Agricul-tural Labour Force	Output per head of Agricul-tural Labour Force	Manu-factur-ing Labour Force	Output per head of manu-facturing Labour Force
1875–1895	2·3	2·9	1·7	1·1	3·5	1·7
1895–1915	1·9	2·2	0·6	1·4	3·3	1·4

Calculated from Tables 9, 16 and 19, in S. Kuznets, *Long Term Changes in the National Income of the United States since 1870.* Income and Wealth, Series II.

the rate of growth of the agricultural labour force declined by about two-thirds from what it had been earlier. Part of this was due to a decline in the rate of growth of the total labour force, but it is clearly evident that the main factor was a relative shift of labour towards manufacturing. Even though the rate of increase of total labour force fell by about one quarter, the labour force in manu-facturing continued to grow at only a slightly lower rate than it had done earlier. The decline in the rate of growth of manufacturing output, unlike that of agricultural output, was therefore largely produced by a decline in the rate at which labour productivity rose.

The relative shift of labour from agriculture to manufacturing may have been caused by the greater financial rewards to be ob-tained in industry, although, in the twenty years after 1895, money wages in agriculture rose considerably more than they did in manufacturing.[1] It therefore seems more likely that labour was drawn by the greater attractiveness of urban life. Moreover,

[1] Agricultural money wages rose by about 60 per cent and money wages in manufacturing industry rose by about 40 per cent. See *Historical Statistics of the United States 1789–1945.* It might be thought that the relative rise in farm wages and prices would operate to keep labour on the land. In fact, there is good reason

the rate of settlement on, and exploitation of new land fell off, once all of it had been brought into use.[1] Agricultural growth consequently suffered whilst other sectors of the economy gained. But the greater readiness of labour to work in the towns did not prevent money wages in manufacturing industry from rising, although, no doubt, some check was imposed. In this connection, we should take into account other factors which may have caused money wages to rise. First, despite the shift from agriculture to industry, the manufacturing labour force did not grow quite as fast as it had done earlier, owing to the decline in the growth rate of population and total labour force. Second, around the turn of the century, labour organisations became increasingly active and powerful, thereby playing a larger part in wage determination. Even so, probably the most important factor behind the rise in money wages was the steep rise in food prices which occurred after 1895, which made it more difficult for producers to keep money wages stable. The result was that, in a period when productivity in manufacturing rose less fast than earlier, upward pressures on money wages were greater. In consequence, manufacturing costs of production ceased to fall and began to rise, and a general rise in the price level had to follow.

A significant feature of the improvement in agriculture's terms of exchange after the mid 1890's is that it was large enough to produce a rise in the share of agriculture in national income: normally one would expect a progressive decline in the agriculture's share owing to a less than unity income elasticity of demand for agricultural products. From the 1870's to the 1890's, agriculture's share did, in fact, decline from about 20 per cent of national product to 17 per cent despite a 20 per cent improvement in the terms of exchange, but by the outbreak of the First World War it had risen again to 18 per cent.[2] This check to the decline in agriculture's share may possibly throw some light on a rather puzzling feature of United States economic development at this time.

to believe that migration of labour *from* the land is directly related to the movement of farm prices, rising when the latter rise. See T. W. Schultz, *The Economic Organisation of Agriculture* (McGraw-Hill, 1953).

[1] In addition to the decline in the rate of growth of total output there also occurred a shift in land use away from wheat production to the production of feeding stuffs for animals, and to the production of raw materials for industry, in particular, cotton. See Freund, op. cit.

[2] If relative price changes are ignored agriculture's share fell by almost one-third from the 1870's to the '90's and by almost another third from the '90's to the 1910's. See Kuznets, op. cit., Tables 14 and 17

Professor Kuznets has shown that whereas in the period 1870 to 1895 net capital formation in the United States averaged about 15·2 per cent of national product, in the following two decades it averaged only 13·2 per cent. More significantly, the ratio rose from 14·3 per cent in the 1870's to over 16 per cent in the 1890's, but by the decade 1909–18 it had fallen to 12·5 per cent.[1] Neither the increase in the ratio in the last quarter of the nineteenth century, nor the decline that followed, is satisfactorily explained; nor is it certain that the decline contributed to a fall in the United States rate of growth after 1895 which is recognised to have taken place. Moreover, the decline in the ratio seems to run counter to the view taken by some investigators[2] that income distribution became more inequitable after 1895 than before since, if the latter was the case, a rise in the propensity to save might ordinarily be expected.

The argument that income distribution became more inequitable after 1895 is, however, based on the fact that whilst net national product *per capita* continued to rise, real wages in manufacturing industry remained constant. Hence, it is argued, the share of non-wage income must have risen. But this view overlooks the importance of distributional changes between agriculture and other sectors of the economy. It is true that average money wages in non-agricultural employment rose by the same amount as the cost of living,[3] but the failure of real wages to rise was the consequence of a steep rise in the price of food, which rose by over 60 per cent in the course of twenty years. In terms of the product he produced, the industrial worker succeeded in raising his real wages, since money wages rose by more than the price level of manufactured goods.[4] Thus the industrial workers' loss was largely the farmers' and farm workers' gain. It is not even certain that the distribution of income within the non-agricultural sector itself became more unequal. From 1895 to 1914, for instance, average hourly earnings in manufacturing rose by about 43 per cent whilst productivity rose by about 30 per cent.[5] The implication is that labour costs rose by

---

[1] Kuznets, op. cit., Table 34.

[2] For instance, Handfield Jones and Weber, 'Variations in the Rate of Economic Growth in the U.S.A. 1869–1939', *Oxford Economic Papers*, June 1954.

[3] Average hourly earnings in manufacturing industry rose by about 43 per cent; unskilled workers' weekly earnings by about 36 per cent; and the cost of living by about 40 per cent. See *Historical Statistics of the United States*.

[4] Manufactured good prices rose by about 22 per cent.

[5] Calculated by dividing the increase in manufacturing production by the increase in labour employed in manufacturing industry.

about 10 per cent. Given the fact that farm prices (and therefore perhaps agricultural raw material prices) rose by about 60 per cent whilst manufactured good prices rose by only 22 per cent, whether wages were squeezed relatively to profits depended on what proportion agricultural raw materials were to total costs. The higher this proportion, the less likely it is that the share of profits rose and the more likely it is that it fell; but this we cannot determine with any degree of certainty. In fact, it is probable that the distribution of income outside the agricultural sector changed very little during this time.

The increase in agriculture's share of national income, however, may have increased the equality of income distribution, (and thereby perhaps have contributed to a smaller propensity to save) by virtue of the fact that income distribution *within* the agricultural sector probably tends to be more equal than in other sectors of the economy.[1] Moreover, it is also possible that it lowered the propensity to invest. Farmers are notorious hoarders and/or are very often in debt to banks so that an increase in their income often leads to a rise in idle balances or retirement of bank debt, rather than to further investment in agriculture or industry. Furthermore, when the terms of exchange are moving very substantially in favour of agriculture, the general price level is likely to be rising, so that unless the supply of money is sufficiently elastic interest rates will be rising: accordingly investment generally may be discouraged.

It is impossible to prove that the rise in agriculture's share of national income in the two decades prior to the First World War produced the fall in the ratio of investment to national income: a rise from 17 to 18 per cent, is certainly too small to carry much significance, although of course the mere fact that the share *did not fall* despite the much slower growth of agriculture in real terms may have been important. In any case, even if we could prove this, we still cannot prove that the fall in the investment-income ratio in turn produced a slower rate of economic growth: technical progress can render the employment of capital more efficient so that growth does not suffer. Nonetheless, United States economic growth *was* slower in the two decades after the mid 1890's, than it

[1] By 1910, almost as many people were engaged in agriculture as in manufacturing, construction, transportation and public utilities combined: hence a shift of income towards the agricultural sector could assume considerable importance if the propensities to save of the various sectors differed.

was during the two or three decades prior to this time. Obviously, the decline in the growth of agriculture itself had a *direct* effect on the growth of the economy as a whole. But it is clear that the growth rate of the rest of the economy also fell. Whilst it is possible that the two were interconnected in the fashion we have described, it is not possible to demonstrate the connection in any certain way.

III

THE INTER-WAR YEARS

When we turn to the period after 1914 it is not possible to apply our thesis in so straightforward a fashion. The main reason for this is the extremely unsettled character of the whole period which renders it difficult to pick out longer term trends. There were the two world wars, both of which were followed by slump and recovery in production; and there was, of course, the severe peacetime slump of the early 1930's. Both wars produced substantial increases in production and prices, production rising more in the second than in the first whilst prices rose less.[1] The smaller inflation of the 1939–45 war is, however, somewhat misleading, since prices were largely restrained by controls. When these were removed at the end of the war, prices rose very sharply indeed: moreover, they did not subsequently fall, as was the case after the First World War.

Leaving aside the war years, the 1920's comprised a period of very rapid peacetime economic growth. From 1921 to 1929, manufacturing production rose by about 85 per cent, a rate of increase not often excelled in United States growth experience. Net national product also rose very fast (by over 50 per cent), as did national product *per capita* (by 35 per cent). The latter, indeed, rose at a faster rate than during any of the pre-war decades. This rapid peacetime growth took place in an environment of comparative price stability. Wholesale prices, which had fallen sharply at the end of the war, rose a few per cent until 1925 or 1926 when production was growing fastest, but by 1929 had fallen back to the 1921 level; and retail prices behaved very similarly. However, from

---

[1] From 1914 to 1917, which was the 'peak' output year of the First World War, manufacturing production rose by about 40 per cent, whereas from 1939 to 1943, the 'peak' year of the Second World War, it rose by 133 per cent.

the point of view of the thesis we have been developing, it is the relative price changes which are of most interest.

Comparative general price stability was produced by a fall in manufactured good prices, offset by a rise in farm prices. The latter fell very steeply in the post-war slump, but they began to rise again after 1921. By 1929 they were about 20 per cent above the 1921 level. Manufactured good prices also fell steeply in the post-war slump, but they continued to fall, although at a much slower rate, until 1929. If the prices of metals and metal products can be taken as an indication, manufactured good prices fell by 13 or 14 per cent below their 1921 level. Thus the terms of exchange moved in favour of agricultural products and against manufactures by something like 35 per cent.

The improvement in agriculture's terms of exchange in the 1920's is perhaps readily understandable. Whilst manufacturing production was increasing at a very fast rate, farm production lagged well behind. From 1922 to 1929 the latter rose by less than 9 per cent, which was not very much different from the rise in population at this time, and barely a tenth of the rise in manufacturing production. Taking a longer view, however, the relationship between agricultural growth and manufacturing growth is less unbalanced. From 1914 to 1929, manufacturing production rose by about 75 per cent whereas farm production rose by about 15 per cent, i.e. a fifth as much. Even so, the increase in agricultural output was less than the increase in population in the same period. Whilst this does not necessarily mean that consumption of farm produce per head fell, since net imports of food and agricultural products increased substantially in these years, it remains true that by 1929 farm prices were almost 50 per cent above their 1914 level, as against a rise of only half as much in manufactured good prices.

But, as in the pre-1895 period the substantial improvement in agriculture's terms of exchange in the 1920's, which was quite as large as had occurred in the earlier periods, did not cause the general price level to rise very much. The factor which seems to have prevented it was a very substantial rise in labour productivity in manufacturing industry. The increase in production in the 1920's was almost solely due to a rise in the efficiency with which labour worked, very little being due to an increase in the numbers of employed. Hence there was a considerable fall in manufacturing

K

costs of production,[1] and considerable room for a fall in prices, without adverse effects on profitability. The improvement in agriculture's terms of exchange, was therefore able to take place with a smaller rise in agricultural prices, and hence in prices in general.

Nor was the improvement sufficient to increase agriculture's share of national income, which continued to fall in the 1920's, from about 15 per cent at the beginning to less than 12 per cent at the end. Of course, for reasons we have discussed earlier, a decline in the share of agriculture is to be expected, as economic growth takes place. The point we are making is that, whereas in the immediate pre-war decades an improvement in agriculture's terms of exchange was sufficient to check the long-term decline and even reverse it, this was not the case in the 1920's. On the other hand, the decline in agriculture's share was not associated, as it had been in the '70's and '80's of the last century, with a marked rise in the ratio of capital formation to national product, although we have suggested a possible relationship between the two. In fact, from 1919 to 1929, net capital formation averaged about 9½ per cent of net national product, a proportion somewhat lower than in the first decade and a half of the twentieth century when agriculture's share was substantially higher, and economic growth was somewhat slower. In large part, however, the lower ratio of net investment to national product in the 1920's is somewhat misleading; and it by no means follows that the increase in productive capacity in the 1920's was at a lower rate than during the previous fifty years. *Net* capital formation was a much smaller proportion of *gross* capital formation than during the earlier years,[2] in other words *gross* capital formation was not much lower in the 1920's than earlier. The point is relevant since it is unlikely that equipment installed in the 1920's had the same productive performance as equipment installed say 10 or 15 years earlier. Hence the mere replacement of depreciated equipment probably raised the capacity to produce, quite apart from additions to the capital stock; and less *net* capital formation was therefore required to obtain a given rate of growth. World War I also stimulated great technological progress which

---

[1] Money wages of production workers in manufacturing industry rose by 10 per cent from 1921 to 1929, whereas productivity rose by more than 40 per cent.

[2] In the first twenty years of the twentieth century, capital consumption averaged about 45 per cent of gross capital formation, whereas in the 1920's, it averaged nearer 55 per cent. See Kuznets, op. cit., Table 35.

was exploited in the 1920's: in particular, this was the era of the development and mass production of the internal combustion engine and the motor car in America.

The boom years of the 1920's were followed by the massive slump of the 1930's and manufacturing production fell by 50 per cent. Agricultural production, on the other hand declined much less, although, as was to be expected, agricultural prices fell by more than manufactured good prices. This is not the place to go into the causes of the 1930 slump; but it can be argued that its effect was to allow agricultural production to catch up somewhat. Even though in the subsequent recovery from 1933 to 1937, manufacturing production again increased relatively to agricultural output, the relationship between them in 1937 was closer than it had been in 1929. Whereas manufacturing production was almost 100 per cent greater than in 1914, agricultural production had risen by 23 or 24 per cent. In *per capita* terms there was even a slight rise in the latter.

The Second World War again produced a massive increase in manufacturing production (130 per cent in four years). This time, however, agricultural production also showed a substantial rise (30 per cent) as well. Controls limited the rise in prices to some extent, but, even so, they did not prevent agricultural prices from rising by about 75 per cent and manufactured good prices by about 20 per cent in the war years. It appears, however, that price controls were more effective in restraining manufactured good prices than agricultural prices.[1] When they were abolished, all prices rose substantially, but metal and metal product prices rose the most. Taking the war period 1939 to 1948 as a whole, agricultural prices rose by 200 per cent, metal prices by 90 per cent and textiles (in which the agricultural cost component would have been important) by 125 per cent. Afterwards there was some fall in agricultural prices, whilst manufactured good prices continued to rise.

We wish to examine the period 1948 to 1959 in somewhat more detail, but it will be of interest to close this section by summing up the broad picture of United States economic development from 1914. If we compare the average annual production and income

[1] This was partly the consequence of the nature of the price legislation. Farm prices were related to an index of costs incurred by farmers for materials; but many of these materials were also farm products. Hence the rise in farm prices became both cause and effect of itself. See T. W. Schultz, *Agriculture in an Unstable Economy* (New York, 1945), p. 123.

figures of the decade 1909–18 with those of the decade 1939–48 we get the results shown in Table VI.

Table VI

United States Growth 1914 to 1944

Popula-tion	Net National Product per capita	Agricul-tural Output	Agricul-tural Output per capita	Manufac-turing Produc-tion	Manufac-turing Production per capita
(Percentage Increases from Decade 1909–18 to Decade 1939–48)					
41	53	50	6·5	217	125
	Percentage Rate of Growth				
1·2	1·4	1·4	0·2	4·0	2·8

SOURCE: Calculations from Kuznets, op. cit.

Comparing Table VI with our earlier Table IV, we see evidence of a progressive slowing down in the growth rate of the American economy. Real income per head, which grew at about 2½ per cent per annum in the last quarter of the nineteenth century and at less than 2 per cent per annum in the two pre-war decades, grew at less than 1½ per cent per annum in the thirty years following the outbreak of the First World War. Manufacturing production *per capita*, however, seems to have maintained a consistent rate of growth, at a little less than 3 per cent per annum throughout. But, from our point of view, the most significant fact to emerge from Tables IV and VI is that, although agricultural production *in toto* grew at a slower rate in the later period than in either of the other two, if the growth of population is taken into account, growth *per capita* was faster in the third period than in the second, although still much slower than from 1870 to 1895. Moreover, the relationship between the growth of real income per head and the growth of agricultural output per head seems to have been more favourable for price stability in the last period than in the second. Thus, national income per head grew 4 times as fast as agricultural output per head in the 1870–95 period, 18 times as fast from 1895 to 1915 and 7 times as fast from 1915 to the 1940's. Similarly the relationship between the growth rate of manufacturing output per head and the growth rate of agricultural output per head bears this out: the former was 5 times the latter from 1870 to 1895, 28 times from 1895 to 1915 and

14 times from 1915 to the 1940's. These relationships suggest that terms of exchange would have moved more strongly in favour of agriculture in the second period than in either of the other two. This, indeed, is the case. We noted earlier that from 1870 to 1895 agricultural prices rose relatively to manufactured good prices by about 20 per cent,[1] whilst from 1895 to 1915 the relative improvement was as much as 30 per cent. From 1915 to the 1940's, however, *relative* prices remained pretty constant, both agricultural prices and manufactured good prices rising by about 130 per cent.[2] It is, of course, not surprising that the terms of exchange moved more favourably to agriculture in the last quarter of the nineteenth-century than they did in the thirty years after 1915, even though the relationship between the agricultural growth rate and the manufacturing growth rate seems more unbalanced in the later period: the fact is, of course, that real income *per capita* was much higher in the period after 1915 than in the earlier one, so that the income elasticity of demand for, and the propensity to spend on agricultural goods was lower: consequently we could expect a larger gap between the growth rate of agriculture and the growth rate of manufacturing.

On the other hand, if our thesis connecting changes in the terms of exchange between agricultural products and industrial products, on the one hand, and the behaviour of the general price level, on the other, is correct, why did prices rise over the long run in the period 1914 to 1945, even though there was no substantial change in the terms of exchange? The explanation is obvious, and lies in the two world wars which placed enormous *short-term* pressures on the price level. Admittedly, prices fell substantially at the end of the First World War, but even so it required the massive slump of the early 1930's to pull down prices to anywhere near their 1914 level. In the post 1939–45 war period, price declines have been very small, and as yet there has been no slump of the 1930 severity to put strong deflationary pressures on prices. Thus it is possible to infer that if there had been no wars the general price level would have risen much less in the thirty years after 1914, than in fact it did. Indeed, it is a reasonable hypothesis that since, apparently, no

[1] It will be remembered that both agricultural and manufactured good prices were falling at this time.
[2] As an indication of the change in manufactured good prices, we make use of the price change of metals and metal products, and of textiles: the former rose by about 115 per cent, the latter by 150 per cent.

substantial long-term change in the terms of exchange between agriculture and industry was required, United States economic development might have occurred in the context of long-term price stability if the wars had not taken place; but it is a hypothesis that can hardly be proved.

To sum up at this point. We have argued that the secular behaviour of the United States price level in the period 1870 to 1914 is explicable in terms of the comparative rates of growth of agriculture and industry. In the early years of the period, an acceleration in the rate of growth of agricultural output relatively to that of manufacturing output caused prices to fall steeply. In the 1880's and '90's, however, agricultural growth began to slow down and agricultural prices ceased to fall. At first, an acceleration in the rate of growth of manufacturing kept other prices falling; but from about the late 1890's on, the progressive decline in agricultural growth produced a wide gap between the growth rate of agriculture and the growth rate of industry. In consequence, the terms of exchange moved strongly in favour of agriculture, and the general price level began to rise. The long-term rise in the price level since 1914, however, cannot be explained in these terms. Variations in the comparative rates of growth of agriculture and industry produced severe short-term fluctuations in prices in peace and war: but in the long run, the rates of growth of agriculture and industry seems to have been such that no substantial change in the terms of exchange of agriculture was required. The long-term rise in the price level must therefore be explained by the inflationary pressures generated in the two wars, in combination with the fact that prices have become increasingly rigid in the downward direction. This has become particularly true in the post second war period, and it is to a closer examination of these years that we now turn.

IV

THE POST-WAR YEARS, 1948–58

Manufacturing production reached a wartime peak in 1944: thereafter it declined, until by 1946 it had fallen to less than two-thirds of its earlier level. Some recovery then followed as consumers' demand, which had been severely restrained during the war, took the place of orders for defence; and production rose by about 11 per cent in the course of the next eighteen months.

Prices, which had continued to rise in the years 1944 to 1946 when production fell, now rose at a faster rate than before — indeed at a faster rate than at almost any time during the war years. But this intensification of inflation cannot be attributed solely to the pressure of the consumer good boom: rather, it was the result of the removal of many price controls which had suppressed inflationary forces during the war. Prices had become seriously out of line with both costs and demand, and adjustment was therefore required, which rapidly took place with the removal of controls. By 1948, it can be said that the United States economy had returned to a more normal peacetime shape, with resources distributed according to the pattern of consumers' demand rather than according to wartime needs.

The course of events since the middle of 1948 is depicted in Table VII. In the latter half of 1948 and in the first few months of 1949 a small recession stabilised the American price level. Demand was already picking up, however, when the outbreak of the Korean War subjected the economy to further pressures. Production rose substantially in the course of 1950, stabilised during 1951, and surged upwards again in 1952 and the first few months of 1953. At first, prices rose very rapidly: from the last quarter of 1949 to the last quarter of 1950, wholesale prices rose by about 20 per cent and consumer prices by about 10 per cent. It does not appear, however, that this substantial inflation was the result of excessive overloading of the economy. Unemployment, which was about $5\frac{1}{2}$ per cent of the labour force in 1949, still averaged 5 per cent in 1950, indicating that the economy was by no means fully employed. The main factor seems to have been the building up of stocks of primary products and foodstuffs on a world-wide scale, which forced up their prices to very high levels. Part of the reason for this was the fear of a new world war, but there was an important speculative element as well. When the speculative boom was pricked, as it was in the latter half of 1951, primary product prices fell, although not by as much as they had earlier risen. Thereafter, the rise in prices, both at wholesale level and retail level, was very moderate, even though production was rising fast, and unemployment was falling to its lowest peacetime level.[1]

[1] From the middle of 1952 to the middle of 1953, manufacturing production rose by about 20 per cent, and unemployment fell to about $2\frac{1}{4}$ per cent of the labour force. Prices, however, rose by only 2 per cent.

The boom in production came to an end in the middle of 1953, and production fell. Prices, however, did not follow suit but continued to rise at about the same rate as before. Nor did prices fall in the recession that followed yet another boom in 1955 and 1956. Indeed, in the course of 1957 and 1958, retail prices rose at quite as fast a rate as they had done in the earlier booms of 1952/3 and 1954/6. It became evident therefore that other forces were at work.

In brief, the post-war period was characterised by a persistent tendency for prices to rise both at wholesale and retail level, through boom and slump alike, particularly in the more peacetime conditions after 1953. Taking the period 1948 to 1958 as a whole, consumer prices rose by about 30 per cent (see Table VIII). A third of this occurred in 1950 at the time of the Korean boom, but a substantial part also occurred during the recession years of 1957 and 1958.[1] Prices of raw materials at the wholesale stage pursued a more fluctuating course, but, in general, rose by much less than consumer prices in the period as a whole. By far the largest rise in prices was those of finished producer goods, and the intermediate materials required for their production. Moreover, to repeat, there was no fluctuation in boom and recession, prices rising steadily from year to year.

The absence of price reductions in the recessions of the post-war period, and the opposite tendency for them to rise instead, cannot easily or satisfactorily be explained by the smallness of the recessions or their short-lived nature. That recessions in production *were* limited *and* short-lived was naturally an important factor in the post-war inflation, as we shall argue later. But production did decline by over 10 per cent in each of the recessions of 1953/4 and 1957/8; and declines of a similar magnitude in earlier periods had produced a fall in prices. Nor can we resort to the explanation with which we have made great play in the earlier sections of this chapter, namely a failure of agricultural production to rise at a sufficiently fast rate relatively to other production. Agricultural output, under the influence of government price support policies, rose very substantially in the post-war period, indeed not greatly less than the increase in manufacturing production itself.[2] Correspondingly there was no tendency for the

[1] From 1956 to 1958 consumer prices rose by about 6 or 7 per cent.
[2] The increase in manufacturing production from 1945 to 1958 was about 35 per cent, whilst farm output rose by about 28 per cent. See *Statistical Abstract of the United States*.

Table VII

Prices and Production in Boom and Recession: United States, 1948–1958

(Percentage Change)

	I Recession Mid 1948 to 4th Qtr. 1949	II Boom 4th Qtr. 1949 to 4th Qtr. 1950	III Plateau 4th Qtr. 1950 to end 1st Qtr. 1952	IV Boom Mid 1952 to Mid 1953	V Recession Mid 1953 to March 1954	VI Boom March 1954 to end 1956	VII Recession End 1956 to Mid 1958	VIII Boom Mid 1958 to 1st Qtr. 1960
Industrial Production	$+12\frac{1}{2}$	+31	0	+20	−10	+19	−13/14	+22
Durable Manufactures	−24	+53	$+2\frac{1}{2}/3$	+41	−12/13	+24	−21	+33
Non-durable Manufactures	−14	+28	−5	+12	−6/7	+15	−4/5	+15
Wholesale Prices								
All	−12	+22	−3	+2/3	$+1/2$	+4/5	+3	+1
Machinery		+3/4	0	+2		+15/16	+4/5	+3
Furniture	−2	+16	−2/3	+2	+1	+4/5	−1	0
Fuel Power	−3	+4	0	+1/2	+1	+5	−3	+2
Farm Produce	−18	+24		−11	+2	−10	+6/7	−8
Processed Food				−5/6	+2	−3	+9	−3
Chemicals	−12	+27	−5	0	$+1\frac{1}{2}$	+1	+2	0
Metals	+6	+12	0	+5/6	+1	+21/22	−2/3	+4
Textiles	−9	+32	−13	$-2\frac{1}{2}$	−3	+1	−2/3	+3
Retail Prices								
All	−4	+10	$+1\frac{1}{2}$	+2	+1	+3	+4/5	+2
Food	−5	+13	0	0	+1	0	+6/7	−3
Services	+5	+3/4	+3/4	+1	+1/22	+3/4	+4/5	+4
Rent	+3	+9	+4	+7	+5	+5	+2/3	+3
House Furnishings	−5	+10	−1	−1	−1/2	−2	0	0
Hourly Earnings (All)	+7	+11	+7	+8	+3	+13/14	$+3\frac{1}{2}$	+8
Weekly Earnings (All)	+6	+14	+5	+9	−1	+20	−5	+8
Weekly Earnings Durable Ind.	+6	+15	+4	+10	−2	+21	$-4\frac{1}{2}$	+10
Weekly Earnings Non-Durable Ind.	+5	+11	+2	+4/5	0	+15	−1	+6
Av. Unemployment in Period (%)	4·6	5·0	3·0	2·5	5·4	3·7	7·3	5·7

Source: U.S. Dept. of Commerce: *Survey of Current Business.*

Table VIII

United States Price Movements 1948–1958

	Percentage increase
Consumer Price Index	
All items	23
Food	15
Rent	37
Household furnishings	0
Transportation	40
Medical care	44
Miscellaneous Services	27
Wholesale Prices	
All commodities	20
Farm Products	−5
Wholesale Prices by stage of processing	
Crude foodstuffs	−17
Raw materials for manufacturing industry	1
Intermediate materials for manufacturing industry	23
Producer goods for manufacturing industry	50

SOURCE: U.S. Dept. of Commerce, *Statistical Abstract of the United States.*

terms of exchange of agricultural products to improve, quite the reverse. Farm prices at the primary stage fluctuated sharply at times, but, in the period as a whole, they fell rather than rose. Prices of manufactured goods on the other hand, particularly those of a durable kind, rose considerably. Admittedly, prices of foodstuffs to consumers rose by about 25 per cent in ten years, but it is clear that this was due to a rise in processing and distribution costs, and not due to a rise in prices at the farm stage. Food prices at the consumer stage fluctuated somewhat more in the course of boom and recession than did the prices of most other consumer goods, but often the stability of the price of food at the raw material stage was an important factor in restraining a general rise in prices.[1] There is little doubt that considerable excess supply of farm products existed in most of the post-war years; and in the absence of

[1] In the booms of 1952/3 and 1954/6 wholesale prices of foodstuffs at the raw material level declined

government support, farm prices would have fallen substantially. If they had, the rise in the general price level would have been less: indeed, it may even have fallen over the period as a whole. On the other hand, a severe fall in farm prices might have given rise to the danger of a larger general depression than in fact occurred during the post-war years: hence it was perhaps wiser policy to keep up farm prices than to let them fall. Nonetheless, this aspect of government policy was an important factor underlying the general rise in prices. But there were other reasons as well.

In Chapter V, it was argued that prices of a large range of products produced by a relatively well developed economy are very unresponsive to the pressure of demand, particularly when it is declining. The larger and more capitalistic industry becomes, the less are the prices of the goods it produces determined in competitive markets by the interplay of demand and supply, particularly in the short run. Producers fix their prices, obviously in some relation to their direct costs, and with a view to obtaining satisfactory profits, but they do not repeatedly adjust them in response to the changing pressures of demand. Even when demand is proving excessive, prices are not always raised to take advantage, although if attempts to raise production to meet demand result in a significant rise in direct costs, prices will at some stage almost certainly follow. When demand is deficient, producers do not customarily resort to price cutting to attract demand away from their competitors. The reluctance of firms to compete by price cutting is readily understandable in the case of those with large fixed costs per unit of output, but smaller firms also seem to feel it. Competition is carried on between them more by means of advertising and product differentiation than through prices. Similarly, in the field of wage fixing, it is clear that demand and supply are not crucial in the short run. Money wage rates rise, even when there is no excess demand for labour, and trade unions and social pressure erect strong barriers against wage cuts.

The fact that prices tend to fall less readily when demand and costs fall than rise when the latter rise has important implications for the longer term behaviour of the price level. It means that prices are likely to rise more in booms than they fall in slumps:[1] hence, in the long run, prices will tend to rise. This development is

[1] This is quite apart from the behaviour of agricultural production and prices which we have stressed earlier.

reinforced by the fact that governments of modern states are increasingly determined, and able, to take corrective action against slumps: it is unlikely that severe depressions of the 1930 variety will again occur. Thus, downward pressure on prices and wages is not likely to persist for long. Of course, if extensive excess demand can also be avoided, then the danger of prices rising is much less; but it was argued in Chapter V, that even the absence of aggregate excess demand would not necessarily prevent prices from rising. The cost-determined nature of prices and their downward rigidity are not just macro-phenomena: they apply to individual industries as well. Hence excess demand for the output of some industries will raise prices in some sectors, but excess supply in others will not necessarily produce an offsetting fall. Moreover, wage increases tend to be determined in the expanding sectors and quickly spread to others, whether expanding or not. In consequence, since an essential characteristic of a dynamic economy is that relative demands and outputs will be changing over time, it is clear there will be a persistent upward pressure on the price level.

What evidence should we look for to show that these forces have been important in the United States economy in the post-war period? We should, of course, expect to find production and employment consistently high and an obvious willingness of governments to take prompt corrective action when falling production and employment threatened. We should expect to find no close connection between the changes in level of employment and changes in the level of money wage rates, either macrowise or in respect of individual industries: we should certainly not expect to find money wage rates falling when unemployment was rising, although they may rise faster when the latter is falling. Similarly, we should find that the prices of a large range of manufactured goods, particularly of a durable kind, were insensitive to changes in demand, perhaps even rising when production was falling. And finally, we should expect to find a persistent rise in prices of many goods and services produced in conditions in which labour productivity, for technical reasons, can rise but slowly.

There is in fact plenty of evidence of this nature in the history of the United States post-war inflation; and in the accompanying Tables (Tables VII and IX) we set out some pertinent statistics relating to the movement of prices and production during the course of boom and recession.

The most obvious feature is the persistently low level of unemployment as compared with pre-war. In the eleven years 1948 to 1958, unemployment averaged about 4 per cent of the labour force. When production was rising strongly, as in 1952/3, it fell below 3 per cent, but even when production was falling it seldom rose above 5 per cent. The only exception to this is during the recession of 1957/8 when unemployment rose to about 7 per cent.[1] It is possible that the United States government was less willing to take corrective measures than at earlier times owing to its increasing concern at the persistence of post-war inflation: but it is significant that, despite this reluctance, prices continued to rise at the same rate as before. Certainly, the high level of unemployment did not prevent money wage rates from rising. If we accept *hourly* earnings in industry as a satisfactory index of wage rates, we see that the latter rose persistently through boom and recession (Table VII). It is true that they rose more strongly when production was rising and unemployment was falling, but at no time during recessions did they rise less than 3 per cent. *Weekly earnings* naturally fluctuated more, and in the two recessions after 1953 declined; but in each case the decline was small, and did not match the rise in the preceding boom. The manufacture of durable products — capital equipment, machinery, for example — fluctuated most in the course of boom and slump (see Tables VII and IX): correspondingly, weekly earnings of labour employed in these industries also fluctuated most. But hourly wage rates paid in these industries continued to rise, even when production declined substantially. In the recession of 1957/8, for instance, the production of primary metals and of machinery declined by about 25 per cent and 18 per cent respectively, yet hourly money wages in both rose by about 15 per cent.

Productivity in most industries tended to rise steadily through boom and recession, thereby moderating the effects of money wages on costs. But prices were not prevented from rising in either boom or recession. The prices of some products at wholesale level, for instance, furniture and textiles, did generally move in the same direction as production, but it is evident from Tables VII and IX that prices of many important products, components and services persistently rose, despite substantial declines in production. This

---

[1] Note, however, that in the recovery after the recession of 1957/8, unemployment remained above the 5 per cent mark.

is particularly true of many metal products. The point is strikingly brought out if we examine the course of prices and production of iron and steel, and motor cars, presented below.

U.S. Prices and Production: Iron and Steel, 1947–59

	1947	1948	1949	1950	1951	1952	1953	1954	1955	1956	1957	195
Production mil. tons	84·8	88·6	77·9	96·8	105·2	93·1	111·6	88·3	117·0	115·2	112·7	85
Percentage of Capacity Output	93	94·1	81·1	96·9	100·9	85·8	94·9	71	93	89·8	84·5	60
Wholesale Prices (1947/9＝100)	89·7	104·3	106	113	123·2	124·7	131·3	132·9	140·6	154·7	166·2	168

U.S. Prices and Production: Automobiles, 1947–58
1947/9＝100

	1947	1948	1949	1950	1951	1952	1953	1954	1955	1956	1957	195
Index of Output	85	93	122	159	127	103	146	131	190	138	146	101
Wholesale Price Index	91·3	100·8	107·9	107·2	112·9	119·6	118·9	119·3	122·9	129·8	135·4	139

SOURCE: U.S. Dept. of Commerce, *Statistical Abstract of the U.S.*

At no time did steel prices fall, even when production declined substantially. Up to 1955, however, they tended to rise more when production relatively to capacity increased. But in the next three years, despite a fall in the ratio of production to capacity from 93 per cent to 60 per cent, prices rose by about 20 per cent. In the case of motor cars, prices seemed to rise even more when production fell than when it rose; and only on one occasion, 1949 to 1950, did prices fall and that when production rose substantially.

The downward inflexibility of prices, at the wholesale stage, of a number of important products is, in fact, amply demonstrated in United States post-war experience. Similarly, the prices of many items appearing in the consumer price index have shown no tendency to fall. Rents of houses, the price of fuel and power, the cost of medical and other personal services have shown a persistent and substantial rise in the post-war period.[1] Food prices fluctuated to some extent, but only in response to sharp fluctuations in prices at the farm stage. It is evident that costs of processing and distribution were exerting a strong upward pressure throughout, which was

[1] Each of these items rose in price by between 30 and 50 per cent in the course of ten years.

quite independent of the cost of food at the raw material stage and also largely independent of the general level of economic activity. Only the prices of clothing and house furnishings showed significant year to year fluctuations in prices and it is noteworthy that over the whole period these prices rose the least.

The persistent tendency for prices to rise since the end of the war cannot satisfactorily be explained by a sustained overloading of the economy. It is probably true that during the years 1946 to 1948 and 1950 to 1953, aggregate excess demand was an important factor causing prices to rise; but it was not important in the years that followed. Even in the boom years of 1954 to 1956, unemployment barely went below 4 per cent, and there was no real shortage of goods. In the following years, unemployment, at over 7 per cent of the labour force, was unsatisfactorily high. Nor can it be argued that the booms set up such strong price raising forces that many years were required for them to be worked out; or that, correspondingly, if the recessions had been allowed to last somewhat longer, eventual stability would have been achieved. After all, the 1954–6 boom was by no means excessive — it was already beginning to tail off quite sharply in 1956 — and the recession that followed lasted almost two years, during which time prices continued to rise. In fact, in almost all respects the period 1954 to mid-1958 itself provides striking confirmation of the arguments set out in Chapter V, and therefore warrants a closer examination on our part. We shall therefore conclude this chapter with a somewhat more detailed account of these years.

In the recovery from the 1953/4 recession, expanding demand for consumer durables, particularly motor cars, and residential house building led the way; but, at a later stage, investment in manufacturing industry began to expand as well. When the demand for cars and houses tailed off towards the end of 1955, and began to fall in 1956, investment kept the boom going. As a result, industrial production rose strongly through 1955, and by the end of the year was 16 per cent above the low point of mid-1954. Under-utilised equipment was rapidly pulled into use and the output of manufacturing industry reached over 90 per cent of capacity.[1] Correspondingly, unemployment of labour declined from over 5 per cent at the middle of 1954 to less than 4 per cent at the end of 1955. Hence it can be said that the United States reached a point of full

[1] McGraw-Hill Dept. of Economics and *Fortune* Magazine.

Table IX
Prices, Wages and Productivity: U.S. 1950–59
(1950 = 100)
Durable Manufactures

	1950	1951	1952	1953	1954	1955	1956	1957	1958	1959
Primary Metals										
Production	100	109	100	112	90	119	117	112	87	101
Prices	100	110	110	114	115	123	135	137	136	142
Hourly Money Wages	100	110	115	125	127	136	143	151	160	169
Productivity	100	100	100	103	95	113	111	106	101	114
Fabricated Metals										
Production	100	107	105	118	106	115	115	120	109	124
Prices	100	110	110	114	115	123	135	137	136	136
Hourly Money Wages	100	108	113	121	124	129	135	142	148	155
Productivity	100	100	101	103	102	107	106	111	111	120
Machinery										
Production	100	114	125	135	120	133	147	143	121	147
Prices	100	110	112	114	115	118	127	135	140	143
Hourly Money Wages	100	109	115	122	125	130	137	142	148	155
Productivity	100	95	102	108	110	120	122	119	121	135
Transportation equipment										
Production	100	111	130	162	150	180	174	190	160	185
Prices	100	105	111	110	111	113	120	126	130	133
Hourly Money Wages	100	107	113	120	123	129	135	144	146	153
Productivity	100	94	101	108	116	130	133	141	147	162

Non-durable Manufactures

	1950	1951	1952	1953	1954	1955	1956	1957	1958	1959
Furniture										
Production	100	94	98	101	106	120	124	121	117	140
Prices	100	108	106	108	109	110	113	116	117	117
Hourly Money Wages	100	108	115	120	122	126	132	136	139	142
Productivity	100	98	102	101	116	125	124	121	130	140
Food and Kindred Products										
Production	100	102	105	106	108	113	116	116	118	123
Prices	100	111	109	105	105	102	102	105	110	107
Hourly Money Wages	100	108	114	121	125	132	137	145	151	158
Productivity	100	102	105	106	111	117	120	123	131	136
Apparel										
Production	100	99	103	106	102	112	116	117	118	141
Prices	100	110	100	98	97	96	96	96	95	96
Hourly Money Wages	100	107	108	111	112	112	120	125	126	127
Productivity	100	99	103	102	102	109	112	117	123	137
Chemicals										
Production	100	113	118	128	127	146	157	166	166	187
Prices	100	115	109	110	111	110	111	113	115	115
Hourly Money Wages	100	108	113	121	126	132	133	147	153	160
Productivity	100	105	109	114	118	130	140	148	160	174

SOURCE: U.S. Department of Commerce, *Statistical Abstract of the United States*, 1960. The productivity index is obtained by dividing the production index by a production worker index.

employment of both labour and equipment. On the other hand, there was little sign of *over-full* employment and demand was not excessive in relation to production.[1] The expansion of demand and production in 1955 was accompanied by very little rise in prices, the index of wholesale prices rising by less than 1 per cent. Admittedly, this very great stability was permitted by a significant fall in raw food prices (9 per cent): even so, finished good prices rose very little, by no more than 1 or 2 per cent, and consumer good prices on average rose not at all.

In 1956, industrial production rose much less rapidly — by only 2 to 3 per cent in the course of the year — whilst prices rose more rapidly. To some extent, the latter was due to a reversal of direction of the movement of food prices, but manufactured good prices also rose at a faster rate, particularly prices of producers' durable goods.[2] It might therefore be thought that the United States economy, having reached a point of full employment, could increase its production very little more, hence prices had to rise. But closer inspection reveals that this is not a correct interpretation of events. The fact is that whilst demand was certainly excessive in some sectors of the economy, in others it was deficient, hence output had to fall.

During 1955, the demand for consumer durables expanded very vigorously indeed. This is reflected particularly in the output of cars which rose by over 50 per cent, but it is also seen in the expansion of house building and in the associated rise in output of house furnishings etc. But the consumer good boom was declining in the last quarter of 1955, and in 1956, demand and output fell off steeply. The production of cars for instance, fell by over 15 per cent, leaving considerable excess capacity in the industry. On the other hand, the investment boom continued its way. In consequence, the production of many types of machinery and of fabricated metals increased strongly in 1956 (see Table IX). Thus, a feature of economic activity in 1956 was a wide dispersion in the movement of demand: there were as many industries experienced contracting demand and output as there were experiencing expansions. Moreover, the investment boom itself was adding to manufacturing capacity at a fast rate: between 1955 and 1957, capacity in all manufacturing industry rose by about 12 per cent,[3] a sub-

---

[1] Unfilled orders of manufacturers rose in the course of 1955 but at no time reached the high levels associated with the boom of 1951–3.
[2] Rose by 10 per cent in course of the year.
[3] McGraw-Hill Dept. of Economics.

stantial part of which, however, remained unutilised. By the end of 1956, manufacturing industry was operating at only 86 per cent of capacity, on average, as compared with over 90 per cent at the beginning of the year.

Despite clear signs of excess capacity in many sectors of the economy, prices continued to rise, indeed, at a faster rate than during the previous twelve months. Prices rose more in those sectors where demand and output were rising most rapidly: machinery prices, for instance, which had risen by only 2 or 3 per cent in 1955, rose by 8 or 9 per cent during 1956; and prices of producer goods in general rose by nearer 10 per cent. But prices also rose significantly in sectors where demand and output were not increasing and where it was even falling. This was particularly true of many products whose processes of production were tied in some way to iron and steel — for instance, forge products, tin cans, motor cars, etc. It can be seen from the table on page 150 that when iron and steel production was declining, and excess capacity was rising during 1956, steel prices rose by over 10 per cent; and they continued to rise sharply in 1957 and '58 when output had fallen to less than two thirds of capacity. The story is the same with cars, prices rising less in 1955 when production was rising than in 1956 when it was falling. But, quite apart from iron and steel products, inspection of wholesale price indexes for a wide range of manufacturing industry reveals how few instances there were in which falling or stationary output was accompanied by falling prices: the general picture is that prices rose irrespective of what happened to output and demand.

The behaviour of final product prices was conditioned partly by the behaviour of material prices, partly by the behaviour of money wages rates. The spread of wage increases throughout the economy is particularly evident. From 1954 to 1955, money wages rose on average by about 4 per cent in manufacturing industry, and somewhat more in industries producing consumer and producer durables. In 1956, however, the rise in money wage rates was highly uniform, at about 10 per cent, throughout most industries, durable and non-durable producing sectors alike. The rise in money wage rates was clearly unconnected with changes in employment: the expanding industries tended to increase their employment somewhat whilst the contracting industries reduced their employment more; money wage rates rose about the same in all cases. Moreover, since productivity per man hour also tended to rise less in the contracting or stagnating industries than it did in the expanding ones, unit labour costs rose more in the former than in the latter. To this, was often added the burden of rising overhead costs per unit of output as production fell off; and to some extent the rise in prices was purely the consequence of firms attempting to maintain their profits by raising their gross mark-up; but this was inevitably self defeating, since rising prices tended to deter demand even more and unit overhead costs continued to rise.

In sum, in the events of 1955/6 there is unmistakeable evidence that the absence of aggregate excess demand is by no means a sufficient condition for prices to remain stable. If any more is required, it is necessary only to look at the following period 1957 and early 1958 in which demand and output in *all* sectors of the economy were declining, yet prices and wages continued to rise. These latter years clearly indicate that the United States economy is faced with a secular price raising force of considerable importance; for, if aggregate demand and its composition cannot be sufficiently controlled at all times (as it clearly cannot) so as to prevent prices from ever rising then it is clearly going to be very difficult to force them down again, save at the expense of a serious slump which lasts long enough to break down all normal pricing behaviour. It is likely that these upward pressures have always been in existence to some extent, which only the onset of severe depressions has temporarily destroyed. Moreover, in the past, agricultural prices have played a more important role in determining the long run behaviour of the price level, in the way we have indicated earlier. Now, however, agricultural output is a much smaller proportion of total output than formerly. Furthermore, and this is perhaps more important, the normal downward flexibility of agricultural prices, which at times in the past operated to pull down the general price level, can no longer be relied on. For better or worse, on an international as well as national scale, governments are increasingly pursuing farm price support policies. Thus an important element of flexibility in the system has been removed.

Important implications for policy are therefore raised; these, however, we shall not consider until a later chapter. First, we shall go on to examine the relationship between prices and growth in the more 'open' economy of the United Kingdom.

Chapter VII

THE UNITED KINGDOM

I

PROFESSOR HAMILTON'S THESIS CONCERNING THE SIXTEENTH AND SEVENTEENTH CENTURIES

The thesis that inflation played an important role in the early economic development of England was advanced by the distinguished American economic historian, Earl J. Hamilton. In an early article,[1] Hamilton pointed to the importance of the discovery of America and the opening up of the East Indies trade route for the rapid growth of capitalism and industrialisation in England, France and Spain in the sixteenth and seventeenth centuries. He recognised, of course, that other factors independent of the discovery — for example, agricultural improvements and enclosures, the growth of national states, simplification of public administration and unification of legal systems — as well as those stemming from it, were also important at this time: but it is clear that he put greatest emphasis on the influx of gold and silver from the New World into Europe. The influx of precious metals, according to Hamilton, had two major effects: first, it financed trade with East India, which proved very productive of speculative gains and profits, a large proportion of which found its way into commerce and industry; and, second, it led to a great and prolonged rise in prices. During this inflation, wages and rents lagged well behind the rise in prices of goods so that profits were the main beneficiary. As a result, saving and investment were stimulated and capitalism and industrialisation prospered.

Keynes lent his support to Hamilton's views in the historical chapter of his *Treatise on Money*.[2] 'It is the teaching of this Treatise that the wealth of nations is enriched not during Income inflations, but during Profit inflations — at times, that is to say, when prices are running away from costs.'[3] During these times, according to

[1] E. J. Hamilton, 'American Treasure and the Rise of Capitalism', *Economica*, 1929.
[2] J. M. Keynes, *Treatise on Money*, Vol. II, Chapter 30.　　　[3] Ibid., p. 154.

Keynes, profits, saving and investment are all rising at the expense of current consumption, so that capital wealth is being accumulated. Wiebe's statistics of prices and wages, as adapted by Hamilton, obviously supported Keynes's theory, especially since the sixteenth and seventeenth centuries were recognised by historians generally as being years of rapid industrial development in France and England. Keynes, indeed, attempted to quantify the argument so as to bring out the extent to which profits were inflated at this time. Taking Hamilton's statistics of prices and wages at their face value,[1] and assuming that money wages constituted one half of costs of production whilst the other half moved parallel with product prices, Keynes calculated price/costs ratios for England, France and Spain, over the two centuries. From these calculations it appeared that the ratio of prices to costs in England was about 16 per cent higher in the second half of the sixteenth century than it had been in the first half, and it rose to a peak (40 per cent higher) by about 1625. Thereafter it fell, but even by 1700 it was still some 14 per cent higher than two hundred years earlier. In France, the price/costs ratio reached its highest point in the last quarter of the sixteenth century, being about 40 per cent above what it was in 1500. The rise in the ratio was less great in Spain, being about 25 per cent higher in 1550 than in 1500, thereafter falling; and in this lower ratio Keynes sees the explanation of Spain's lagging development as compared with what was going on in England and France.[2]

Hamilton's thesis did not go without early criticism. Professor J. U. Nef, for instance, compared industrial growth in France with that in England in the sixteenth and seventeenth centuries,[3] and concluded that no simple interpretation of the great price revolution was possible. Both the rise in prices and the fall in real wages were as great in France as in England yet France developed more slowly. Nef did not deny the coincidence between the fall in real wages and very rapid industrial development in England between 1550 and 1620, but he pointed out that the coincidence did not exist in France. In fact, France developed more slowly between 1575 and 1600, when real wages were falling most rapidly, than it

---

[1] It is clear that Keynes was disturbed by the implications for real wages of these statistics, but he also pointed out that real wages were exceptionally high in 1500.

[2] Ibid., pp. 159–61.

[3] J. U. Nef, 'Prices and Industrial Capitalism in France and England 1540–1640', *Economic History Review*, 1936–7.

did during the next twenty-five years when real wages were probably higher. Nor did Nef accept the implications of Hamilton's price and wage data which seemed to suggest that real wages in England fell by a half during the last half of the sixteenth century and first quarter of the seventeenth. 'Had the standard of living among the English working people really fallen by anything approaching half, the advantages which employers derived from hiring labour cheaply might have been offset by the reduction in the amount workmen could have spent on manufactured goods.'[1] In fact, he argued, money wages probably rose more than Hamilton's index would suggest: furthermore, payments in kind to workmen were probably very common in this period, and many workmen and their families were able to cultivate small holdings in their spare time. In addition, town prices were probably very unrepresentative of those in the country as a whole, being much higher than in the rural areas. Finally, whilst not denying that profits rose substantially during this period, Nef pointed to the striking progress made in industrial technology which was the main factor in keeping labour costs down.

Hamilton, however, does not seem to have accepted the substance of Nef's criticism, and re-affirmed his thesis in later writings.[2] Now, however, he applied his thesis to eighteenth-century development in France and Spain, and particularly to the early stages of the industrial revolution in England. Once again, Hamilton explicitly recognises the presence of 'other' factors, but these seem to slip more into the background, and increasing emphasis is given to the price-wage lag. The steady rise in prices from 1750 to 1800 is attributed to the increase in silver output from Mexico and to gold discoveries in Brazil. Money wages lagged behind prices, so that profits were inflated, and as result, the rate of capital formation in industry was once again vastly accelerated.[3]

However, Hamilton's interpretation of the facts relating to prices and growth in England and France of the sixteenth and seventeenth centuries and latter part of the eighteenth century is

[1] Ibid., p. 184. Nef suggests that the fall in real wages in France in the last quarter of the sixteenth century probably checked development for this reason.
[2] E. J. Hamilton, 'Profit Inflation in the Industrial Revolution', *Quarterly Journal of Economics 1942*; and 'Prices and Progress', *Journal of Economic History, 1952*.
[3] The most rapid rise in prices occurred in the last decade of the eighteenth century at the time of the Napoleonic Wars; but even if this is excluded, prices rose by about 30 per cent during the forty years up to 1790, that is to say, at about the same rate as in the fifteenth and sixteenth centuries.

not the only one possible. For his account of the earlier period, Hamilton made use of price and wage indices constructed by G. Wiebe.[1] These showed that in England prices rose by about 250 per cent in the 200 years following the end of the fourteenth century. Wages, however, rose by only about 130 per cent. In France, prices rose by about 150 per cent in the sixteenth century, and although there was some tendency for them to fall during the next century, they still remained 130 per cent above the level of the year 1500. Wages rose by some 20 per cent in the sixteenth century and by a further 35 per cent in the seventeenth. Hamilton therefore concluded that there must have been an enormous rise in profits in both countries, with consequential favourable results for industrial growth. It seems clear, however, that besides being of somewhat limited coverage,[2] Wiebe's overall price indices obscure more than they reveal. If they are broken down and a distinction made between agricultural and industrial product prices, then it becomes evident that agricultural and wood product prices are mainly responsible for the steep rise in the overall index.[3] In England unprocessed agricultural products (largely raw food) rose by about 400 per cent in price, during the course of inflation, and wood and wood product prices rose by about 300 per cent. Industrial product prices, on the other hand, rose by only 140 per cent and within this category, textile prices rose by no more than 50 per cent. Similarly in France during the sixteenth century, industrial product prices rose much less than agricultural prices, the former by about 50 per cent as against 300 per cent by the latter. If the change in industrial product prices is compared with the change in money wages over the same period, the evidence for profit inflation in industry at least is rapidly seen to diminish in significance. Furthermore, it must be borne in mind that industrial costs of production were affected by the steep rise in the price level of agricultural raw materials; hence the fact that prices rose relatively to money wages cannot be taken to indicate that they rose to quite the same degree relative to costs. On the other hand, the rise in money wages is not an indication of the rise in labour costs, for

---

[1] Georg Wiebe, *Zur Geschichte der Preisrevolution des XVI und XVII Jahrhunderts* (Leipzig 1895), pp. 374–7.

[2] Wiebe's price and wage series for England consist of a simple average of 79 commodity prices and 8 wage rates.

[3] See D. Felix, 'Profit Inflation and Industrial Growth', *Quarterly Journal of Economics*, August 1956, Tables I, II and III.

there is substantial evidence that widespread improvements in labour productivity took place in both countries during this period. Unfortunately, the evidence is not of a quantitative nature nor do we have information concerning the relative importance of raw material costs in industry. But at least it seems reasonably certain that profit margins were by no means so inflated as Hamilton's interpretation would warrant. Indeed, if we rework Keynes's calculations of price/costs ratios in England, now, however, assuming that raw material costs moved more in line with agricultural and timber prices whilst industrial product prices rose much less, then it becomes clear that a substantial rise in labour productivity was required, particularly after about 1550, in order to keep the price/costs ratio from falling, let alone to contribute to its rise. No doubt, a substantial rise in productivity did occur, but clearly there is room to doubt whether it was sufficient to cause a significant rise in profit margins.[1]

Once the changing relationship between agricultural prices and industrial prices is observed, a different interpretation of the great price revolution of the sixteenth and seventeenth centuries becomes possible. Hamilton explained the inflation of this period in terms of the quantity theory of money: the influx of precious metals from the New World increased the quantity of money in Europe which in turn caused prices to rise through the effect on demand. Wages lagged behind, hence profits, saving and investment rose. An alternative explanation, however, would put rising food and agricultural raw material prices in the leading role with industrial costs and prices following suit. Industrial costs and prices did not rise by as much as agricultural prices, partly because industrial money wages did not rise as fast as food prices. Industrial money wages were kept in check by the rapid growth of the labour supply which itself stemmed, first, from rising total population,

---

[1] Price/costs ratios, as calculated by Keynes, reached their maximum in the first quarter of the seventeenth century; but if we recalculate them on the basis of Felix's breakdown of Wiebe's price series — taking timber prices as indication of raw material costs — then it seems probably that price/costs ratios in industry were lower at this time than during the first half of the sixteenth century, and lower even than they were around 1500.

On this basis the price/costs ratios would be:

1500–1550	..	100 (100)	1640–1650	..	75 (133)
1550–1560	..	92 (116)	1670–1680	..	53 (124)
1580–1590	..	80 (120)	1690–1700	..	63 (114)
1610–1620	..	74 (135)			

N.B.—Keynes's ratios are given in brackets.

and second, from developments in agriculture, such as the en-
closure movement, which pushed labour off the land into the
towns. At the same time, however, the rise in *money* wages was
sufficient to encourage industrialists to seek for labour-saving
methods, thereby inducing a rise in labour productivity which
helped to check the rise in costs of production and prices in
industry. It is quite likely that many producers were able to increase
their profit margins at the same time, but probably the largest
gainers in this process of inflation were the sellers of food, that is,
the farmers, and the owners of land on short leases who were able
to raise rents. Some of these gains were no doubt channelled into
industry, although the general view seems to be that industry did
not obtain much capital from agriculture at this time.[1] On the
other hand, rising agricultural incomes provided a market for the
products of industry, thereby contributing to development through
the demand side rather than through supply.

This interpretation of inflation, of course, leaves unexplained
the rise in food and agricultural prices in the first place, but a
sufficient explanation would seem to be the growth of population
at this time — it about doubled between 1500 and 1700 — plus
the income effect on the demand for food as real incomes rose in
some sectors of the economy. The rise in population also helps to
explain the source of demand for the rapidly growing industrial
output, although the real wages, and therefore purchasing power,
of a substantial proportion of the population were falling. The
losers in the inflation were in fact the landless labourers who were
unable to insulate themselves against food scarcity by cultivating
small holdings; and it has been estimated that this class of persons
constituted about 30 per cent of the population.[2]

The price inflation of 1750 to 1790 is open to a similar interpretation. Hamilton's price index suggests that prices rose by about
30 per cent during this period, but when it is broken down, it is at
once obvious that agricultural prices took the lead. From 1750 to
1790 (that is, excluding the Napoleonic Wars) prices of agricultural
products and of commodities produced from domestic agricultural
materials probably rose by about 50 per cent whereas industrial
product prices rose by considerably less — about 10 or 11 per cent,

[1] E. Lipson, *The Economic History of England* (London 1947–8) 164, III, p. 208.
[2] Phelps Brown and Hopkins, 'Wage Rates and Prices: Evidence for Population Pressure in the Sixteenth Century', *Economica*, August 1957.

that is, somewhat less than money wages which rose by about 15 per cent.[1] Once again, therefore, it appears that inflation was accompanied, if not caused, by a change in the barter terms of trade between agriculture and industry; and it seems reasonable to suppose that the process was initiated by the rapid growth of population at this time[2] which put pressure on food prices, and therefore on money wages, industrial costs and prices. Rising wage costs was no doubt one of the stimulants to technological development, which was extensive at this time, and if profit margins were not squeezed, this was due to the success which employers had in raising labour productivity.

This interpretation of price inflation must not be taken to deny that economic development in the sixteenth and seventeenth centuries and latter half of the eighteenth, was very significant. But in stressing that prices tended to rise because industrial development and population growth were outstripping the development of agriculture, our interpretation does run counter to the view that economic growth was promoted by an increase in the supply of monetary metals which raised prices, and thereby stimulated saving and investment. Moreover, the general thesis connecting inflation with rapid economic development in this manner receives a further blow if we survey the path of Britain's economic development during the first half of the nineteenth century.

II

PRICES AND GROWTH IN THE NINETEENTH CENTURY

Between the end of the Napoleonic Wars and the mid-century Britain's economy grew at a faster rate than at any time before or after. Yet the general level of prices was falling or stable, and real wages were rising. In assessing the implication of this we need of course to take into account the effects of the Napoleonic Wars. From 1790 to 1812 the price level of domestically produced goods rose by about 150 per cent.[3] At the end of the wars, however, prices collapsed and by 1822 they were back to their pre-war level. The sharp rise and fall from 1790 to 1822 can easily be explained

---

[1] Felix, op. cit., Table IV, p. 456.
[2] Population rose by about 1·4 per cent per annum during this period.
[3] See Gayer, Rostow, and Schwartz, *The Growth and Fluctuation of the British Economy, 1790–1850* (Oxford 1953), pp. 486/7, and Fig. 97, pp. 471–2.
If 1821–25 = 100, then prices moved as follows:

with reference to the wars, but the continued stability of the domestic price level, and the fall in the total price level (domestic plus import) up to 1849, have to be considered independently. Indeed it might be more sensible to view the whole period 1790 to 1850 as one of a long-term fall in the price level, interrupted only by war inflation from 1793 to 1815.

It is generally recognised that the war years constituted a period of rapid economic development in Britain: to this extent, therefore, Hamilton's thesis is given empirical support. A great volume of investment took place, in agriculture, in mining and in industrial plant.[1] The iron industry was naturally stimulated by wartime orders, but also by restrictions on imports which forced the industry to become independent of foreign supplies; and of course during this period the cotton industry made extraordinary progress, partly through the introduction of the cotton gin which enlarged supplies of raw materials, partly through the expansion of markets overseas. But any judgment of the effects of inflationary fiscal policy pursued at this time must take into account also the fact that the government was the principal, and large-scale, borrower, and that interest rates were rising. Investment and production were therefore directed into channels satisfying wartime rather than peacetime requirements. Cannon were produced rather than machinery, and export markets stimulated by government loans and subsidies, given largely for political reasons, relatively to markets at home. Whilst of course it cannot be known what would have happened if there had been no wars, a considered view is that progress in the British economy would have been even greater.[2] What is certainly true, however, is that rates of growth of

	1790/2	1812/14	1822	1824	1850
Domestic Prices	76	189	79		74
Import Prices	85	180		92	52
Domestic plus Import	85	177	85		71

[1] Ibid., p. 647.

[2] 'It may, however, be tentatively inferred that technological advance would probably have been more rapid; that the increase in exports would have been less rapid; and that the increase in producers' goods production would have been greater, with the brick index rising more sharply, and the increased production of iron turned more largely to machinery, bridges, and other domestic uses rather than to cannon and materials of warfare. In individual markets, demand curves might have shifted somewhat less to the right, but the long run cost curves would have shifted farther down and to the right. The increase in total output would have been differently distributed as among industries. And above all, the tendency for prices to fall would have been more strongly and sooner felt.' Ibid., pp. 648/9.

industrial production were higher after 1815 than during the previous twenty-five years.

Hoffman's index of industrial production in Great Britain, used by Gayer, Rostow and Schwartz in their study of the British economy in this period,[1] indicates that total production rose at the rate of 3½ per cent per annum from 1815 to 1847 as against 2 per cent per annum from 1793 to 1815. The production of capital goods grew singularly fast, at about 4·3 per cent per annum, and faster relatively to the output of consumption goods in the second period than in the first.[2] Moreover, production was no longer devoted to war purposes and less of it went to export markets. Hence capital formation in domestic industry, and living standards of the domestic population received the main benefit. Technical progress continued at a great rate and there is little doubt that labour productivity rose fast. It is pertinent to Hamilton's thesis to note that the expansion of industry after 1815 was not at the expense of real wages. Indeed, whereas real wages had been falling steadily throughout the war period, from 1815 onwards they rose by more than ½ per cent per annum. It is also significant that the rise was much greater in terms of industrial products — that is, the prices of industrial goods fell faster than money wages — than in terms of agricultural goods, the price level of which fell only slightly more than money wages.[3] Superficially, therefore, it could be argued that profit margins in industry, at least, must have been falling in these years, in which case, if we accept Hamilton's thesis, we have to explain how the saving arose to finance the undoubtedly massive rate of investment. The fact is, of course, that movements of final product prices and money wages over a long period of time do not provide a reliable guide to the movements of either profit margins or total profits in the same period. Industrial prices were falling between 1820 and 1850, partly because the cost of industrial raw materials was falling, but largely because labour productivity was rising fast. The stability of agricultural prices in general and of food prices in particular was important, in this context, because it made possible the stability of money wages,

---

[1] Ibid., Vol. II, Chapter IV, Table 77.

[2] Between 1793 and 1815 the output of producers' goods rose at 2·3 per cent per annum and the output of consumers' goods at 1·9 per cent per annum. The latter rose at 3·2 per cent per annum between 1815 and 1847. Ibid., Vol. II, Chapter IV, Table 77.

[3] The Corn Laws, of course, were an important influence checking the rise in real wages in terms of agricultural products.

thereby permitting increases in productivity to be reflected in rising profit margins or falling prices, or both. Evidence concerning industrial profit margins in the first half of the nineteenth century is neither full nor satisfactory, but even if, as some suspected,[1] profit margins per unit of product were falling, it does not follow that either gross profits or profits relative to capital employed were also falling. What is clear is that 'profits (were) still sufficient to allow of a great accumulation of capital in the manufacture, as is evident from the continual erection of new mills, and the remarkable extension and improvement of the towns where the business is carried on'.[2]

The downward trend of prices was reversed after 1850, but although prices rose in the 1850's, this had ceased by the end of the decade. Thereafter, prices remained fairly constant until the 1870–73 boom, but after this had collapsed, the general downward trend was resumed until the mid-1890's. In fact, the general long run course of prices throughout the nineteenth century, apart from the inflation of the Napoleonic War years and the short price boom of the 1850's, was downward, the value of money probably being higher in 1895 than in 1820. After 1895, however, prices began to rise persistently, and the rise was given further impetus by the 1914–18 war. It is significant that growth in this later period, whether measured in terms of real income *per capita*, output *per capita*, or total industrial production, was slower than in the previous forty years,[3] when prices were either falling or stable. In fact it seems reasonably clear that development in Britain after 1850 gives no more support to Hamilton's thesis than it did pre-1850. Nor can the development be seen in terms of prices running away from money wages. Apart from a check in the early 1850's, real wages rose throughout the nineteenth century; and, if anything, they rose faster when growth was faster, rather than the other way round. It was not until the first two decades of the

---

[1] E. Barnes, *History of the Cotton Manufacture* (London 1835) and G. R. Porter, *Progress of the Nation* (London 1847), quoted in Gayer, Rostow and Schwartz, op. cit., pp. 653/4.

[2] Barnes, op. cit., quoted in Gayer, Rostow, Schwartz, ibid., pp. 653/4.

[3] In the last quarter of the nineteenth century, real national income per head rose by about 2 per cent per annum, whereas in the pre First World War decade and a half, the rise was less than 1 per cent per annum; cf. S. Kuznets, 'Quantitative aspects of the Economic Growth of Nations', in *Economic Development and Cultural Change*, October 1956, and Jefferys and Walters, 'National Income and Expenditure of the United Kingdom, 1870–1952', in *Income and Wealth*, Series V.

twentieth century that real wages began to fall and as we have seen, growth at this time was probably slower.

Thus, it appears that as far as the period 1815 to 1915 is concerned, British economic development refutes the general thesis that rapid economic growth tends to go hand in hand with secular inflation. Apart from the Napoleonic war years and the decade of the 1850's, prices tended to fall secularly throughout the nineteenth century, yet there can be no doubting the massive economic growth that took place. Moreover, after 1895, when prices began to rise persistently, growth was slower than at almost any time during the previous century. Nonetheless, the question remains: why did prices behave as they did, and what was the connection with the rate of growth?

Up to 1850 domestic wheat harvests were probably the most important factor determining the behaviour of the price level. In the first half of the century, domestic agriculture provided the bulk of food requirements (largely grain products), although marginal amounts were pulled in from abroad when domestic harvests were poor. During the Napoleonic wars, Britain was partly cut off from foreign grain supplies: moreover, the wars forced freight and insurance rates to high levels. It was this more than any other factor that caused prices to rise so steeply from 1793 to 1815. Admittedly, government war expenditure, financed by an elastic money supply, contributed to inflation, but its effect was confined to a relatively few products, for instance, iron, wool and timber.[1] When harvests were poor, however, wheat prices rose strongly, since foreign supplies were uncertain or could only be obtained at high cost; and although they fell in years of better harvests, they seldom fell by as much as they had earlier risen (see Chart I). Other prices were affected by the fluctuations in wheat prices, but it was the latter that largely determined the behaviour of the domestic price level. Thus, at the close of the wars, when foreign sources of supply became more certain and cheaper to import, a substantial fall in wheat prices occurred, bringing them down to about their pre-war level. Thereafter, although wheat prices continued to fluctuate, the extent to which they rose was limited by the availability of imports;[2] and in the years up to 1850, they tended to fall in the

---

[1] See Gayer, Rostow, Schwartz, op. cit., Vol. II, Chapter IV.
[2] Without the Corn Laws, of course, the amplitude of the fluctuations would have been much less.

course of fluctuations at least as much as they rose. Moreover, in this period, in addition to the greater accessibility to foreign sources, the available supply of wheat to the domestic market was receiving the benefit of considerable investment in agriculture which had taken place during the war years. Thus, there was a considerable expansion of domestic food output in the first half of

Chart I. Wheat Prices, 1790–1850

(Annual percentage change)

SOURCE: Gayer, Rostow, Schwartz, *The Growth and Fluctuation of the British Economy, 1790–1850* (Oxford), Vol. II, p. 826.

the nineteenth century, which at first, at any rate, kept pace with the growth of population. When the growth of agriculture threatened to fall seriously behind the growth of population and other production towards the middle of the century, the repeal of the Corn Laws increased the elasticity of supply, and fluctuations in grain prices diminished, producing greater stability in the domestic price level until the end of the century.

The *secular* stability of food prices from 1820 to 1850 was an important factor underlying the secular fall in the domestic price level at this time. It permitted secular stability of money wage rates in manufacturing industry, so that the gains in labour productivity which took place were reflected in falling manufactured good prices rather than in rising money incomes. The price level of manufactured goods also benefitted from a secular fall in raw cotton prices. The latter fell steeply at the close of the Napoleonic wars, partly as a result of a fall in freight and insurance freights. Afterwards, the movement of raw cotton prices depended principally on the relationship between the growth of American supply and the growth of

British demand. In the 1820's and early '30's, supply grew faster than demand, and cotton prices fell steeply; but in the late '30's, demand more than caught up, so that prices rose. In the 1840's and '50's, however, the growth of demand and supply were roughly in balance, so that, despite year to year fluctuations, raw cotton prices remained relatively constant in the longer run.

In brief, the slight secular fall in prices which occurred in Britain in the thirty-five years following the end of the Napoleonic wars was the consequence of an adequate growth of domestic food supply relatively to the growth of population and industrial production, plus a rapid rise in labour productivity in industry, and a fall in the cost of its most important raw material. The terms of exchange moved in favour of domestic agriculture, not because agricultural output was greatly deficient in relation to demand, but because of the enormous growth in manufacturing output. After 1850, however, the behaviour of import prices played an increasingly important role in the determination of the domestic price level, largely because imported foodstuffs began to figure strongly in domestic diet.[1]

This is brought out in Table Ia and Chart II in which we present various indexes of prices, on an annual basis, from 1860 to the outbreak of the First World War. We see that, apart from the boom of 1868 to 1873, in which strongly rising money wages produced by booming employment conditions appear to have been the major pressure affecting manufactured good prices, fluctuations in the cost of living were normally related fairly closely to fluctuations in the price level of imported foodstuffs. The latter, however, were not at all correlated with fluctuations in domestic activity. Moreover, the amplitude of fluctuations in the cost of living index in the second half of the century was much smaller than it was in the first half, owing, largely, to the greater elasticity of supply of grain products which had appeared as the consequence of the repeal of the Corn Laws. There is also an obvious connection between the behaviour of the imported raw material price index and the behaviour of the manufactured good price index; but in

---

[1] In the twenty-five years prior to the repeal of the Corn Laws the volume of food imports into Britain doubled. They doubled again in less than half this time once the Corn Laws had been repealed, and further doubled in each of the next two decades. Thus whereas in the mid 1840's food imports were roughly double what they had been in 1820, by 1860 they were 5 times as large, and by 1870 almost 8 times as large. See W. Schlote, *British Overseas Trade* (Blackwell 1952), Table 8.

Table Ia

Prices and Production, United Kingdom 1860–1913

Year	(1) Industrial Production (excl. building) (1913 = 100)	(2) Manufactured Good Prices (1913 = 100)	(3) Import Prices Raw Materials (1913 = 100)	Food	(4) Cost of living (1890–9 = 100)	(5) Money Wages
1860	34	95	103	135	130	68
1	33	94	110	130	129	68
2	31	108	152	123	130	68
3	33	125	171	114	133	70
4	34	137	180	119	133	73
5	37	129	159	118	130	75
6	38	131	144	124	131	78
7	37	119	123	136	131	77
8	40	111	122	135	130	75
9	40	112	128	123	128	75
70	43	109	123	121	127	78
1	46	110	109	126	130	80
2	47	120	120	131	138	89
3	49	121	119	131	141	96
4	50	114	113	130	133	100
5	49	109	109	126	128	100
6	50	100	105	122	127	99
7	51	96	101	131	127	98
8	48	93	95	119	120	95
9	46	88	90	113	116	93
80	54	92	97	117	121	93
1	54	87	95	118	119	93
2	58	88	94	119	118	93
3	60	86	91	114	118	94
4	58	83	89	105	112	94
5	56	80	83	98	105	93
6	55	76	77	92	103	93
7	57	76	77	91	101	93
8	62	77	81	93	101	93
9	66	77	81	95	103	96
90	65	82	81	92	103	100
1	66	82	78	97	103	100
2	63	79	75	93	104	100
3	61	78	75	92	103	99
4	65	74	75	83	98	99
5	67	72	66	80	96	98
6	70	74	71	79	96	99
7	71	73	70	80	98	100
8	74	72	67	83	91	102
9	77	76	73	81	99	104
1900	77	85	84	82	105	108
1	76	84	79	84	104	107
2	77	80	77	85	104	107
3	77	82	81	85	105	106
4	77	84	83	84	106	105
5	82	85	82	87	106	105
6	85	89	91	87	107	107
7	87	94	95	91	110	107
8	82	93	85	93	107	107
9	83	90	86	96	108	107
10	86	93	100	98	110	107
13	100	100	100	100	118	115

SOURCES: Column (1): W. Hoffmann, *British Industry 1700–1950*, Blackwell. Table 54.
Columns (2) and (3): W. Schlote, *British Overseas Trade*, Blackwell, Table 26.
Columns (4) and (5): Phelps Brown and Hopkins: 'Wage Rates in Five Countries, 1860–1939', *Oxford Economic Papers*, June 1950.

M

this case, fluctuations in the former are, to some extent at least, also correlated with fluctuations in domestic economic activity. This latter correlation clearly does not hold in the 1860's when the strong rise in imported raw material prices and manufactured good prices was the result of the restriction of cotton supplies arising from the American civil war.

Table Ib

Percentage Change in Production and Prices in Boom and Slump. United Kingdom, 1860–1913

Period (*)	Industrial Production	Manufactured Good Prices	Import Prices Raw Materials	Food	Cost of Living	Money Wages
1860 to 1862	− 8	+14	+50	−10	0	
1862 to 1866	+22	+21	− 4	0	0	
1866 to 1868	− 3	−15	−15	−10	− 1	
1868 to 1873	+25	+12	− 1	− 4	+ 9	+33
1873 to 1879	− 8	−26	−20	−15	−17	− 7
1879 to 1883	+28	− 2	+ 1	+ 1	+ 1	+ 1
1883 to 1886	−12	−11	−16	−20	−13	− 1
1886 to 1890	+18	+ 8	+ 5	0	0	+ 7
1890 to 1894	− 6	− 7	− 7	−10	− 5	− 1
1894 to 1900	+18	+15	+27	0	+ 7	+ 8
1900 to 1904	− 1	0	0	+ 2	+ 1	− 3
1904 to 1907	+13	+11	+14	+ 8	+ 4	+ 2
1907 to 1908	− 4	− 1	− 6	+ 2	− 3	0
1908 to 1913	+16	+ 8	+16	+ 7	+10	+ 8

* The periods are chosen with reference to the annual turning points of British trade cycles, given by Rostow in *British Economy in the Nineteenth Century* (Oxford), Table II.

It is also clear from Table Ib that, in the period 1870 to 1895, prices tended to fall much more in the slumps of economic activity than they rose in the booms, whilst the opposite was true from 1895 to the outbreak of the First World War. Hence a clear reversal of secular price behaviour occurred in the mid-1890's. Since British prices were largely conditioned by the behaviour of the price level of imports, it is to developments in the international economy that we must probably look for the explanation.

The explanation of secular international price behaviour in the nineteenth century, which has longest standing, is that which stresses changes in the supply of precious metals. On the assumption that precious metals provide the basis of other forms of

Chart II

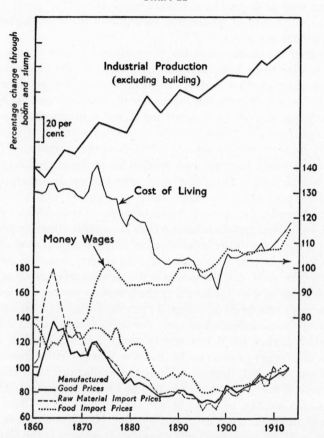

money, changes in the supply of the former are reflected in changes in the volume of the circulating medium. The latter, in turn, cause changes in monetary demand for goods and services, and therefore in prices and output. Prices are seen to change first, inducing a later change in output. But, as was pointed out in the introductory chapter to this book, the theory is no longer so widely or firmly held as it once was, because convincing arguments have been set against it. In addition to the arguments set out in Chapter I, there is also the fact that the 'gold' explanation is not really consistent with the shorter run behaviour of prices. There is little evidence, for instance, that, in the periods 1815 to 1850 and 1870 to 1875, booms were brought to an end by a shortage of money or slumps were prolonged by it, both of which one might expect if the secular behaviour of prices was successfully to be explained in purely monetary terms.

Another explanation that has been advanced turns on the fact that secular price behaviour can be related to the character of investment and other outlays at various times.[1] If expenditure is being directed towards the expansion of plant and machinery or to the expansion of raw material and factor of production supply, although prices may tend to rise at first as a result of current money incomes being increased relatively to the current supply of consumer goods, they will later tend to fall as the expenditure begins to bear fruit in terms of a rising output of goods and services. On the other hand if the expenditure is essentially 'unproductive' — for example, if it arises as a result of wars — then no future yield can be expected and therefore no later favourable effect on prices. Even if the expenditure is 'productive' the gestation period of investment must also be considered. The shorter it is, the sooner appears the yield, and the sooner is the upward pressure on prices abated. Conversely, the longer is the gestation period, the longer are prices likely to go on rising. Typically, British foreign investment of the nineteenth and early twentieth centuries had a long gestation period, for it was largely directed into expanding new areas of primary production in the New World. With this sort of argument in mind, Rostow explains the secular price movements in terms of wars and the distribution of British investment. Thus, from 1789 to 1815, prices in Britain rose because expenditure was largely directed towards financing the Napoleonic Wars. In addition, there was considerable foreign investment in the form of government subsidies to other countries. After 1815, investment turned inwards and domestic capital formation of short gestation period became predominant. Absence of wars further contributed towards a falling price level. In the 1850's a greater share of investment outlays went overseas, being connnected with the opening up of America and the accompanying railway boom there; furthermore the Crimean War and American Civil War caused much expenditure between 1850 and 1870 to be 'unproductive', so that prices either rose or did not fall. The last quarter of the nineteenth century was similar to the second quarter, in that investment was

[1] W. W. Rostow, *British Economy in the Nineteenth Century* (Oxford).

predominantly domestic and prices were falling, whereas in the first two decades of the twentieth century, both wars and a large-scale foreign investment boom (directed towards Argentina and Canada) once again produced a rising price level.

In later discussion of the subject[1] Rostow put more emphasis on the effect of investment outlays devoted to the opening up or extension of areas of primary production on the balance between world demand and supply of primary products. When investment was directed towards this end, the flow of primary products tended to rise relatively to the demand for them and consequently their prices fell. Costs of production in manufacturing countries therefore tended to fall, hence the price level of manufactures tended to move in sympathy with primary products prices. Conversely, when the supply of primary products became scarce relatively to the demand for them the price level generally would tend to rise. Rostow further saw the possibility of periods of primary product abundance alternating with periods of primary product scarcity. Thus if we started off with a situation in which the demand for primary products, as conditioned by the growth of industrial production, was tending to outstrip the growth of supply,[2] prices would rise. This would induce extensive investment in the areas of primary production, eventually leading to an increase in supply. But the nature of this investment and the conditions of primary production would often involve 'over-shooting' of production. The opening up of new areas of production or the extensive development of older areas required large-scale investment outlays rather than marginal, divisible expenditure. The gestation period of this investment tended to be very long and no quick or short run checks on the profitability of investment outlays were possible; investment outlays therefore often continued beyond the point where the future would show that they could be profitable. Hence over-production materialised, and a long period of falling prices set in. This would now discourage investment in primary production until once again demand had caught up with supply, producing a rise in the price level. This explanation has been criticised on grounds that available statistical data for the latter part of the nineteenth century and early years of the twentieth do not show significant secular fluctuations in the rate of growth of

---

[1] W. W. Rostow, *Process of Economic Growth* (Oxford).
[2] Wars would also play a part in producing these periods of scarcity.

output of primary products.[1] If this is true secular fluctuations in primary product prices must be explained with reference to demand, that is, with reference to variations in the rate of growth of world industrial capacity, which would determine variations in the growth of demand.

It is perhaps not too difficult to explain the secular fall in world primary product prices in the last quarter of the century in terms of changes in both demand and supply of primary products. Earlier decades had witnessed the opening up and exploitation of new areas of production in America and elsewhere which had borne fruit in a vast expansion in the supply of raw materials and foodstuffs to the trading world. It is possible, too, that Britain's own industrial development had lost some of the impetus of the previous half century. From 1870 to the mid-'90's industrial production grew at barely half the rate achieved during the 50 years following the end of the Napoleonic wars[2]; and since, at this time, Britain was by far the most important importer of primary products, this development must have affected the balance between the growth of demand and growth of supply. At any rate, Britain's import prices of food and raw materials fell by between a third and a half in the course of twenty-five years.[3]

The more difficult task is to explain the upturn in primary product prices after 1895, at a time when the rate of growth of both Britain and America showed no sign of increasing, in fact, may even have declined, as compared with the previous quarter century. As was pointed out in an earlier chapter,[4] however, Professor Phelps Brown and Mr. Ozga have shown that constant rates of growth of individual industrial countries are quite consistent with a rise in the rate of growth of world industrial capacity: all that is required is that some countries should be growing at a faster rate than others. It is possible, therefore, that rate of growth of demand for primary products accelerated after 1895 because of this; and since there are no signs that the growth of supply of primary products accelerated at the same time, a rise in primary product prices could be expected. But whilst it is not denied that this mechanism may

---

[1] See Phelps Brown and Ozga, 'Economic Growth and the Price Level', *Economic Journal*, March 1955.

[2] 1·6 per cent p.a. as compared with between 3 and 3·5 per cent p.a.

[3] The real costs of transportation also fell during this period, but this is not sufficient to account for all of the fall in British import prices.

[4] Chapter IV.

have contributed to the upturn in prices, it will be remembered that in Chapter VI we argued that a decline in the rate of growth of United States agricultural output also played a part. There is clear evidence that United States agriculture grew very much more slowly after the turn of the century than during the previous twenty-five years. The rate of growth of demand for agricultural products in the United States, if it declined at all, did not decline anywhere near to the same extent. Hence, there was a smaller surplus to export overseas, and, as far as foodstuffs are concerned, the United States even became a net importer. It is true that supplies of foodstuffs from other areas, such as Australia, Canada, and Argentina increased during this period, but apparently not sufficiently to offset the loss of American supplies.[1] Britain was the main sufferer, since by far the largest part of American exports of agricultural products had gone to the British market. It seems likely therefore that both an acceleration in the growth of world demand for primary products and a retardation in the growth of supply contributed to the upturn in British prices in the 1890's.

Turning now to the effect of a secular change in prices on the rate of economic growth, it was argued in an earlier theoretical chapter that a secular rise or fall in primary product prices might affect the rate of growth of an industrial economy, as well as its price level, through the influence it would have on its net barter terms of trade.[2] In the nineteenth century, however, it was not always the case that falling primary product prices were associated with an improvement in the terms of trade, or rising prices with worsening terms of trade. The most notable period in which the former association did not hold covers the thirty-five years from the end of the Napoleonic wars to the mid-nineteenth century. Even if we discount the sharp fall in import prices which occurred at the end of the war, import prices fell by more than a half between 1816 and 1852.[3] The downward trend was persistent, apart from some rise in the 1830's. But export prices fell faster than import prices, and by 1851 were only about one third of their level in 1816. The commodity terms of trade therefore deteriorated by over 30 per cent in the course of this period, and the deterioration continued throughout the 1850's, although now because import prices

[1] See the articles by Freund, cited in footnote 1, p. 129, Chapter VI.
[2] See Chapter IV.
[3] A. H. Imlah, *Economic Elements in the Pax Britannica* (Harvard), Chapter IX, Table 8.

rose faster than export prices. The events of the first half century can be interpreted in a way that suggests that the fruits of Britain's early industrial revolution were being passed on to overseas countries; but this should not obscure the fact that real wages in Britain rose substantially in this period. In fact, the deterioration in the terms of trade in this period arose out of two things: first, from the fact that technological progress in both the production of raw cotton and the manufacture of cotton finished goods lowered the cost of producing cotton goods; and second from the fact that cotton manufactures had a larger weight in British exports than imports of raw cotton had in British imports. The price of raw cotton probably fell by as much as the price level of finished cotton manufactures, so that the net barter terms of trade of cotton commodities alone did not deteriorate.[1] But because of the greater weight of cotton exports in total exports than cotton imports in total imports,[2] average export prices fell by more than average import prices. Rising productivity in the cotton manufacturing industry no doubt contributed most to the reduction in cotton export prices and therefore contributed to real incomes overseas; but at the same time it enabled a unit of British labour to increase its real purchasing power over other imported goods and services.

After 1865, however, import prices increasingly dictated the longer run movements in Britain's terms of trade. Import prices fell steadily until the mid 1890's except for a rise in the 1870 boom; and, apart from the effects of the collapse of the 1870 boom on export prices, which fell steeply after an equally precipitate, but short-term, rise, the commodity terms of trade improved. Another sharp boom and slump in both import and export prices at the turn of the century was associated with a favourable movement in the terms of trade; but from about 1903 until 1912, import prices rose and the terms of trade deteriorated, although only slightly. We have noted earlier that Britain's economic growth was probably slower after 1900 than it was in the previous twenty-five years; and it is of interest now to find out to what extent the factors associated with rising or falling primary product prices contributed to this result. This cannot, of course, be established with any certainty, but some reasonable inferences are possible.

The rate of growth of real income *per capita* in the last quarter

[1] Imlah, ibid., p. 106.
[2] In 1840, 40 per cent as against 20 per cent. See Imlah, ibid., Table 9, p. 104.

of the nineteenth century varied between 2 and $2\frac{1}{2}$ per cent per annum, whereas in the pre-war decade and a half, it was less than 1 per cent per annum.[1] (See Table II.) By 1895 the net barter terms of trade were about 10 or 11 per cent more favourable than in 1870, so that, even given the great weight of foreign trade relative to Britain's national product in this period, it seems reasonably clear that the *direct* effect of the terms of trade on real income *per capita* cannot have been great, contributing only a fraction of the

Table II

U.K. Net National Income 1912–13 prices
Percentage change per Decade

Interval	Net National Income	Net National Income per capita
1860–69 to 1870–79	18·4	5·9
1865–74 to 1875–84	21·1	7·7
1870–79 to 1880–89	29·8	16·1
1875–84 to 1885–94	37·6	24·3
1880–89 to 1890–99	36·9	23·5
1885–94 to 1895–04	29·2	16·2
1890–99 to 1900–09	19·2	7·6
1895–04 to 1905–14	16·5	6·1
1900–09 to 1910–19	11·5	3·2
1905–14 to 1915–24	−0·8	−3·1
1910–19 to 1920–29	7·3	2·5
1915–24 to 1925–34	21·1	12·4
1920–29 to 1930–39	22·7	17·6
1925–34 to 1935–44	30·7	24·5
1930–39 to 1940–49	24·4	18·5
1935–44 to 1949–53	22·7	17·4

SOURCE: S. Kuznets: 'Quantitative Aspects of the Economic Growth of Nations: Levels and Variability of Rates of Growth', *Economic Development and Cultural Change*, Oct. 1956. Appendix, Table 1.

annual rate of growth of the latter. The change in the terms of trade after 1903 was so slight as to give no direct effect on real income in this period. Hence, if import prices and the terms of trade had an important effect on the British economy during these periods, they must have done so indirectly, that is, by affecting the rate at which domestically produced income grew. If movements in industrial production are any guide to the movements of domestic

[1] The price index used to deflate National Income estimates is heavily weighted with foodstuffs: hence it is probable that the increase in real income *per capita* from 1870 to 1895 is over-estimated whilst the increase from 1895 to 1913 is under-estimated.

real income, it is clear that the growth of the latter after 1900 was less than what it was before: between 1870 and 1895 industrial production rose by about 60 per cent (i.e. by about 1·9 per cent per annum), whereas from 1895 to 1913 the rise was only 35 per cent (i.e. by about 1·2 per cent per annum). The slower rate of growth of total production was not solely due to a slower rate of growth of labour engaged in industry: output per operative was more than 20 per cent greater in 1900 than in 1870, whereas in 1913 it was probably below its 1900 level.

One factor that might have played an important part in reducing the rate of growth after the 1890's, as compared with the previous quarter of a century, was a severe check to the rise in real wages. From the mid '90's to the outbreak of the First World War money wage rates rose by about 15 per cent. The cost of living on the other hand rose by nearer 20 per cent, so that real wages fell by about 5 per cent. In contrast to this, money wages in 1895 were about 33 per cent above their level in 1870 whilst the cost of living to wage earners had fallen by more than a quarter. Hence real wages rose by some 60 per cent in the course of twenty-five years.[1] (See Table III, column 5.) The behaviour of imported food prices was the determining factor, so that given an inelastic demand for food, it is possible to infer that the rise in real wages prior to 1895 must have greatly stimulated the demand for manufactured goods. Conversely, the check to real wages after 1895 must have held back the demand for manufactured goods. Moreover, building activity, too, was probably affected, not only because falling food prices would be likely to shift money expenditure away from food to other necessities (conversely when they were rising) but also because interest rates were falling in the pre-1895 period and rising afterwards. It is certainly true that a marked relative decline in building activity took place in the first decade of the twentieth: indeed, this decline was wholly responsible for the slower rate of growth of industrial production after 1895.[2] However it is unlikely that a relative fall in the demand for houses was solely responsible.

To some extent the rise in real wages from 1870 to 1895 was at

---

[1] Phelps Brown and Hopkins, 'The Course of Wage Rates in Five Countries. 1860–1939', *Oxford Economic Papers*, June 1950.

[2] Including building, industrial production grew at 1·9 per cent p.a. in the 1870–94 period and 1·2 per cent p.a. in the 1895–1913 period. Excluding building, however, the rates of growth are 1·6 per cent and 1·8 per cent respectively. See W. Hoffman, *British Industry 1700–1950* (Blackwell 1950), Table 54, Part B.

the expense of other income earners, whilst the later fall benefited them. Thus the share of wages in national income, which had risen strongly in the 1870's, remained relatively high in the 1880's. It began to fall in the '90's and continued to do so during the first decade of the twentieth century.[1] Shifts in the distribution of national income pre- and post-1900 were reflected in the realised saving-income ratio, but the difference is not very great. Net capital formation (including foreign investment) between 1900 and 1915 was running at about 10·5 per cent of national income, whereas in the last quarter of the nineteenth century it averaged about 9·6 per cent of national income.[2] It seems to follow from this that the gains in real income resulting from improving terms of trade from 1870 to 1895 did not benefit saving and investment so much as real consumption; and the corresponding loss (or absence of gain) from the terms of trade after 1900 did not reduce saving and investment but rather consumption. This, of course, is not surprising. Real wages and consumption depend much more on the price and quantity of imported primary products (given the large weight of food in workers' consumption) than does the level of real invest-ment, so that if the terms of trade are very dependent on what happens to import prices, then changes in the terms of trade must bear more on real wages than on investment. But if the rate of capital formation, expressed as a proportion of national income, does not seem to have varied greatly as between 1870–1900 and 1900–15, its distribution between home and foreign sources of supply certainly does.

From 1900 to 1913, foreign investment absorbed nearly a half of Britain's total net capital formation, whereas during the previous twenty-five years only about a third was directed in this way.[3] It has been pointed out earlier that the distribution of investment between home and foreign sources of supply might well be depen-dent on the course of primary product prices; and the fact that the latter were falling pre-1900 and rising post-1900 seems to fit with the distribution of Britain's investment over the whole period. But this direct relationship between primary product prices and

[1] Phelps Brown and Hart, 'The Share of Wages in National Income', *Economic Journal*, June 1952.
[2] Jefferys and Walters, op. cit.
[3] Net domestic capital formation averaged about 6·6 per cent of net national income in the period 1870–1900, whilst net overseas lending averaged about 3 per cent. From 1900 to 1913, the proportions are 6·5 per cent and 5 per cent respectively. cf. Jefferys and Walters, op. cit., Table VIII.

foreign investment does not get 100 per cent support from the facts pertaining to British investment in the period *before* 1900. Chart III shows the movement of British import prices, export prices and the terms of trade between 1870 and 1913, and also the movements of the ratio of foreign investment to total investment over the same period. We find that the foreign investment proportion fell in the periods 1872 to 1878 and 1890 to 1900 when import prices were falling, and that it rose after 1902/3 when import prices were rising. But it is evident that from 1878 to the late 1880's the relationship between import prices and the foreign investment proportion ran the other way, that is, contrary to the assumed relationship.[1] It remains true, however, that investment at home and investment abroad varied inversely to each other over the long run, if not in the short. This is brought out in Chart III and Table III where the course of domestic capital formation (measured in real terms) and foreign investment are plotted. In fact, there is not much doubt that the great foreign investment boom which took place after 1905, when in real terms investment overseas was probably more than double what it had been during the earlier foreign investment boom of the 1880's, was at the expense of additions to capital equipment at home. In real terms, average annual gross investment in domestic capital between 1905 and 1913 was probably less than two-thirds of the average annual level of 1895 to 1900, and, more significantly, probably no greater than the average annual level for the whole of the 1880's and 1890's.

Theoretically, it is possible to explain the relative decline in building activity after 1900 (which was the main factor causing Britain's slower rate of growth) in terms of a rise in primary product prices which, on the one hand, increased the profitability of investment overseas,[2] and on the other hand, through its effects on the pattern of consumption and the rate of interest, reduced the demand for houses and lowered the profitability of investment in

---

[1] There seems more evidence for a positive relationship between import price and foreign investment than for the inverse relationship between foreign investment and the terms of trade suggested by Cairncross in his *Home and Foreign Investment 1870–1913* (Cambridge). Note also that the change in the direction of investment probably lagged behind the change in import prices. Thus if the 1870–3 boom can be disregarded, the fall in import prices can be dated from the mid-1860's and the fall in the foreign investment proportion from 1872; whilst at the turn of the century import prices began to rise after 1895 and foreign investment after 1902/3.

[2] It seems likely that the boom in investment overseas was the main factor maintaining the rate of growth of industrial output excluding building.

domestic industries. The explanation is not completely satisfactory since earlier swings in building activity cannot be explained in these terms. For instance, in the late 1870's and early 1880's when primary product prices were falling, building activity also showed a relative decline, suggesting that the foreign investment boom of

Chart III. U.K. Export, Import Prices and the Terms of the Trade, 1870–1913

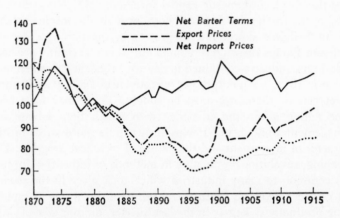

Ratio of Net Overseas Investments to Total Net Investment (Home Plus Overseas)

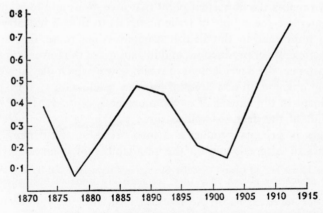

SOURCE: Imlah, *Economic Elements in the Pax Britannica* (Harvard), Chapter IX.

the period was the important factor.[1] Nor can it be argued with any certainty that rising primary product and import prices were, in fact, the main cause of the foreign investment boom after 1905. It has been suggested that the flow of investment at this time was partly the product of inertia and institutional bias in the British capital market, although this explanation by itself does not seem sufficient to account for the wide fluctuations in the ratio of foreign to total investment over the whole period from 1870. Nor does the check to domestic capital formation, which was the obverse of the foreign investment boom, provide the whole explanation of Britain's slower rate of growth in the pre-1914 decade. Professor Phelps Brown has pointed out[2] that real capital per head in domestic industry continued to rise after 1900, and was certainly higher in 1912, when output per operative was *lower*, than in 1900. Other causes, therefore, must be sought. There may have been some falling off in the efficiency with which both labour and management worked, but Phelps Brown puts more stress on the character of investment and the nature of technical progress. The sweeping, revolutionary changes in methods of industrial production common to many industries which took place in the second half of the nineteenth century and bore fruit in terms of rapidly rising productivity largely in the last quarter, did not take place in the period that followed. Technical progress continued but not at the same massive rate as earlier, and investment took the form of extending known, existing methods more widely. But Phelps Brown makes the important point that inventions and investment that increase the supply of basic materials to British industry are more important to the British economy than those that affect domestic costs of production; and inventions of the former type — for instance, the development of steam power which played a vital part in opening up new areas of primary production — were predominant in the latter half of the nineteenth century.[3] If we take account of this fact, as well as those pertaining to the effect of changes in primary product and food prices on the demand for manufactured goods and on the profitability of overseas invest-

[1] See Lewis and O'Leary, 'Secular Swings in Production and Trade, 1870–1913', *Manchester School*, May 1955, for some discussion of fluctuations in building activity.

[2] Phelps Brown and Weber, 'Accumulation, Productivity and Distribution in the British Economy, 1870–1938', *Economic Journal*, June 1953.

[3] Phelps Brown and Handfield Jones, 'The Climacteric of the 1890's', *Oxford Economic Papers*, October 1952.

Table III

United Kingdom: National Income, Home and Overseas Investment and Real Wages 1870–1913

	1 Net National Income (£m) (Current Prices)	2 Foreign Investment (£m) (Current Prices)	3 Gross Domestic Fixed Capital Formation (£m) (Current Prices)	4 Gross Domestic Fixed Capital Formation (£m) (1912/13 Prices)	5 Real Wages (1890–9 = 100)
1870	965	38·7	72·9	70	61
1	1,023	57·7	87·6	83	62
2	1,078	75·7	96·6	85	64
3P	1,171	68·1	106·1	88	68
4	1,173	57·0	129·1	115	75
5	1,124	31·3	110·4	104	78
6	1,125	2·1	115·4	112	78
7	1,130	−16·3	125·8	128	77
8	1,106	0·2	120·7	127	79
9T	1,051	8·7	105·5	115	80
1880	1,104	6·7	109·1	114	77
1	1,144	41·3	114·3	125	78
2	1,188	39·7	119·6	132	79
3P	1,216	28·1	113·8	129	80
4	1,169	49·2	98·0	114	84
5	1,149	39·5	82·9	99	89
6T	1,164	60·9	72·6	92	90
7	1,193	67·8	76·9	97	92
8	1,276	74·6	83·1	104	92
9	1,364	72·5	101·9	124	93
1890P	1,431	94·4	101·8	120	97
1	1,419	52·3	102·5	122	97
2	1,393	37·4	99·9	125	96
3	1,360	42·1	95·0	122	96
4T	1,406	30·9	98·8	130	101
5	1,472	36·1	105·6	143	102
6	1,500	33·5	117·3	156	103
7	1,551	23·2	137·4	183	102
8	1,633	19·9	173·0	227	101
9	1,706	32·5	195·0	240	105
1900P	1,791	31·1	203·2	225	103
1	1,759	18·1	205·2	233	103
2	1,775	15·1	201·4	233	103
3	1,751	20·9	184·7	212	101
4T	1,779	22·1	181·9	204	99
5	1,857	65·3	177·5	197	99
6	1,978	99·4	170·7	184	100
7P	2,076	138·0	150·0	154	97
8T	1,967	120·6	118·1	127	100
9	2,016	109·4	117·9	128	98
1910	2,108	142·2	114·5	124	97
1	2,185	177·3	125·8	133	96
2	2,318	190·8	136·6	139	97
3P	2,424	210·1	158·5	155	97

SOURCES: Columns 1, 2 and 3: *Jefferys and Walters*, 'National Income and Expenditure of the U.K., 1870–1952', *Income and Wealth* Series V.

Column 4: Column 3 deflated by capital goods price index given in *Jefferys and Walters*, op. cit. Table XVI.

Column 5: *Phelps Brown and Hopkins*, 'Wage Rates in Five Countries, 1860–1939', *Oxford Economic Papers*, June 1950.

N.B. Peak and Trough years are marked with a P and T respectively.

ment, then it seems possible to believe that the apparent association of falling primary product prices with high rates of economic growth in the period 1870 to 1900, and the apparent association of rising primary product prices with slower growth after 1900, were not purely coincidental.

III

THE INTER-WAR YEARS

Despite the high level of unemployment that persisted throughout, and despite the impact of the major economic slump of the early 1930's, secular rates of growth of real income *per capita* in the inter-war period tended to be greater than those that prevailed in the decade and a half prior to World War I — although they were not as high as those that ruled in the 1870's and '80's.[1] This is shown in Table II, taken from Professor Kuznets's essay on 'Quantitative Aspects of the Economic Growth of Nations'. Whereas national income *per capita* rose by about 1 per cent per annum in the two decades prior to 1914, it rose by about 1·5 per cent per annum in the decade and a half before World War II. Admittedly, in the 1920's, the growth of output represented recovery from a post-war low level of activity, neither real national income nor industrial production regaining its 1914 level until about 1927. But in the course of the '20's, industrial production rose by more than 80 per cent, a rate of expansion not often achieved in earlier times.

Despite the rapidity of the growth of output, wholesale and retail prices fell substantially, the former by somewhat more than a third, the latter by a little less than a third.[2] (See Table IV.) There can be little doubt that the operative cause of the fall in domestic prices was the sharp fall in the world price level of foodstuffs and raw materials, particularly in the first two or three years of the 1920's. The war, and the immediate post-war boom in manufacturing production, had stimulated an enormous expansion of primary product output in many parts of the world, which in the event

---

[1] Population grew at a slower rate after the First World War than before. Even so, the rate of growth of real national income was higher in the 1920's and 1930's than in the 1900–15 period; although not as high as in the 1870–1900 period. See Kuznets, op. cit. and Jefferys and Walters, op. cit.

[2] The fall is reckoned from 1921. If 1920 were taken as the initial year, the fall in prices would be considerably greater.

Table IV

Prices and Production, United Kingdom, 1920–1939

	(1) Total Industrial Production (1913 = 100)		(2) Wholesale Prices of Manufactured Products (June 1939 = 100)	(3) Import Prices (1938 = 100)	(4) Wholesale Prices of Raw Materials (1938 = 100)	(5) Cost of Living (1938 = 100)	(6) Money Wages (1938 = 100)
	Excluding Building	Including Building					
1920	91	95	254	279	278	159	138
21	57	95	163	186	161	144	137
22	78	96	131	149	138	117	105
23	85	98	131	146	140	112	94
24	91	100	137	152	153	112	96
25	89	102	131	152	150	112	96
26	76	104	122	139	137	110	96
27	100	106	117	133	134	107	96
28	98	109	116	135	130	106	96
29	106	112	113	132	123	105	95
1930	99	116	99	116	101	101	94
31	91	119	87	94	84	94	93
32	91	122	84	87	84	92	92
33	97	124	85	84	86	90	90
34	110	127	87	87	88	90	90
35	114	129	88	88	88	92	91
36	123	141	93	93	95	94	93
37	131	150	107	107	115	99	97
38	117	137	100	100	100	100	100
39	—	—	101	101	107	103	101

SOURCES: (1) W. Hoffman, *British Industry 1700–1950*. Table 54.
(2), (3), (4), (5) and (6) *London and Cambridge Economic Service Bulletin*.

N

proved to be excessive in relation to the world's demand; and prices fell sharply. Britain gained very much from this development, although its export trade suffered from falling primary producer incomes overseas. At any rate, the falling price of food made it possible to keep money wages very stable after their sharp fall in the post-war slump, so that the substantial gains in labour productivity which took place in the 1920's were reflected in falling manufactured good prices rather than in rising incomes.

The onset of the great slump in 1929 accelerated the fall in world primary product prices, and British import prices fell by almost 40 per cent from 1929 to 1933. Industrial production also declined, largely as a result of a fall in demand for British exports; but in this respect Britain suffered less than most other industrial countries of the west.[1] Moreover, industrial production picked up strongly in the second half of the 1930's as recovery from the slump set in. Rising import prices, both of food and raw materials, caused a rise in money wage rates and in the general price level despite substantial unemployment which continued to exist.

In the period as a whole, both import and domestic prices fell far more than they rose: in 1938, for instance, import prices averaged only two-thirds of their level in 1922, whilst retail prices had fallen by over 15 per cent.[2] As in the 1870's and '80's labour incomes benefitted most from the long-term fall in the price level, the real wages of those who remained in employment rising by some 13 or 14 per cent up to the mid-1930's. The share of wages in national income rose to about 42 per cent in the late 1920's as against 38 per cent in the pre-war decade,[3] and it was generally higher in the 1920's and 30's than in earlier decades. Real wages, of course, had fallen during the war years, but they quickly recovered to their pre-war level which was reached in 1921/2.[4]

The rise in the share of wages in national income had its expected obverse in a fall in the investment-national income coefficient. This rate averaged about 6·5 per cent in the inter-war period, being particularly low at the time of the 1930 slump. But the fall was

---

[1] For instance, industrial production in the U.S.A. and Germany declined by over 45 per cent, and in France and Belgium by about 30 per cent, as against a fall of only 16 or 17 per cent in Britain.

[2] Leaving aside the post-war slump, the cost of living fell by 30 per cent from 1921 to 1934; and, even if the slump of the 1930's is also set aside, the fall in the cost of living up to 1929 was still nearly 20 per cent.

[3] Phelps Brown and Hart, op. cit.

[4] Phelps Brown and Hopkins, op. cit.

almost wholly due to the cessation of *foreign* investment which was negligible in the 1920's and '30's. Whilst this development fits in with the hypothesis that the movement of primary product prices and the flow of foreign investment are directly connected, it hardly seems plausible to explain the decline in the latter by the decline in the former — although the war years had seen considerable expansion of food and primary product production in many parts of the world which turned out to be excessive for the world's peacetime needs. Probably, however, the fall in foreign investment stemmed from the breakdown of the international capital market, the causes of which were probably as much political as economic.[1]

Investment in the domestic economy measured as a proportion of national income, was as high in the inter-war years as in the earlier 1870–1914 period; and in real terms, annual investment in real capital rose substantially, particularly in the second half of the 1930's (see Table V). But it seems that a substantial proportion of domestic investment was absorbed by the great housing boom of the period. Phelps Brown's figures suggest that whereas the stock of industrial capital rose by not much more than the size of the occupied population — 13 per cent as against 11 per cent in the period 1924 to 1938 — the stock of revenue-yielding building rose by as much as 30 per cent.

It would seem, therefore, that the inter-war years period in British economic history presents a rather paradoxical picture. First, we see that high unemployment persisted throughout the period, being never less than 9 per cent of the working force and at times as much as 20 per cent. Second, the period contained one of the most serious slumps of British industrial history. Third, the rate of *industrial* capital accumulation was low and only barely kept pace with the growth of the labour force. Yet, despite these things, real income *per capita* grew faster during this time than in the first two decades of the century, and not greatly slower than in the last quarter of the nineteenth century which is now recognised as a period of very substantial economic progress. How did this come about? One factor of considerable importance so far as the rise in real income *per capita* is concerned was the substantial improvement in the terms of trade in the inter-war period. This improve-

[1] To the extent that (1) the decline in British overseas investment was caused by Britain's export difficulties and (2) that the latter were caused by the world fall in primary product prices, then the direct connection between import prices and foreign investment remains.

ment took place namely in the early 1920's and again in the early
'30's, and by the second half of the 1930's the terms of trade were

Table V

United Kingdom: National Income and Capital
Formation 1924 to 1938

	Net National Income £m (current prices)	Investment Overseas £m (current prices)	Gross domestic fixed capital formation		Real Wages (1890-9 = 100)
			£m (current prices)	£m 1912-13 prices	
1924	4004	72	347	173	93
5	4066	46	372	196	97
6	4055	− 14	388	204	98
7	4242	82	432	233	103
8	4251	123	414	230	101
9	4275	103	419	231	102
30	4051	28	414	239	105
1	3757	− 104	394	234	113
2	3659	− 51	343	214	112
3	3823	0	343	217	113
4	3980	− 7	384	245	112
5	4213	32	434	263	112
6	4498	− 18	515	300	110
7	4730	− 56	594	324	114
8	4867	− 62	600	324	113

For SOURCES: *see* Table II.

about 20 per cent more favourable than at the beginning of the
period, and a third more favourable than in 1913. But whilst an
improvement of this magnitude clearly made a significant contribution to the rise in Britain's real income (particularly real wages)
at this time, it hardly provides the whole explanation. Perhaps
more important was the character of capital accumulation in the
1920's. Although capital accumulation in industry proceeded at a
slow rate, it was accompanied by the introduction of new and more
productive techniques and equipment. Considerable technical development had taken place in many processes and machinery of
industry — for instance in connection with electricity, the internal
combustion engine, chemical engineering, etc. — in the early part
of the century. In the main, however, these were not applied in
industry until after the 1914–18 war, so that it was in the inter-war
period that the fruits of technical progress which had taken place

earlier were harvested. The result was that, although unemployment was high, industrial production and labour productivity increased very greatly.[1] Hence it turns out that Britain's real income
was kept rising by a fortuitous improvement in the terms of trade
and by technical developments that had taken place earlier.

Unlike the 1870's and 1880's, however, the fall in primary product prices which made such a substantial contribution to Britain's
living standards in the 1920's and particularly in the 1930's, proved
a mixed blessing. Its obverse was a decline in primary producer
incomes which reacted back on the export sales of manufacturing
countries. The volume of British exports fell off disastrously during
the slump of the 1930's, worsening the employment situation
in this sector of the economy. This development had serious effects
on industrial production since resources were very immobile, and
therefore must have served to check the growth of the British
economy as a whole. But Britain's export troubles did not stem
only from the collapse of primary producer incomes. Even in the
1920's when world trade was increasing, the volume of British
exports fell. This happened largely because of shifts in the composition of world trade to which the British economy did not
readily respond. In the nineteenth century world trade mostly took
the form of the exchange of consumer goods for primary products,
but producer goods began to displace consumer goods as the century reached its close; and the trend continued on into the twentieth
century. British exports, however, were largely consumer goods, in
particular textiles, and coal, and the economy was slow to adapt
itself to changing world demand for manufactures. The position of
the traditional export industries was also made worse by the unrealistic foreign exchange policy of the time which aimed at the
restoration of the Gold Standard at pre-war parity. It thus seems
likely that if resources in Britain had been more mobile — between home and export production, and within the export sector,
itself — the British economy would have benefited far more from
the relative abundance of primary products in the 1920's and 1930's
than in fact it did.

This brief survey of the growth of the British economy from
1800 to the mid-1930's indicates pretty clearly that the British

---

[1] It has been estimated that output per wage earner in British manufacturing
industry rose by 37 per cent from 1924 to 1937, and industrial production rose by
50 per cent in the same period.

economy did not grow faster when the price level was showing a long term tendency to rise: on the contrary, a secularly falling price level seems to have been more conducive to growth.[1] Superficially at least, history does not support the theory that secular inflation is good for growth. It is reasonably certain, however, that secular movements in the British price level have been closely connected with the underlying trend of the world price level of primary products: furthermore, theoretical reasons can be advanced to suggest that the British economy benefits more from a fall in primary product prices than from a rise. Even so, it does not emerge unequivocally from a study of Britain's growth history that in fact her fastest rates of growth were *caused* by a relative abundance of primary products and a consequential fall in the price level. As was emphasised in an earlier chapter, the causal connection is more likely to be present when this relative abundance is produced by factors operating on primary product supply — for instance, the opening up of new areas of primary production — than when it is produced by a slackening in the rate of demand. It is plausible to think that the last half of the nineteenth century was in fact a period when industrial production benefited from a rapidly rising output of primary products. The same may have been true to some extent in the 1920's, but, in the 1930's, the fall in primary product prices was produced more by a check to world industrial growth arising from forces independent of primary product supply. In such circumstances the trend of primary product prices is clearly not acting as a stimulant to world industrial production, although of course it may act as a stimulant in a particular country whose industrial growth has been unaffected by the forces which have operated generally to slow down growth, or in which these forces have been offset (for instance, Japan in the 1930's). But even in this case, a favourable change in the terms of trade with which manufactures can be exchanged for primary products requires mobility of resources in the industrial country if the benefit is to be fully reaped.

---

[1] Since 1946, if industrial production is taken as the measure, the British economy has enjoyed very significant economic growth, although for much of the time import prices and the general price level have been rising, and the terms of trade have tended to worsen. But this raises questions concerning the relation between prices and economic growth in a 'full employment' economy (i.e. an economy in which full employment is an end of government economic policy) which will be dealt with later.

It is perhaps safer to argue that a rising price level of primary products tends to check industrial growth, because, despite considerable elasticity between the input of raw materials and the output of manufactures, the growth of an industrial economy must be to some extent limited by the supply of primary products to it. It is hardly likely that the rate of growth of output of primary products would at all times be appropriate for the rate of growth of potential industrial output, even if the technological factors determining raw material input relative to finished good output remained constant. The rate of growth of potential industrial output can vary independently of primary product supply; and of course, the pattern of demand for industrial product can change over time, altering the composition of production and therefore the demand for raw material input per unit of industrial good output. But if demand for primary products is tending to grow faster than supply, forces are set up which must eventually slow down the growth of industrial output, to bring demand and supply of primary products together. Moreover, it tends to cause a rise in the general price level.

What this suggests, however, is that to examine different periods of world economic history, or even different periods of a particular country's economic history, with a view to comparing growth performance is to take too short a view of the process of development. Periods can seldom be considered independently of each other. In one period the demand for primary products, as determined by the growth of industrial capacity as well as other factors, is tending to outstrip supply: forces are set up tending to check the rise in demand and perhaps increase supply: as these forces work out in the next period, primary product supply catches up with demand, removing the checks on industrial growth; and so on. Thus instead of studying British economic history of the nineteenth and twentieth century period by period, we should look at it as a whole. The British foreign investment boom of the 1850's, for instance, contributed greatly to the rapid economic advance (particularly in living standards) of the last three decades of the century by increasing the supply of primary products; and the foreign investment boom of the early twentieth century probably had an important effect on living standards in the 1920's and 1930's. Analagously, the rising price level of the 1850's cannot be considered independently of the falling price level of the 1880's and 1890's, nor can pre-First World War price history be divorced completely from that of the 1920's and 1930's. In fact, it would seem that the secular movements of prices have very little to do in a causal way with the rate of economic development: rather they and the rate of economic growth are the product of more important underlying causes.

In another sense, of course, a comparative study of the secular behaviour of the British and American economies takes too long a view of the process of development. Although it can be argued that the secular movement of prices had very little to do with the rate of capital accumulation or the rate of growth, it can still be argued that in fact capital accumulation did typically take place when prices were rising. Not only was the development of both economies characterised by secular movements in prices and in *rates* of economic growth, it was, as we have seen, also characterised by fluctuations of shorter duration in the absolute level of money (and often real) national income. We referred earlier to the well-known fact that the rising trend of economic growth had superimposed on it an apparently cyclical fluctuation, the length of an individual 'cycle' measured from the peak of one cycle to the peak of the next, varying between seven and ten years. It is not the place here to consider the extent to which this cyclical development was produced by forces inherent in the economic system or in the process of growth, or whether it was just an accidental feature of economic history.[1] But if statistics relating to income, prices, production and employment, etc., are reliable, then they show as a matter of fact that British and American economic development was not a smooth process but rather one in which increases in income and production took place in short bursts, each of which was followed by a period of reaction in which income and production ceased to rise, or even fell (see Table I). Usually prices were rising in the later stages of the booms and were falling or stable after the boom had broken; furthermore, a most consistent feature of this cyclical development was the concentration of long-term investment decisions and of actual investment in the late stages of the boom (see Table III). Rostow has put it: 'On the whole, the impression one receives is that the industrial revolution, regarded as a process of plant expansion and the installation of new industrial methods and techniques, lurched forward in a highly discontinuous way, with a high concentration of decisions to expand, or

[1] cf. R.C.O. Matthews, *The Trade Cycle*, Chapter 12.

to improve technique, occurring in the later stages of the major cycles.'[1]

But although it seems clear that capital accumulation did typically take place at a faster rate when prices were rising — the latter probably being the effect of the former — some important qualifications have to be borne in mind before we interpret the development in terms of inflation and forced saving. In the first place the rise in prices was never very great in the course of the boom,[2] and in the ensuing slump prices often fell more than they had risen — particularly before 1900. Thus, confidence in the value of money was never lost. Second, in neither country was the faster rate of capital accumulation invariably at the expense of real wages. Table III shows quite clearly that real wages in Britain often remained unchanged or even rose when prices were rising in the boom: for instance, they remained unchanged in the upswing of 1885/6 to 1890, and rose in the upward swings of 1879 to 1882/3 and 1894 to 1900. But this tended to be less true in the periods pre- and post- the 1870–1900 period, which suggests that the movement of primary product, in particular food, prices was the crucial factor. The fall in real wages in the upswing of 1904–7 and 1908–13, for instance, was no doubt caused more by rising import prices than by any shift of income to profits. On the other hand, it is quite likely that in manufacturing industry at least, profit margins were inflated during the booms: manufactured good prices rose relatively to money wages at these times. In this connection it is reasonable to believe that the longer term trend of primary product and food prices had important implications for development. When this trend was downward, money wages were more easily restrained in the course of the boom: inflation of profits and saving in industry was therefore achieved with a smaller rise in the price level of manufactured goods. With the collapse of the boom the fall in the price level also tended to be greater, so that despite occasional periods of rising prices, the longer-term trend of the general price level was downward. Conversely, if the trend of primary product and food prices was upwards, money wages and industrial costs were subject to a persistent upward pressure, so

[1] W. W. Rostow, *The British Economy in the Nineteenth Century* (Oxford), p. 54. The major cycles are defined as those in which, during the upswing, full employment is reached.
[2] The booms of 1870–3 and 1896–1900 in Britain, and those of 1896–1902 and 1904–7 in the United States, were exceptional in this respect.

that in the booms prices tended to rise more or profits and saving rose less. *Mutatis mutandis* prices fell less during the downswing, and the longer-term trend of the general price level was therefore rising. Taking the period 1870 to 1913 as a whole, however, it remains true that even though real wages often rose with the rate of capital accumulation in the course of booms, they tended to rise at a much faster rate in the downswings, when the rate of capital accumulation was lower. To this extent, therefore, investment and real wages were competitive; and in so far as a higher rate of investment and inflation tended to go together, it might be said that saving was being forced.

IV

THE POST-WAR YEARS,
1946–58

We now turn to a brief review of price behaviour and the rate of economic growth in the post-Second World War period. This period is notable for the persistence of inflation over the course of some thirteen or fourteen years: as Table VI shows, in no year did the general price level fail to rise, and, on average, prices rose by about 5 per cent per annum. Probably at no other time in British history have prices risen at so fast a rate for so long a period. Even in the two decades prior to the First World War, prices rose on average by only one or two per cent per annum, and there were some years in which they fell. On the other hand, economic growth was particularly fast in the post-Second World War years, compared with the previous half-century. Between 1946 and 1959 gross domestic product in real terms rose by about 41 per cent, population increased by about 10 per cent so that real income *per capita* rose by about 28 per cent, a rate of growth of about 2 per cent per annum. This was almost twice as great as in the early decades of the twentieth century, and not greatly less than in the last quarter of the nineteenth century.

The behaviour of prices suggests that Britain enjoyed a continuous boom in the post-war period. This view is supported by statistics of industrial production, also shown in Table VI. On average, industrial production rose by about 4 per cent per annum, and in one year only (1952) was there a noticeable fall in production; even here, the decline in production was by no means general,

Table VI

Prices and Production: United Kingdom, 1946–60
(1954 = 100)

	(1) Industrial Production	(2) Final Product Prices	(3) Import Prices
1946	67		
7	72		
8	79	78	73
9	83	80	74
50	88	83	85
1	91	93	113
2	89	98	111
3	94	99	101
4	100	100	100
5	105	104	103
6	105	109	105
7	107	113	107
8	106	115	99
9	112	116	98
1960	120	117	99

SOURCES: Column (1) *National Institute Economic Review* (N.I.E.S.R.).
Columns (2) and (3) *National Income and Expenditure* (Blue Book) C.S.O.

being largely confined to a few consumer good industries such as textiles and house furnishings. On the other hand, the longish period of industrial stagnation, between 1956 and 1959, should be noted, which suggests that a plateau had been reached: hence the notion of a continuous post-war boom must be qualified.

One normally expects strong booms to be associated with excess demand and rising prices, and it certainly appears that prices tended to rise fast when industrial production was rising fast, for instance, between 1946 and 1951, and 1952 to 1955. It is also reasonably clear that excess demand generally existed at these times (see Chart IV) which could be expected to raise the prices of both goods and labour. But, obviously, pressure on resources does not provide the whole explanation of the persistent post-war inflation. Prices did not cease to rise when excess demand was negative or when industrial production was falling or stagnating, for instance, in 1952 and in the years 1956 to 1959. The fact that prices continued to rise sharply in 1952, when there was deficiency of demand in some sectors of the economy, causing production to fall, can no doubt be explained by the delayed working through of the severe inflationary pressures which had been generated during the previous two years; but this does not hold for the continued rise in prices in 1957 and 1958. Moreover, even the connection between steeply rising prices, on the one hand, and excess demand, on the other, in the years 1946–8 and in 1950–1, was by no means so direct or obvious as at first appears. It seems likely that domestic prices were more affected by a rise in the world price level of raw materials and foodstuffs than they were by purely domestic pressure of demand.

The part played by import prices in the first half of the post-war period is unmistakeable. The abandonment of price controls in the United States at the end of the war led to a steep rise in world commodity prices from 1946 to '48. As a result British import prices rose by over a third, a rise which could hardly fail to affect the domestic cost and price level significantly, despite the extensive use of price controls and subsidies. It is, of course, clear from our Chart that considerable excess demand for goods and labour also existed at this time, so that it is likely that prices were affected by demand as well as by rising raw material costs. But without the rise in costs it is doubtful whether prices would have risen as much as they did, if only because price controls are usually more effective in restraining pressure on prices when it comes from the side of demand than when it comes from costs: the price regulating authority must take into account the need to maintain profitability of production, hence if costs of production rise as a result of forces not under the control of the producer, prices must be allowed to rise in compensation. Moreover, as we have implied in an earlier chapter, the existence of formal price controls may not be crucial in this matter, for even without them, prices do not always rise when there is excess demand, unless at the same time there is a rise in costs.

However, it seems likely that excess demand for goods was in fact the main factor behind the continued rise in prices in 1949 and during the first nine months of 1950, if not during 1946–8, since in these years import prices remained reasonably stable. Furthermore, despite the apparent excess demand for labour, (see Chart IV) labour costs do not seem to have contributed to the rise in prices at this time; both wage *rates* and wage *earnings* seem to have risen less than labour productivity in the course of 1949 and

Chart IV

Excess Demand and Prices. United Kingdom
1946–58

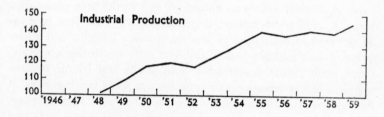

Industrial Production

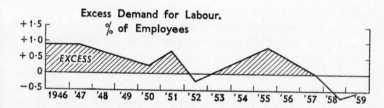

Excess Demand for Labour. % of Employees

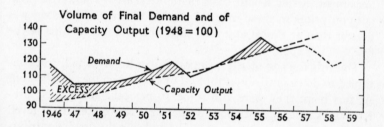

Volume of Final Demand and of Capacity Output (1948 = 100)

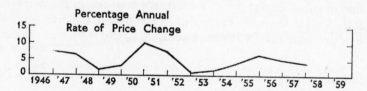

Percentage Annual Rate of Price Change

SOURCE: Memorandum of Evidence submitted by J. C. R. Dow to the Radcliffe Committee (Volume 3, p. 103).

1950.[1] But the fact that the rate of increase of prices fell off markedly in 1949 and 1950 is a reflection of the greater stability of costs.[2]

The story repeated itself in the last quarter of 1950 and through 1951 and part of 1952. Devaluation of sterling in September of 1949 led to some rise in Britain's import prices, by about 8 per cent,[3] but the main factor was the outbreak of the Korean War in June 1950 which led to an enormous and world-wide speculative boom in commodity prices. Britain's import prices rose by over 40 per cent in the course of less than twelve months, and a new burst of cost inflation was introduced into the British economy. Once again excess demand for both goods and labour became apparent as a re-armament programme was set in train; even so, it does not seem to have reached the proportions of 1946 or 1947. Yet, significantly enough, prices rose at a greater rate in 1951 and 1952 than in the earlier years, a fact that can be taken as indicative of greater cost pressures which now existed. These cost pressures did not stem only from rising import prices. Money wages rose strongly, partly as a result of excess demand for labour, partly as a result of rising food prices. At the same time, the rate of productivity growth in manufacturing industry fell off as the composition of industrial output was readjusted to meet the needs of re-armament. Rising labour costs therefore exerted a powerful pressure on prices in these months, so that the rate of inflation was greater than at almost any time since the first few months of the war.

Towards the end of 1951, import prices began to fall, and continued to do so until about the end of 1953 when they levelled off. At this point they were still some 16 per cent above their pre-Korean War level, and about 80 per cent above their 1946 level. It is the latter figure that gives the best idea of the direct contribution of rising import prices towards the total rise in the domestic price level in the 1946–52 period. In this period, the price level of final products rose by about 42 per cent, so that if we take the cost

---

[1] Productivity in manufacturing industry seems to have risen by about 4–4½ per cent per annum whereas wage rates rose by about 2½ per cent and wage earning by 4 per cent per annum.

[2] Prices rose at the rate of 7 per cent per annum in 1947 and 1948, but at only 3 per cent per annum in 1949 and 1950.

[3] If devaluation had been caused by overseas trade deficit, itself the consequence of excess demand in the home market, then the resulting rise in imports costs could be said to be the direct consequence of excess demand in the domestic economy; but this does not seem to have been the case.

of imports to be about one fifth of the total price of final products, then two-fifths of the rise in prices was directly due to the rise in import prices. But the total contribution was clearly greater than this, for it seems reasonably certain that money wage rates would have risen less if import prices had been more stable; and if money wage rates had risen less so would the final product price level.

If import prices played a prominent, indeed vital, role in the course of inflation up to 1952, they did not do so afterwards. Taking the period 1953 to 1959 as a whole, import prices fell rather than rose, and hence made no *direct* contribution to the continued rise in the price level. It is true that they rose somewhat in the course of 1954/55 boom, but the rise amounted to no more than 6 or 7 per cent, and can have affected final product prices only insignificantly. Moreover, the continued rise in the domestic price level between 1957 and 1959 must be considered against the background of a *fall* in the price level of imported products at this time. Thus the behaviour of domestic prices seems to be more determined by purely domestic pressures than during any of the previous post-war years.

Excess demand for both goods and labour associated with a large-scale investment boom was clearly the most important factor underlying the rise in prices from 1954 to 1956. Dow's indexes, reproduced in our Chart IV, clearly show that excess demand for labour rose strongly in 1954 and 1955 and remained positive in 1956: at one point, it was markedly greater than in 1951, and almost as great as in the immediate post-war years. Unemployment fell to about one per cent of the labour force, the lowest level of the post-war period. In the beginning money wages did not rise much more strongly than they had done in the previous two years, but in 1955 and '56 the rise accelerated, producing a sharp rise in labour costs (see Table VII). During these years prices of final products rose at the rate of about 5 per cent per annum as against a rise of only 1 per cent per annum in the previous two years. As was to be expected, prices of capital goods rose more than did the prices of other goods.

The boom came to an end in 1956. Total industrial production levelled off and did not begin to rise again until the second quarter of 1959. The stability of *total* production, however, was the result of different movements of production of various industry groups. The output of some industries — for instance metal manufacture, shipbuilding, marine engineering and textiles, declined in 1957 and 1958, whilst the output of others, in particular vehicles,[1] increased. But in many industries, production remained rather stable. However, no matter how production behaved in these years, prices, generally, continued to rise. Between 1956 and the beginning of 1959, final product prices rose on average by a further 6 per cent, both consumer goods and capital goods sharing in the increase. The prices of only a very few domestically produced products fell, textiles and paper products being conspicuous examples, and these largely because the price level of a basic material used in their production fell. The prices of many other products continued to rise, even when their output was falling. An important example of this somewhat contradictory development is to be found in the metal industries, particularly iron and steel. During the boom years (from 1953 to 1957) ferrous metal manufacturing output rose by about 16 per cent: in the same period iron and steel prices rose by about 25 per cent, about half of the rise, however, taking place in the course of 1957, when production was rising only slightly. But during 1958, production fell by about 10 per cent whilst prices continued to rise by another 3 or 4 per cent. Prices at wholesale level of many other goods behaved similarly, although they tended to rise less than this.

The continued rise in prices in 1958 cannot be attributed to the persistence of excess demand for goods and labour: industrial production did not cease to rise because resources had been pushed to the limit, preventing any further rise. On the contrary, it ceased to rise because the growth of demand had been checked, in some cases even, sufficiently to cause a fall in production. Unemployment rose quite strongly in 1957 and '58, whilst unfilled vacancies declined: thus excess demand for labour, which had been characteristic of the boom years 1954–6, quickly disappeared. Moreover, owing to the nature of the 1954–6 boom, the capacity of industry had been greatly increased; and there were plenty of signs, particularly in 1958 and early 1959, of excess capacity in many industries.

Undoubtedly an important factor contributing to the continued rise in prices was rising labour costs. Despite the absence of excess demand for labour, despite rising unemployment, money wage

---

[1] The output of vehicles declined sharply in 1956 when the output of many other industries was still rising; but it rose strongly in 1957 and 1958.

Table VII

Output, Wage Rates and Productivity in Manufacturing Industry, U.K. 1948-60

(1954 = 100)

	1948	1949	1950	1951	1952	1953	1954	1955	1956	1957	1958	1959	1960
Output	77·3	82·2	87·8	91·6	88·2	93·7	100	106·4	105·9	108·3	106·9	114·1	122·9
Employment	90·7	92·0	94·6	97·0	96·2	97·4	100	102·6	103·1	103·1	101·7	102·1	105·9
Productivity	85·5	89	93	94	92	96	100	104	103	105	105	112	116
Weekly Wage Rates	73·7	75·8	77·3	84·4	91·5	95·7	100	106	115	121	125	128	131
Unemployment (% total labour force)	1·50	1·52	1·53	1·19	1·99	1·64	1·34	1·08	1·19	1·43	2·10	2·17	1·60
Unfilled Vacancies (% total labour force)	2·30	1·95	1·77	2·01	1·34	1·33	1·56	1·91	1·66	1·27	0·90	1·02	1·40
Excess Demand for Labour (Index)	0·68	0·42	0·27	0·69	-0·27	-0·04	0·29	0·73	0·46	0·01	-0·67	-0·62	-0·08
Year to Year Change in Productivity and Wage Rates (Per Cent)													
Productivity	—	+4·0	+4·5	+1·5	-1·5	+4·3	+4·1	+3·8	-1·0	+2·2	0	+6·5	+3·5
Weekly Wage Rates	—	+2·9	+2·0	+9·2	+8·4	+4·5	+4·5	+6·0	+8·4	+4·3	+3·3	+2·4	+2·4

SOURCE: *Annual Abstract of Statistics* (C.S.O.);
National Institute Economic Review (N.I.E.S.R.).

Table VIII

Output, Employment Productivity and Wage Rates: Selected Industries, U.K., 1948–59

	1948	1949	1950	1951	1952	1953	1954	1955	1956	1957	1958	1959
Food Drink and Tobacco												
Output	87·4	90·9	90·1	93·1	94·7	98·5	100	102·7	105·5	106·9	109·4	113·6
Employment	84·0	89·0	91·6	94·0	96·4	97·3	100	100·9	102·3	102·9	103·9	103·9
Productivity	104	102	98	99	99	101	100	101	103	104	105	109
Wage Rates	74	77	78	84	92	96	100	107	115	121	126	130
Price Level	—	72	—	85	96	100	100	102	106	107	105	107
Chemical and Allied												
Output	68·0	70·2	79·7	83·7	79·6	89·1	100	106·2	110·6	115·0	115·0	131·2
Employment	88·4	91·0	94·5	97·2	97·5	98·0	100	104·0	106·0	107·0	107·6	107·6
Productivity	77	78	84	86	81	91	100	102	104	107	107	122
Wage Rates	73	74	77	84	92	95	100	106	113	120	123	128
Price Level	—	76	79	92	100	100	100	99	103	106	106	107
Metal Manufacture												
Output	83·2	83·6	87·9	93·2	95·9	93·7	100	108·4	110·1	111·3	101·1	105·6
Employment	95·7	96·1	97·5	98·5	100·8	99·0	100	102·9	104·6	104·6	101·1	98·0
Productivity	87	87	90	94	95	94	100	105	105	106	100	107
Wage Rates	75	77	78	86	93	96	100	109	119	125	131	135
Price Level	—	71	72	80	97	100	100	105	113	125	130	129

Shipbuilding and Marine Engineering												
Output	116·5	106·1	93·5	96·2	99·2	105·1	100	108·5	117·4	107·9	108·8	101·1
Employment	—	—	100	96·4	98·6	100·1	100	99·8	101·7	100·8	99·2	96·0
Productivity	—	—	93	100	101	105	100	108	116	107	109	105
Wage Rates	73	76	77	84	92	96	100	108	116	122	125	129
Mechanical and Electrical Engineering												
Output	69·4	75·9	84·5	90·5	92·4	93·6	100	107·4	107·0	111·0	111·5	117·0
Employment	—	—	90·5	93·8	98·4	97·3	100	106·3	108·0	109·9	117·5	117·5
Productivity	—	—	93	97	95	96	100	101	99	101	95	100
Wage Rates	73	76	77	84	92	96	100	106	115	119	125	129
Vehicles												
Output	61·4	71·2	76·4	79·9	79·5	90·4	100	114·6	107·2	114·9	118·4	130·8
Employment	82·5	83·9	86·6	89·1	93·9	95·9	100	104·9	106·0	104·5	105·2	106·0
Productivity	74	85	88	89	84	94	100	109	101	110	112	123
Wage Rates	74	76	76	82	90	95	100	106	115	119	122	125
Textiles												
Output	85·5	92·1	100·1	99·8	81·9	97·4	100	97·5	96·4	96·5	87·1	92·0
Employment	94·1	97·6	102·0	104·4	91·0	97·8	100	96·1	94·3	94·0	87·1	84·0
Productivity	91	94	98	95	90	100	100	101	102	103	100	109
Wage Rates	74	78	80	87	93	97	100	105	111	115	119	122
Price Level	—	76	100	136	103	100	100	98	98	101	98	96
Building and Contracting												
Output	86·7	90·7	90·8	87·3	90·0	96·3	100	100·3	105·8	105·5	105	—
Employment	99·6	98·3	98·3	99·4	98·6	98·6	100	102·1	105·7	104·3	102·3	105·0
Productivity	86	92	92	87	92	97	100	98	100	101	103	103
Wage Rates	73	75	77	83	90	96	100	106	115	120	125	129
Price Level	—	81	82	95	102	100	100	106	110	114	115	113

SOURCES: C.S.O.: *Annual Abstract of Statistics*: and Crossley, 'An Index of Wage Rates by Industries', *Manchester School*.

rates continued to rise. Admittedly, the rate of increase in 1957 and 1958 was only half of what it had been during the previous two years — $3\frac{1}{2}$ per cent per annum as against 7 per cent per annum — but it tended to occur in most industries, whether their output was rising or falling (see Table VIII). Unfortunately, although the disappearance of excess demand for goods and labour slowed down the rise in money wages, it also reduced the rate of increase of productivity. Productivity in manufacturing industry had risen by about 4 per cent per annum during the course of the boom. In the next two years, it rose by barely 1 per cent per annum (see Table VII): moreover in some industries, for whose product demand declined, productivity fell. Since money wages in most industries continued to rise, there was a sharp rise in labour costs which was translated into a rise in prices.

The development of labour costs and prices through 1954 to 1958 brings out clearly the difficulty of combining high employment of labour and other resources with price stability. There is little doubt that labour costs are an important determinant of the behaviour of prices; and their behaviour is the result of money wage changes and productivity changes. The post-war period has shown that productivity tends to rise faster when total demand and output are rising fast, as for instance, from 1946 to '50 and again from 1952 to '55. Usually, however, in an economy in which the *average* level of employment tends to be high, fast rising production tends to be associated with excess demand for goods and labour. Recent investigations into the post-war behaviour of money wages indicate quite clearly that the demand for labour has a considerable influence on money wages: it is suggested, for instance, by one investigation that a one point change in the percentage level of excess demand for labour (roughly equivalent to a change of one point in percentage unemployment) is associated with a change of 3 or 4 per cent in the percentage annual rate of wage change.[1] It follows that when productivity is rising fast, money wages are usually rising fast also: more often than not, the latter are rising faster than the former, so that labour costs and prices tend to rise in the course of the boom. On the other hand, when excess demand for goods and labour is eliminated, productivity growth falls off.

---

[1] See Dow and Dicks-Mireaux, 'The Determinants of Wage-Inflation: United Kingdom, 1946–56', *Journal of the Royal Statistical Society*, Series A (General), Vol. 122, Part 2, 1959.

The rate of increase of money wages also declines, but the investigation referred to above indicates that it does not fall to zero even when excess demand for labour is zero. In addition to being influenced by the demand for labour, money wages are also affected by price changes and by the 'aggressiveness' of trade unions; and it has been shown that even in the absence of price changes and excess demand for labour, money wage rates in Britain tend to rise by about $2\frac{1}{2}$ per cent per annum. Thus if the rate of productivity growth falls off very sharply when excess demand is eliminated, the rate of increase of money wages may still exceed it, causing a continued rise in labour costs and prices, even when the boom has come to an end. All this, of course, assumes that employment remains at a high level when the economy is not booming. Given 'full employment' policies, this seems to be a likely state of affairs; but the implication is that attempts to reduce the rate of inflation by holding back demand and production are self-defeating, in that they tend to cause a larger fall in the rate of increase of productivity than in the rate of increase of money wages. Moreover, since wage changes are affected to some extent by price changes,[1] a price change introduced by forces independent of labour costs — for instance, introduced through a large rise in import prices — has repercussions on wages, causing them to rise faster than they otherwise would, *given* the demand for labour. There is not much doubt that the large rise in import prices in 1946–8 and 1950–1, for instance, contributed greatly to the large rise in money wages relatively to productivity growth. On the other hand, when there is no independent pressure causing prices to rise, political pressures or influence can often produce 'restraint' on the part of trade unions, even when excess demand for labour is high. Money wages and prices then rise less than would be expected, *given* the demand for goods and labour. The period 1948–9 seems to provide a clear illustration of this. There was no such 'restraint' in the late 1950's: indeed, it seems clear that the aggressiveness of trade unions, as manifested in their autonomous demands for higher money wages, increased markedly over the post-war period:[2] hence, although there was no serious independent force, such as import prices,

---

[1] Dow and Dicks-Mireaux, op. cit., suggest a wage-price co-efficient of about 0·5.
[2] See Dow and Dicks-Mireaux, op. cit., p. 8, for an index of trade union aggressiveness.

causing final product prices to rise, money wages rose by more than demand for labour would lead us to expect.

Taking the post-war period as a whole, however, there can be no doubt that excessive demand for goods and labour has been the most consistent force causing wages and prices to rise. To some extent this pressure was hidden in the early years of the period by the strong upward movement of raw material and food prices throughout the world, which, by raising British import prices, caused costs and prices to rise independently of domestic demand. But after 1952, the latter was the main factor causing prices to rise. In other words, it might be said that Britain enjoyed a prolonged boom in the post-war period, in the course of which prices rose — as in the past they have always tended to do at such times. Towards the end of the period, however, there have been signs of more persistent inflationary pressure, not associated with booming demand and production.

These signs do not emerge so clearly in British post-war experience as they do in the United States. This is because post-war recessions in demand and production have occurred less frequently in Britain than in the United States, and have been less deep and less prolonged. Nonetheless, the last few years of the 1950's do indicate fairly clearly that neither excessive demand for goods and labour nor a rise in import prices is a necessary condition for a continued rise in prices. In an earlier chapter (Chapter V) we have given reasons for this, and in general they seem to hold for British experience as well as for that of the United States. There are obvious signs of reluctance on the part of manufacturers to reduce their prices when demand is deficient or when costs are falling: instead they prefer to spend more on non-price competition. Similarly, there is a clear tendency for wage claims to be made and granted irrespective of the level of demand for labour — provided of course there is no serious fall in employment. This applies not only to industry as a whole but also to industries considered separately; there is a clear-cut tendency for wages paid in all industries to rise proportionately, independently of particular demands or particular productivity growths. These two tendencies, when taken in conjunction with the technological fact that productivity increases do not take place evenly throughout the economy, operate to produce a rise in the general price level through time.

The behaviour of retail prices clearly indicates the changing importance of the various forces which have contributed to post-war inflation (see Table IX). Up to 1952, prices which rose the most were those of goods containing a substantial element of imported materials, namely food and clothing. Prices of durable household goods also rose considerably, partly due to rising labour costs (themselves linked indirectly to rising import prices through the cost of living), and partly due to the immediate post-war pressure of excess demand, which probably allowed producers to pass on to consumers more than the increase in their costs. On the other hand, housing costs (rent and rates) were held down by social policy, whilst drink and tobacco prices were purely determined by taxation policy. But the movement of the price level of 'services' probably accurately reflects the rise in labour costs throughout these early years. After 1952, however, import costs contributed very little to inflation, as is shown by the movement of textile and clothing prices. It is true that food prices continued to rise strongly, but the increase took place largely in the period 1953 to 1956 and then mainly as a result of government budgetary policy which aimed at the reduction of food subsidies. Similarly, Government policy with respect to rents and to nationalised industries was largely responsible for the steep rise in two other components of the retail price index, housing and fuel and light. Durable household good prices however remained very stable, except for a rise towards the end of the 1954-6 boom, when labour costs were probably rising sharply: otherwise, rising productivity kept labour costs reasonably stable despite rising money wages, and it is doubtful whether any serious shortage of household durables remained after 1952, once the pent-up demand arising during the war had been satisfied. Significantly, however, 'services' (including transport) prices continued to rise at the same rate as before, reflecting the slow rise in productivity and faster rise in wage rates. It is obvious that the inflation of 'service' prices contributed more to the total rate of inflation after 1952 than it did in the years before; and it seems clear that this trend is likely to continue. Indeed in the future it may become the most important factor causing retail prices to rise.

We conclude therefore that in a relatively fully employed economy, such as the United Kingdom economy in the post-war period, there are pressures tending to produce inflation independently of excess demand for goods and labour. These pressures are not easy to contain by restrictions on demand, since if the latter involve restrictions on the growth of output, as they almost necessarily do, then as much is lost by a fall in productivity growth as is gained by a decline in the rate at which money incomes rise. In any case, restricting growth is not a desirable policy in the long term, although the forces producing a gradually rising price level are essentially long run. There are clear indications, for instance, that although restrictive measures did succeed to some extent in

Table IX

Retail Prices, United Kingdom, 1947–60

	All Items	Food	Rents and Rates	Fuel and Light	Dur-able House-hold Goods	Cloth-ing	Drink and Tobacco		Ser-vices
				(June 1947 = 100)					
1947 (June)	100	100	100	100	100	100	100		100
1948	108	108	99	110	107	109	109		104
1949	111	114	100	113	108	117	108		105
1950	114	122	101	116	112	119	105		108
1951	125	136	103	128	132	138	106		117
1952 (Jan. 15)	132	149	104	140	136	147	108		123
				(15 January 1952 = 100)			Alco-holic Drink	To-bacco	
1952	102	105	102	101	98	97	100	100	103
3	105	111	107	106	96	95	101	100	108
4	107	114	111	111	95	96	101	100	110
5	112	122	115	117	96	96	102	100	115
6	117	127	120	128	102	98	104	106	122
7	120	130	129	137	102	100	107	109	129
8	125	133	142	143	102	101	108	110	135
9	125	135	148	144	100	101	103	110	138
1960	126	135	150	146	100	102	101	114	142
				Percentage Increase 1947–1960					
	68	104	59	106	36	47			80

SOURCE: *Annual Abstract of Statistics*, C.S.O.
The Index of Retail Prices (base 17th January 1956) has been linked to the Interim Index (base 15th January 1952).

stabilising retail prices in Britain in 1959,[1] when demand and output were allowed to pick up strongly again towards the end of the year, prices began to rise yet again.[2] Thus growth had been unnecessarily checked without long-term advantages for price stability being gained.

If these arguments are valid it follows that the growth of a 'full employment' economy is likely to be accompanied by a secular rise in the price level, not so much because prices will rise continually, but rather because there are strong pressures preventing any fall. The rate of secular inflation is not likely to be very significant nor serious for the working of the economy. Nonetheless, as we said at the end of the previous chapter, it does raise certain issues of policy, which, however, will be discussed in more general terms in the concluding chapter.

[1] Even this overall stability was spurious to some extent, since if there had not been a cut in the fiscal duties on beer in the 1959 budget, retail prices would have risen in 1959.

[2] From mid-1959 to mid-1960, the retail price index rose a couple of points.

Chapter VIII

JAPAN AND THE U.S.S.R.

The early economic development of Japan and of Soviet Russia has often been cited as instances of growth being successfully promoted by inflation.[1] Moreover, it is well known that the governments of these countries played a more positive role in economic development than did the governments of Western countries. It might therefore be argued that the growth of Japan and Russia provides a better model for present-day underdeveloped countries, whose governments, it seems clear, are going to play an increasingly active part in promoting growth, than does the pattern of growth in the Western countries. This does not mean, of course, that governments of Western countries had no effect on growth: for instance, the setting up of stable political systems, the establishment of law and order, and the enactment of laws permitting the development of particular types of industrial organisation, were all necessary and important steps in fostering economic growth: but the course of development in these countries and the rate at which it took place depended essentially on the initiative of private enterprise. The State simply created the framework within which the latter worked. Governments, of course, had economic policies, the scope of which steadily increased over time; but certainly during the critical, early stages of development of these countries, these policies were regulatory rather than promotional. But whilst the activities of governments in Japan and Russia can, on this score, be contrasted with those undertaken by their Western type counterparts, the nature of governmental intervention was not the same in the two countries. Japan, for instance, remained an essentially private enterprise economy, in which the profit motive served as a guide to industry. It is true that many industries in Japan came into being as a result of the initiative of the State and under its control and ownership; but as soon as they were established, they were sold off to private buyers and continued their

[1] See, for example, W. A. Lewis, *The Theory of Economic Growth* (Allen and Unwin), p. 405.

development under private ownership. In Soviet Russia, on the other hand, state ownership of the means of production was the rule, and the distribution of resources and production was determined by the provisions of a central plan, rather than guided by the profit motive. Hence, even if the development of many present-day under-developed countries requires the active intervention and leadership of the State, a choice still remains open: between development within the framework of a basically private enterprise economy, as typified by Japan, and development within a fully Sovietised economy in which central planning rather than private initiative determines the character of growth.

Government intervention in both Japan and Russia clearly succeeded in forcing a higher rate of capital formation, and a higher rate of growth, than would otherwise have occurred. Both countries also suffered from inflation, either in the form of a persistent but moderate rise in the price level, as was the case in Japan, or in the form of a shorter period of very steeply rising prices which characterised the 1930 to 1940 development of Soviet Russia. For these reasons, therefore, an analysis of the experience of Russia and Japan should throw some light on the connection between government intervention, growth and inflation. An exhaustive description of development of these countries obviously cannot be attempted in a single chapter. Nevertheless some conclusions can be drawn from the less ambitious and briefer survey that will be attempted here.

I

JAPAN

The development of modern Japan can be said to have started in the late 1860's following widespread political changes that took place at that time.[1] The most important of these changes was probably the destruction of the power of feudal territorial lords and its replacement by a national rather than local administration. A national and unified system of revenue was established in the place of feudal property rights, and restrictions on the internal movement of goods and people were abolished. So were restrictions on individual property rights, including those that applied to

[1] This short account of Japan's economic development relies very much on Mr. W. Lockwood's excellent book *The Economic Development of Japan* (Oxford 1955). Detailed acknowledgement will not be given in the rest of this chapter.

the planting of crops and disposal of harvests; and entrance into
new occupations became very much easier. The political unification and legal emancipation that took place did not, as it did in
France, dispossess the old aristocratic ruling class; but it concentrated leadership into the hands of the abler and more progressive
members of the aristocracy, and produced a liaison between them
and the abler members of the merchant class. Thus conditions
were created for the establishment of modern capitalism which
quickly grew in the course of the next 70 years.

In this development the State, under its new leadership, provided a vital role. In contrast to the growth of capitalism in Western
Europe and America, an authoritation regime took the lead in
promoting economic development, even though the system remained basically private enterprise. Industry and trade, from the
very beginning, was dominated by great financial combines in
which the State was very often a partner; and the growth of middle
class, moderately sized independent business concerns, typical of
early development in Europe, was inhibited. So too was the growth
of trade unionism; the industrial power of great combines, combined with the political opposition of the State, prevented effective
combination of labour, and, in large part, the liberalisation which
accompanied the growth of private capitalism, and of a proletariat
in the West, remained absent. On the other hand, besides establishing a unified system of law and order and a national system of
finance, the State set up advisory and educational services which,
although aimed primarily at benefiting industry and trade, were the
first steps towards a system of national education. An aspect of this
was the training of a powerful and efficient bureaucracy for the
benefit of government and industry; indeed the establishment of
this bureaucracy provided a firm link between the two. Furthermore, in the very early stages of development, the role of the State
was often more direct than this. It set up model factories, opened
coal mines, foundries and machine shops, and established transport and communication facilities. In effect, it undertook the early
risks of industrial development, either by directly engaging in production itself or by entering into financial partnership with large-
scale business; and as industrial development began to spread, it
supported smaller-scale private ventures, financially as well as
technically. As important, if not more important than anything
else, the government provided banking and credit facilities and

pursued monetary and fiscal policies that put purchasing power into the hands of traders and businessmen who would use it productively, that is, invest it in industry.

Perhaps the most important aspect of these financial measures was the reform of the tax system, and in particular the institution of a land tax on the peasants. This tax provided 80 per cent of the revenue of the government up to 1882 and was used both to finance industry and to wage wars. Farmers thus bore the early burden of economic development. After the turn of the century the burden was shifted somewhat and fell more on the shoulders of the general public through the imposition of taxes on goods. Even then the system of taxation was highly regressive, personal and corporate incomes being only lightly taxed until the First World War. Hence the overall incidence of tax was kept relatively small, being only 10–15 per cent of total income.[1] The government also discriminated in favour of certain industries: taxes on them were kept especially light, and in some cases — for instance, mining, iron making, fishing — subsidies were given in order to encourage development. Apart from the steps taken by the State through its revenue policy to force saving, it encouraged voluntary saving. This in any case was promoted by the very unequal distribution of incomes,[2] but the State set out to tap the savings of even the poorer sections of the community. In particular, a postal savings scheme was instituted which attracted substantial sums for investment in government bonds and in other semi-official undertakings. In the last resort, however, the government did not hesitate to create credit whenever shortage of voluntary or tax created saving threatened to slow down economic development, even though the result was inflation. One writer has put it: 'in the early stage of Japan's modernisation, government and banks first created money and credit which stimulated the establishment of various enterprises, and then later collected private savings in money form to augment institutional savings.'[3] Whatever the objections that can be raised against such inflationary methods of financing economic development, the end result in the case of Japan was strikingly impressive; and to these end results we now turn.

---

[1] Farmers probably paid 30 per cent of their incomes.

[2] It is estimated the 50 per cent of household income accrued to the top 16 per cent of the nation, and 10 per cent to the top 0·2 per cent.

[3] S. Okita, 'Savings and Economic Growth in Japan', *Economic Development and Cultural Change*, Vol. VI, No. 1, October 1957.

In the seventy years prior to World War II, Japan's real national income increased by about 9 or 10 fold, that is, at an average annual rate of growth of about 4 per cent. Real income *per capita* rose by

Table I

Japan: Wholesale Price Index, 1878–1942

(1928–32 = 100)

1878	35·9	1911	68·9
79	41·5	12	73·0
1880	49·5	13	73·1
81	54·7	1914	69·7
82	49·9	15	70·6
83	39·0	16	85·3
84	32·5	17	107·4
1885	34·1	18	140·7
86	31·3	19	172·3
87	32·2	1920	189·4
88	32·5	21	146·4
89	35·4	22	143·0
1890	40·6	23	145·0
91	38·0	24	150·8
92	39·0	1925	147·3
93	36·2	26	130·7
94	38·2	27	124·1
1895	41·0	28	124·8
96	44·3	29	121·3
97	49·0	1930	91·2
98	51·6	31	77·1
99	51·9	32	85·5
1900	55·6	33	98·0
01	53·0	34	100·0
02	53·5	1935	102·5
03	56·9	36	106·8
04	59·9	37	129·7
1905	64·2	38	136·8
06	66·2	39	155·3
07	71·4	1940	182·3
08	68·7	41	196·7
09	65·6	42	251·9
1910	66·4		

SOURCE: Ohkawa, K., *The Growth Rate of the Japanese Economy since 1878* (Kimokuniya Book-store Co. Ltd., Tokyo 1957).

more than 400 per cent, at an average rate of about 2·8 per cent per annum.[1] As one would expect, manufacturing production rose at the fastest rate — between 1895 and 1938 it rose 14 or 15 fold — but agricultural and primary product production also showed large

[1] S. Kuznets, 'Quantitative Aspects of the Growth of Nations', *Economic Development and Cultural Change*, Vol. V, No. 1, October 1956.

increases (see Table III). If these statistics of growth are set against the comparable ones for the United States or the United Kingdom, they clearly indicate a very fast rate of growth, unprecedented in the known experience of Western private enterprise economies, and probably only surpassed by that of Soviet Russia in the 1930's. Furthermore, unlike the United States and the United Kingdom, no long-term acceleration or deceleration can be detected: national income and income *per capita* rose at as fast a rate in the last decade of the period as in the first.[1] Prices rose almost continuously throughout the seventy years, there being only two

Table II

Japan: Rate of Growth of National Product
per capita, 1878–1942

Period	Percentage rise in National Product per capita
1878/87 to 1888/97	40·2
1883/92 to 1893/02	40·4
1888/97 to 1898/07	31·6
1893/02 to 1903/12	20·6
1898/07 to 1908/17	15·6
1903/12 to 1913/22	19·2
1908/17 to 1918/27	29·5
1913/22 to 1923/32	42·3
1918/27 to 1928/37	45·8
1923/32 to 1933/42	37·2

SOURCE: Tsuru and Ohkawa, 'Long Term Changes in the National Product of Japan since 1878', *Income and Wealth, Series III* (Bowes and Bowes 1953), Table VI.

significant interruptions, namely in the mid-1880's and the 1920's; and by 1940, prices were about 350 per cent above the level of 1880. Naturally, prices rose most rapidly during the First World War, and again in the late 1930's, during the period of military aggression; but even in peacetime years the rate of inflation was quite striking. Thus from the 1870's to 1914, prices more than doubled (see Chart I and Table I). On the face of it, therefore, whatever general view one might take of the effect of inflation on growth,

---

[1] See Kuznets, ibid., Table 9 and Table 17 Appendix, and comments on p. 42.

there seems no doubt that in the case of Japan, at least, inflation did not retard growth.

Chart I. Wholesale Price Index: Japan 1870–1940

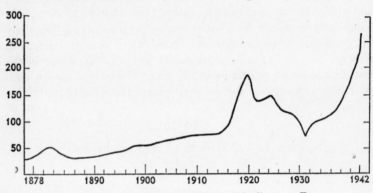

SOURCE: Ohkawa, K., *The Growth Rate of the Japanese Economy since 1878* (Kimokuniya).

Although no long-term acceleration or deceleration in Japan's long-term rate of growth from 1870 to 1940 can be detected, nevertheless growth was not uniform throughout. Whereas the rate of growth of national income *per capita* averaged over 4 per cent per annum in the last quarter of the nineteenth century and also in the 1920's and 1930's, in the first decade and a half of the twentieth century it averaged only about 2 per cent per annum (see Table II). This experience, it will be remembered, is in common with that of the United Kingdom, and to some extent the United States, whose rates of growth also slackened in this period. The suggested explanation of this apparently world-wide development, given in previous chapters, was that the world supply of primary products to manufacturing countries had become relatively scarcer than had been the case in the previous twenty-five years, or was to become the case in the following twenty years. Primary product prices therefore rose which had the effect of imposing a check to industrial growth in individual industrial countries. Furthermore it caused a rise in the price level in industrial countries, so that a slower rate of growth went hand-in-hand with inflation.

There is no doubt that Japan's early development in the 1870's and 1880's benefited to a significant degree from the world abundance of primary products at that time. Japan was enabled to enter world markets with its newly created manufactured goods, and exchange them for industrial raw materials without worsening of its international terms of trade. Indeed, Japan's terms of trade improved quite substantially from the early 1870's to the early 1890's, largely through import prices falling faster than export prices. But imports and exports at this time were barely 5 or 6 per cent of Japan's national product, so that the direct gains of improved terms of trade cannot have been great, and added little to real income or potentialities for growth. At the same time, however, foreign trade and commerce were important for Japan at this early stage of growth. Lockwood has put it 'For Japan, foreign commerce proved to be the key unlocking the door of economic opportunity.'[1] Japan's imports of raw materials and of machinery for its factories increased at a very great rate, and it was fortunate for Japan that it possessed an export commodity, silk, which could be produced with little capital equipment but made use of Japan's abundant labour supply, to finance these imports.[2] Of equal importance was the fact that foreign trade provided stimulus to early manufacturing development. Contacts with foreigners speeded up the application

Table III

Japan: Indices of Growth, 1870–1940

(1910–14 = 100)

Annual average of	Popula-tion	Food Produc-tion	Raw Material Produc-tion	Total Primary Produc-tion	Agricul-tural Produc-tion	Manufac-turing Produc-tion
1875/79	71	—	—	—	—	—
1885/89	77	(57)	(22)	(44)	(55)	—
1895/99	83	67	48	60	69	(37)
1905/09	94	85	78	82	88	69
1910/14	100	100	100	100	100	100
1915/19	107	115	134	121	118	160
1920/24	114	125	140	130	120	217
1925/29	121	135	169	145	129	313
1930/34	131	145	175	150	134	377
1935/39	141	161	205	178	149	600

SOURCE: Lockwood, *The Economic Development of Japan* (Oxford), Tables 2, 3 and 8.

[1] Lockwood, op. cit., p. 306.
[2] It is estimated by Lockwood that between 1870 and 1930 the export of silk products financed 40 per cent of Japan's imports of machinery and raw materials.

P

by industry of the discoveries of modern science and technology, and led to the introduction of modern methods of business organisation. Foreign markets also provided a demand for the output of expanding manufacturing industry which might have been lacking at home, given the very low level of real income which then prevailed. Even so the importance of foreign trade must not be overrated. The early growth of manufacturing industry, for instance, depended far more on domestically produced raw materials than on imported supplies; and Japan's standard of living, at this time largely geared to food supplies, depended more on home agriculture than on foreign sources of supply. From 1885 to 1895 domestic raw material production more than doubled, and food output increased by 20 per cent (see Table III). These increases in percentage terms were no doubt small compared with the growth of imports, but even by 1895 imports of these products provided no more than an eighth of the total supply.[1]

The relative insignificance of imported raw materials and foodstuffs partly, but only partly, explains why Japan's domestic price level did not reflect the world trend of primary product and manufactured good prices in the last quarter of the nineteenth century. Contrary to what was happening in the United Kingdom and elsewhere, Japan's domestic price level rose quite rapidly after a fall in the mid-1880's, despite falling import prices. From 1885 to 1895 prices rose by a third so that Japan experienced a quite considerable inflation at this time. After 1895 the rate of price increase accelerated, prices rising by about 50 per cent in the course of ten years. Some slackening in inflation then occurred, but from 1910 to 1915 the rise in prices again quickened, prices rising by more than 20 per cent. It is reasonable to suppose that after the turn of the century the Japanese price level began to reflect to an increasing extent changes in the world price level. By 1910 imports had grown to about 15 per cent of national income and by 1915 they were nearly 20 per cent.[2] Hence the rise in the world price

---

[1] In 1895, total imports were equivalent to about 10 per cent of Japan's national products, and about half of them were raw materials and foodstuffs. Since about 35 per cent of national product arose in the primary sector (i.e. agriculture, forestry, fishing and mining) of which only a very small part was exported, it follows that raw material and food imports constituted about one-eighth of the total supply of these products to the Japanese economy. See Lockwood, op. cit., Tables 27 and 29.

[2] By 1910, about 20 per cent of Japan's domestic supply of raw materials and foodstuffs came from abroad, and the proportion increased in later years.

level of primary products in the first two decades of the twentieth century clearly had an impact on the Japanese economy. But it is significant that up to the First World War, a rising world price level only accelerated Japan's domestic inflation, it did not cause it, whilst when world primary product prices were falling, this served only to retard Japan's inflation, not prevent it. The explanation clearly lay in domestic monetary and fiscal policies being pursued at this time.

Japan's terms of trade worsened from 1895 to 1900, then recovered to 1906/7. After 1907, a rapid worsening took place, largely the result of a steep rise in import prices. The deterioration continued throughout the war until by 1918, Japan's terms of trade were nearly 50 per cent worse than they had been in 1907. Since imports and exports now constituted about 20 per cent of national product, the impact on Japan's economy must have been severe. As we have seen, the rate of growth of the Japanese economy slowed down very greatly in the decade before the outbreak of World War I, and it seems likely that the relative world scarcity of primary products played a significant part in bringing this about. Raw material imports, which by 1915 constituted probably 50 per cent of Japan's total raw material supply, grew at a slower pace after 1905 than they had done before. Japan's output of domestically produced raw materials also rose at a slower rate than earlier; and, whilst no doubt Japanese manufacturing industry was beginning to turn towards the production of goods requiring less raw material input per unit of output, the slower growth of total raw material supply must have provided some check to Japan's economic development. Domestic food output, however, grew very substantially in the pre-war decade, so that even though Japan's terms of trade worsened so disastrously, real wages rose by some 10 per cent.[1]

From 1914 to 1918 Japan was only technically at war and her own military requirements put little pressure on her industrial capacity. As a consequence she was well placed to take advantage of the withdrawal of the more actively belligerent countries from their normal peacetime trading role. Neutral countries of the Far East turned to Japan to satisfy their needs for manufactured goods which could no longer be supplied by the Western Powers, and the latter themselves placed large orders with Japan for armaments.

[1] From the late 1890's to the outbreak of the First World War real wages rose by about 35 per cent, two-thirds of which occurred in the first 10 years. See Lockwood, op. cit., p. 144.

Thus Japan's economy was given a massive stimulant to which it did not fail to respond. Physical production in all directions rose steeply and the output of manufacturing industry increased by more than 75 per cent during the course of the war. At the same time it became more diversified, and the newer engineering and chemical industries obtained a firm footing both at home and abroad.[1] Exports of finished manufactures, particularly cotton goods, also rose substantially, and although rising industrial production necessitated a larger volume of imports, Japan's balance of trade became very favourable. Japan was therefore able to build up its gold reserves and other short term assets, which were to serve it well in the post-war decade.

All this time, of course, Japan suffered from a violent inflation. Fed by liberal credit policies, wholesale prices rose by 150 per cent in the course of four years, by far the largest rate of increase of prices in Japan's economic development. But even this was turned to Japan's economic advantage; for although industrial production was rising at a very rapid rate, real wages in industry remained rather constant. Part of the increase in national output was absorbed by an increase in population, which rose by about 6 per cent in the war years; but it seems clear that most of the enormous gains in income accrued to the already wealthy classes in the form of rents, dividends, interest and retained corporate profits. In turn, a substantial part of the rise in income was channelled into real capital formation.

Japan enjoyed the boom which swept the Western industrial world, particularly the United States, at the end of the war, but also suffered its collapse. War inflation left a legacy of inflated costs, so that when the world price level began to fall steeply after 1920, some difficulties were created. But Japan recovered more quickly than most Western industrial countries, largely because the government pursued liberal credit and subsidy policies in the interests of industry. By this time Japan had become highly integrated into the world economy. Imports and exports were now about 20 per cent of national product — probably well over half of its raw material supply and 20 per cent of its food supply came from abroad — so that changes in the world price level could not but have effects on Japan's domestic price level. Import

---

[1] It was important for Japan's development that these newer industries required less raw material input per unit of output than did industries established earlier.

prices, which had reached their peak in 1920, fell by 50 per cent in the next twelve years: export prices fell less sharply so that Japan's terms of trade improved. But in the inter-war period they never regained the favourable level of 1910. Japan succeeded in balancing its foreign trade in the 1920's whilst using its accumulated foreign exchange reserves, acquired during the war, to add further to its real capital at home. Wholesale prices followed import prices down, so did the cost of living and money wages: real wages, however, rose by 10 per cent in this period.

Japan's foreign trade position at the end of the 1920's seemed strong enough for it to return to the Gold Standard at its pre-war parity and this step was taken in 1929. In fact, the time proved most inopportune. Costs and prices, despite a fall in the 1920's, were still somewhat out of line with the rest of the world, and some deflationary measures were therefore necessary to prevent gold from flowing out. The Japanese government was prepared for this: but by 1929 the collapse of world trade and prices had begun, and the impact of the slump fell on Japan. Following the departure of the United Kingdom from the Gold Standard in 1931, the yen collapsed to less than 50 per cent of its former value against the dollar. Widespread political consequences ensued, the most important of which was the interruption of incipient trends towards a more democratic regime that seemed to be appearing in the 1920's, and the complete ascendency of the military.

But, as in the early 1920's, the slump in Japan was very short lived, as the government took very active measures to stimulate industrial recovery. Exports were stimulated by the depreciation of the yen, but in addition the government pursued a very aggressive trading policy. As a result the volume of exports doubled in six years. The major increase was in textiles, but other manufactured consumer goods found markets in countries whose incomes had been deflated by the great fall in primary product prices and whose people therefore could not afford the higher priced goods of the Western countries. The government created credit on a liberal scale and financed a rearmament programme, which eventually culminated in war against China and then the West, by running large budget deficits. Devaluation of the yen led to a steep rise in import prices, by 31 per cent from 1930 to 1936; so that both from the demand side and from the cost side considerable inflationary pressure was placed on prices. A number of factors at first operated to limit the rise in prices. For instance, stocks of raw cotton, purchased earlier when prices were low, were drawn on, so limiting the rise in costs. Second, the high level of capital formation which had been maintained in the 1920's bore fruit in terms of rising productivity of labour. And third, agriculture remained relatively depressed even though industry was booming: this meant that food prices were kept stable and that the supply of labour to industry was maintained, hence money wages were kept in check. Wholesale prices therefore rose by only 33 per cent in the six years 1930 to 1936; but in the following two years inflation got out of hand as the pressure of war increased, and prices rose by a further 50 per cent. However, in real terms, the growth of the Japanese economy in the 1930's was very impressive. Diversification continued and manufacturing output rose by more than 65 per cent in six years;[1] and even though agriculture was depressed, net national product rose by 50 per cent. Part of this substantial rise in product was absorbed by a 25 per cent worsening in the terms of trade: even so, a 40 per cent rise in real national income at a time when the rest of the industrial world was suffering from slump conditions was by no means an insignificant performance. But the Japanese worker did not benefit: instead the gains were channelled into further capital formation and into war.

The success of Japan in avoiding the worst effects of the world wide slump of the 1930's pinpoints the important contrast between Japan's economic development and that of the Western powers. This contrast, as we have said earlier, arises from the greater willingness of Japan's governments to intervene actively in the process of growth. The aims of government may of course be criticised: industrialisation was not only an objective in itself, but clearly it was also directed towards building up Japan's military strength: and in the last analysis, all that Japan achieved in the way of economic advancement was destroyed as a result of some of these aims. But it cannot be denied that the combination of aggressive private enterprise and dynamic and pervasive government intervention produced an extraordinarily high rate of growth in the seventy years preceding World War II. To some extent this growth showed one of the characteristics of growth in the purely private enterprise economies: it was accompanied by cyclical fluctuations. But depressions were short lived and booms were prolonged, since

[1] 1930 to 1936.

the State never allowed the inducement to invest by private entrepreneurs to disappear — even if this meant, as it did, the creation of credit and the running of budget deficits to finance new investment. Hence, as compared with the Western countries, the Japanese economy was in a state of almost perpetual boom, at the inevitable cost of perpetually rising prices. Apart from the steep fall in prices in the 1920's, and a minor interruption in the 1880's, prices rose constantly, in peacetime years as well as during wars. If the rate of inflation over seventy years is compared with the rate of real growth over 70 years (4 per cent per annum) it seems reasonable to suppose that the cost was worth it. Inflationary methods of financing growth have often been criticised on grounds that they lead to ill-judged and speculative investment: some no doubt did occur in Japan and was wasteful as far as growth was concerned, but there can be no doubt that most investment was productive in the long run. Social costs of inflation were high: in particular, income distribution was kept highly inequitable by inflation, but this was the obverse of a high rate of capital formation. With a different social and economic organisation no doubt the same rate of capital formation might have been carried out with a less inequitable distribution of income. And in the long run the Japanese worker did not reap the benefits arising from the sacrifice of earlier generations owing to ultimate military defeat in 1945. But when all this is said, there can be no doubt that the inflationary use of the monetary and financial mechanism did succeed in putting purchasing power into the hands of those who used it productively, and did succeed in promoting growth.

Of great significance, too, is the fact that even when prices were rising their fastest, for instance in the 1870's, in World War I, and again in the late 1930's, the danger of hyper-inflation seemed remote. A number of factors contributed to the absence of this danger, as well as to the success of inflation in forcing saving; and these factors must be clearly borne in mind when inferences are drawn from Japanese experience to be applied to the problems of present-day under-developed countries. First, Japan's rapidly growing population and the agricultural reserve tended to keep down money wages in manufacturing industry. In addition, the political and social climate in Japan was against the formation of trade unions. Hence, pressures on industrial costs of production were limited. Second, on the demand side, social and fiscal policy tended to be highly regressive so that a large proportion of income gains was channelled into the hands of the already wealthy classes: saving and capital formation, rather than consumption, benefited. Third, Japan had a high marginal propensity to import which limited short-term booms. Fourth, Japan had considerable success with her exports which found markets at the right time — for instance, silk products in the early stages of industrialisation, and cheap textiles in the 1930's — so enabling her to finance her imports in the long run and in short-term booms. Thus, a combination of high marginal propensities to save and import and checks to the wage-price spiral operated to hold inflation in check, even in extreme boom conditions; and confidence in the value of money was never lost.

But expanding labour supply and weak trade union organisation would not have sufficed to keep the wage-price spiral in industry in check if food prices had got out of hand; and this fact points to one crucial development in Japan's economic growth which perhaps above all others ensured that inflation would be kept reasonably moderate and would successfully force capital formation. This was Japan's success in developing both her own primary product supply in the early stages of industrialisation, and a substantial part of her food supply throughout her growth. A conspicuous feature of Japan's early development was the very rapid expansion of its agricultural sector. Despite the emphasis given to industrialisation, Japan's governments did not neglect agriculture: indeed its expansion accounted for a substantial part of the increase in national income during the first forty years of development.[1] Although the general movement of labour was away from the land towards industry, Japan's governments took active steps to introduce more efficient methods into farming, with considerable success. It is true that Japanese governments resorted to heavy taxation of agricultural incomes so as to siphon off productivity gains in this sector for the benefit of manufacturing industry; but it appears that up to 1900, at least, the development of light consumer good industries which used up relatively little capital and which could be integrated into rural life — as one writer has put it, 'forming an extension of agriculture rather than alternative to it,'[2] — was given

---

[1] Lockwood, op. cit., p. 89.
[2] Ranis, 'Factor Proportions in Japanese Economic Development', *American Economic Review*, September 1957.

priority. Thus agriculture and industry developed side by side, sustaining each other. At any rate, from 1880 to 1910 agricultural output rose by more than 80 per cent, whilst population increased by 44 per cent.[1] Hence output per head rose by 25 per cent. Food output rose sufficiently to maintain a growing population at rising real income standards, and even by the 1930's Japan was producing the bulk of its food supply at home. The former development was an important factor in keeping money wages stable in manufacturing industry: if food supply had not kept pace with population and real income, the pressure of industrialisation would have raised food prices and therefore in turn, money wages, bringing about a spiral of the two; and industrial costs of production would then have suffered. As it was, the pressure of a high level of capital formation and military expenditure financed by credit creation, forced up industrial prices. Industrial costs naturally rose as well, but at a slower rate, so that profits and real capital formation benefited. Inflation in Japanese industry, in other words, bore more the characteristics of a 'demand' inflation than a 'cost' inflation and it was because of this that it contributed to growth. Furthermore, the fact that Japan produced the bulk of its own food supply also meant that the cost of living was relatively insulated from swings in world food prices, so that unlike the United Kingdom for example, a source of pressure on money wages was absent.[2] Moreover, in conjunction with the fact that in the early stages of development, at least, Japan also supplied herself with a substantial part of her raw materials, it meant that export earnings could be used to finance the purchase of capital equipment from abroad, without which Japan's industrial development would have been impossible. As time went on more and more foreign exchange had to be spent on raw materials, and to some extent on food, but at the same time Japan's ability to produce capital equipment was also increasing, so that growth did not suffer.

In brief, in the fifty years up to World War I, the Japanese economy grew in a balanced way, with all the advantages that this implies. The shift of labour from land to factory was accompanied by rapidly growing productivity in agriculture which ensured

[1] Lockwood, op. cit., Table 2, p. 86.
[2] Of course it could be argued that if Japan did not suffer from rising world food prices neither did it benefit when they fell. But money wages tend to rise with food prices but not fall with them. Hence Japan avoided the 'ratchet' effect introduced from overseas.

sufficient food supply for a rapidly growing industrial labour force. At the same time rising agricultural production raised the real income of the Japanese people sufficiently to provide a market for the output of expanding manufacturing industries,[1] the bulk of which was sold in the home market rather than abroad. Indeed, the fact that manufactured good prices tended to rise at least as fast as agricultural and food prices suggests that demand for manufactured goods outstripped supply.[2] This was clearly the consequence of both a high rate of capital formation and large military expenditure, not completely covered by taxation or saving. But the fact that the Japanese worker's need for food was reasonably satisfied kept inflation in check and ensured its success in forcing economic growth. In this respect Japan's early development can be strongly contrasted with industrialisation in Soviet Russia in the 1930's — not on grounds that Soviet Russia's growth at this time was slower, but rather on grounds that it was more unbalanced and was therefore accompanied by inflation of greater severity. Unlike Japan's inflation, the Russian inflation of the 1930's made little contribution to economic development: indeed if it had occurred in a private enterprise economy it would most likely have led to the breakdown of the monetary system and the cessation of growth. But to the facts of Soviet growth and inflation in the 1930's we now turn.

II

THE U.S.S.R. IN THE 1930's

The association of high rates of economic growth and price inflation stands out quite clearly in the case of the U.S.S.R. From 1928/9, when the first Five Year Plan was introduced, until the end of the 1930's, Soviet Russia's national product rose at something like 6 or 7 per cent per annum,[3] so that by 1937, national product had risen by well over 50 per cent. According to Hodgman,[4]

---

[1] Lockwood disposes quite conclusively with the argument that Japan's growth was essentially based on foreign demand for manufactures since its own people were too poor to absorb the output of the manufacturing industries.

[2] See Chapter III, pp. 53–56.

[3] G. Grossman, 'National Income', in A. Bergson, *Soviet Economic Growth* (New York 1953), Table 1.1. If an estimate of Soviet Russia's growth is made using 1926/7 prices, it works out about 8 per cent per annum: if instead 1937 factor costs are chosen, then the result is 5 per cent per annum. Grossman takes a mean, suitably weighted, of the two estimates.

[4] Hodgman, 'Industrial Production' in Bergson, op. cit.

industrial production, to which so much attention was given in the plans of the 1930's, rose by more than 16 per cent per annum, a rate of increase considerably higher than that achieved by the United States at any time since the Civil War. This impressive rise in industrial production was accompanied by a substantial rise in labour productivity which according to Soviet sources, rose by more than 150 per cent during the decade.[1] All industries shared in the progress, but there can be no doubting the emphasis given to heavy industry. Here, if Soviet statistics are taken at their face value, output increased by as much as 450 per cent in ten years; and even if estimates by outside observers are preferred,[2] the rise is still very great (270 per cent). In contrast to the performance of industry, however, agriculture lagged very badly, output rising by no more than 15 per cent in the same period.

If the statistics of industrial growth are impressive, so are those relating to the price level. According to Jasny[3] the cost of living to urban industrial workers rose by about 650 per cent in the ten years up to 1937. Food prices rose almost tenfold, clothing prices sevenfold and household good prices between two and threefold. Against the rise in the cost of living, money wages rose somewhat more than threefold,[4] so that real wages of industrial workers fell by almost a half. On the other hand, the price level of producer goods rose by very much less, by only 75 per cent, but this development was made possible by the extensive use of government subsidies to the producer good industries.[5]

Whilst it is clear that a high rate of economic development and a high rate of price inflation went together, the argument that the former was the effect of the latter cannot easily be substantiated. There is more reason to believe that inflation occurred contrary to the wishes of the government, rather than as the result of deliberate policy. For one thing, Soviet planners seem to have budgeted for a price fall in their Five Year Plans, not a price rise. According to one expert on Soviet economic development, for instance, a fall in retail prices of about 20 per cent was budgeted for in the first Five Year Plan, and a substantial rise in real consumption was antici-

[1] Output per man year.   [2] Hodgman, ibid.
[3] N. Jasny, 'The Soviet Economy during the Plan Era', in *Stanford University Food Research Institute, Misc. Publ. 11A*, July 1951, Appendix, Table III, p. 111.
[4] N. Jasny, ibid., p. 69.
[5] N. Jasny, 'Soviet Prices of Producer Goods', in *Stanford University Food Research Institute, Misc. Publ. 11c*, February 1952.

pated.[1] Nor was there any intention to make use of repressed inflation, that is, to permit the existence of extensive excess demand whilst rationing the available supply. On the contrary, the failure of war communism had persuaded the government to make more use of the market system so far as consumer goods were concerned, and to permit a wide degree of freedom of choice. Indeed, far from being desired by the Soviet government, the inflation of the 1930's must have presented it with enormous difficulties.

Quite apart from these considerations, however, the deliberate use of inflation to finance capital formation hardly seems to be necessary in, nor does it seem compatible with, a fully planned and controlled economy, except as a result of planning errors. The case of a free market, private enterprise economy is of course different. In such a country a government may deliberately pursue easy credit and fiscal policies with a view to inducing private entrepreneurs to expand their businesses. With the purchasing power so made available to them, business men bid for materials and other resources, with the result that, if these are already fully employed in other uses, their prices tend to rise. Provided consumers' incomes lag behind the rise in prices, resources are thus bid away from the consumption good industries, and real capital formation takes place. Inflation has forced real saving. In the case of a fully planned and controlled economy, however, the use of the money and price system to this end, that is, to pull resources out of consumption into investment, does not seem necessary. The government decides at the outset what level of investment is to take place during the period of the plan, and resources are directed, by means of physical controls, according to the prepared scheme of priorities. Resources left over, so to speak, are then available for the production of consumption goods which have a lower priority. It remains necessary, of course, for the government to ensure that demand for what remains does not exceed supply; and for this purpose the Soviet government employed two weapons. First, by virtue of its control over wage and salary incomes in State enterprises, it fixed the level of household income in the appropriate relationship with the anticipated supply of consumer goods, priced according to the plan. Second, prices were divorced from costs and therefore from factor incomes, by the use of commodity or turnover taxes, which

---

[1] M. Dobb, *Soviet Economic Development since 1917* (Routledge-Kegan Paul 1948), p. 235.

were imposed on particular goods at varying rates, depending on the anticipated balance between supply and demand in the consumer market. The two weapons were naturally employed together, that is, factor incomes and commodity taxes were determined simultaneously so as to balance supply and demand. Of course, if it turned out that the planners had miscalculated either supply or demand in the consumer good market, so that excess demand appeared, or if subsequently the investment target had to be revised upwards, then adjustment in household incomes or commodity taxes would become necessary. In practice it would no doubt be easier to raise commodity taxes than to lower household incomes. Hence, if such adjustment had to be made often so that retail prices were constantly rising, then it might be argued that the State was deliberately creating inflation. Even so, it could hardly be argued that the State was doing this in order to attract resources into the capital goods industries; the distribution of resources had already been decided and enforced within the limits of the Plan. In these circumstances, therefore, inflation is the result of error or unforeseen contingencies, rather than of deliberate decision. Moreover, it should be noted that money and credit play no independent role in the process: the volume of money in circulation depends on, rather than determines, the level of money incomes and prices.

Nonetheless, inflation on a massive scale did occur in Soviet Russia during the early Five Year Plans; and it naturally continued through the war years until the decisive currency reforms of 1947. The question then arises: why did it occur?

One explanation has been given by Holzman in his analysis of Soviet finance during the period 1928 to 1939.[1] There seem to be three strands to this. First, Holzman points to the massive increase in short-term credit and currency provided by the State Bank in the 1930's. Currency alone expanded eightfold in the twelve years 1929 to 1941.[2] An increase of this order was clearly incompatible with monetary stability. In the first instance, the expansion of money and credit was reflected in the balances available to the managers of State enterprises. 'It is clear that managers of Soviet enterprises had available to them funds which were more than adequate to meet their needs in the pre-war period, in terms of

[1] Holzman, 'Financing Soviet Economic Development', in *Capital Formation and Economic Growth* (N.B.E.R. 1955).
[2] Ibid., p. 258.

labour, raw materials, and other inputs at planned prices.'[1] The effect of the excess liquidity, which managers were not reluctant to spend for reasons that will be indicated in a moment, differed according to the type of the market. The prices of raw materials and equipment were rather rigidly controlled by the authorities so that the competing demands of enterprises did not result in rising prices. But it led to hoarding of materials on the part of managers, a behaviour on their part quite consistent with conditions of repressed inflation. As far as prices were concerned, the labour market was the weak link, and money wages rose rapidly and continually under the competition of State enterprises. Costs of production of both capital and consumer goods rose more than was planned and the excess purchasing power received by labour forced constant revisions in retail prices.[2] But why did managers of State enterprises behave in this competitive way, which, incidentally, was contrary to Soviet Law? Without the incentive to purchase on their part, excess liquidity would not have mattered. Here Holzman comes to the second strand of his explanation. Managers were driven to behave unlawfully, partly because of the dangers of not fulfilling their planned outputs, and partly because of the rewards they obtained for overfulfilment. Furthermore the penalties attached to non-fulfilment were apparently more severe than the penalties attached to the crime of excess purchase (i.e. excess according to the provisions of the plan) of materials and labour. Again, this behaviour would not have mattered so much if excess purchases by State enterprises had been purely the result of excessive zeal on the part of managers to overfulfil their output quotas. In fact, however, such excess purchases were necessary if the planned output of all State enterprises taken together was to be realised. Holzman argues, in other words, that when summed together, the quotas of raw materials and labour assigned to enterprises implied a greater demand for resources than were in fact available: not all State enterprises could produce their planned output at the same time. In short, Soviet planners went in for what Holzman calls 'over-full employment planning' and inflation was the direct consequence. The provision of ample credit, and pres-

---

[1] Ibid., p. 259.

[2] Holzman suggests that at first upward revisions in the rate of turnover tax were the important factor causing prices to rise. Afterwards, however, the rate of turnover tax was kept fairly constant, so that the rise in prices was due to rising costs of production. Ibid., p. 261.

sure on managers to compete with another to produce their planned outputs were necessary conditions for inflation, but neither of them separately nor both together, were sufficient in themselves. There had also to exist, at bottom, a deficiency of resources in relation to the demands made on them.

A purely monetary explanation of inflation has also been advanced to explain Soviet experience in the 1930's. R. P. Powell[1] has pointed to the existence of a built-in mechanism of cumulative inflation which resulted from the tying of State Bank loans and credit to the value of working stocks held by State enterprises. State managers could always rely on their needs of working capital (i.e. to cover stocks of raw materials, semi-finished and finished goods) being covered by the State Bank. If commodity prices rose, more credit was automatically provided in order to allow the same volume of goods to be carried. Thus, the Soviet government did not attempt to exert financial control over its managers by manipulating the amount of credit available to them. The liberal provision of credit was usually offset by a surplus in the State budget, but the relationship between the budgetary surplus and loans made by the State Bank was by no means stable. In consequence surplus money was often injected into the system. This would cause an increase in expenditure by households and enterprises, commodity prices would rise, and so, automatically, would credit granted by the State Bank. Inflation would then tend to become cumulative. Powell does not deny the presence of 'real' factors behind inflation, but he maintains that no simple or direct dependence of monetary factors on real factors existed: 'to an exceptionally large degree Soviet economic development and Soviet inflation may be regarded as independent phenomena.'[2]

The explanation advanced by Powell is open to the objections that can be raised against all theories emphasising purely monetary factors. It is not sufficient to show that credit was freely available if we want to explain why prices rise. It may equally be the case, and almost certainly was in the Soviet system, that credit was created *because* prices rose. We have to concentrate on expenditure in relation to resources, and an analysis of this requires not only consideration of the supply of purchasing power, but also con-

[1] In a doctorial dissertation, University of California 1952. See a brief summary of his views in a controversy between him and Holzman in *Capital Formation and Economic Growth* (N.B.E.R.).
[2] Ibid., p. 281.

sideration of the motivation of spenders. Holzman's explanation is therefore preferable and no doubt goes some way to explaining Soviet inflation. But it is clearly not the whole story and overlooks a highly important element in the situation.

Holzman emphasises the key and leading role of wages in the inflation. Soviet managers competed for scarce labour, wages were therefore bid up (despite controls and penalties attached to over payment), and costs of production then followed: rising costs plus increased expenditure from rising household money incomes forced an upward adjustment of retail prices. But the facts of the Soviet inflation suggest that even if wages had not been bid above the levels decided on in the various Plans, retail prices would have had to have been adjusted upwards in any case.

A basic element in Soviet economic development in the 1930's was a catastrophic fall in real wages which one expert has put at almost 50 per cent.[1] Far from wages and prices rising proportionately with wages taking the lead, as one would expect in a cost inflation,[2] the latter rose much more than the former. This development seems more compatible with wages lagging rather than leading in time. It seems more likely therefore that Soviet Planners either enormously overestimated the supply of consumption goods that would become available to the civilian population, or that subsequent events caused them to revise their Plans in a way that would reduce the available supply. In fact both error and revision of Plans contributed to inflation.

When the first Five Year Plan was drawn up, there seems to have been no expectation that living standards would have to decline to permit a greater rate of capital formation: in fact, important increases in real wages were expected. But the rising military threat of Germany in the 1930's forced some revision in both the first and subsequent Plans, and more resources were directed towards the building up of military strength. A direct consequence of this was that greater priority had to be given to the development of heavy industry at the expense of light industry which catered more for consumers' needs. Furthermore, as an exporter of raw products and an importer of manufactures, Soviet Russia suffered from the international price movements of the

[1] N. Jasny, op. cit. This estimate of the fall has been disputed by some authors, for instance Dobb (op. cit., p. 286) but there is no doubt that a large fall did occur.

[2] Assuming a closed economy.

1930's. Import prices fell by about 20 per cent and export prices by 30 per cent in the first half of 1931, so that a significant worsening in the terms of trade occurred.[1] Being unwilling or unable to finance an import surplus, and not wanting to cut down imports of essential constructional materials, Soviet Russia cut down on imports of materials for consumer good production: in addition it allocated more home produced consumption goods for export. Hence, military threat and worsening terms of trade forced a revision of plans and a reduction in the supply of consumer goods below what was originally anticipated. But the consequences were made worse by the fact that, in two vital respects, Soviet planners had been over optimistic in their initial drawing up of the Plans, particularly so in the framing of the first.

The first miscalculation related to labour productivity in industry. 'There had evidently been excessive optimism as to the speed with which many of the new plants could be brought into full and successful operation, and yield their fruits in heightened productivity, and as to the speed with which rationalised methods, particularly in building operations, could be achieved.'[2] Instead of doubling, as it was expected to do, from 1928 to 1932, labour productivity in industry increased by only 41 per cent. Costs of production therefore did not fall by as much as had been expected, and more labour had to be employed than was originally intended. This was one of the causes of competitive bidding for labour stressed by Holzman. Hence the wage bill was inflated on two accounts: first, because industrial employment was higher than planned, and second, because money wages per worker were bid up by the competition of State enterprises. Monetary demand in the consumer good market was therefore inflated: at the same time, the supply of goods coming into it was reduced. Hence it is not surprising that inflationary pressure materialised. Even so, it is likely that the second miscalculation of the planners was more vital, since it related to the agricultural sector. Indeed the agricultural crisis of the early 1930's, which completely falsified the predictions of the Soviet planners and brought about a catastrophic fall in food supply, was such an important event in Soviet economic development at this time, that a brief discussion of its background is necessary at this point, if its inflationary significance is to be appreciated.

[1] Dobb, op. cit., p. 238.   [2] Dobb, op. cit., p. 239.

Needless to say, the importance of agriculture in Russia's economic development was well recognised by Soviet Planners. The latter half of the 1920's had been characterised by intensive discussion relating to the nature and pace of Russia's future economic growth. Should the country concentrate on the expansion of heavy industry which promised greater, although delayed, returns? Or should the Russian people be given more immediate benefits through the expansion of light industries producing simple consumer goods? Should resort be made to foreign capital if this were possible? Or should a large export trade in grain and other raw agricultural products be developed so as to facilitate the import of capital goods instead of producing them at home? Such questions occupied the theorists of the Communist Party in the early years following the revolution. But the crucial question centred on the rate at which agricultural production could be expanded, since Soviet economists well recognised the need for simultaneous, if not prior, development in this sector, if successful industrial growth was to take place.

But agriculture had presented a critical problem from the very early days of the revolution. Before 1913, Russia was primarily an agricultural country—'industrialisation had as yet touched little more than the hem of Russia's economic system'[1] — exporting grain and other agricultural products in exchange for manufactures. But agriculture was characterised by primitive methods and employed but little capital. Productivity was therefore low, and supported the mass of the Russian people at not much above subsistence level. The Revolution of 1917, and consequential war and foreign invasion, precipitated an acute crisis that the revolutionary government had to face at the outset. A large area of land was devastated and some, for a time at least, went out of the control of the revolutionary government; and crops and livestock were destroyed. Shortage of food produced a severe inflationary situation in which in three years, from 1917 to 1920, prices rose a hundred fold. The breakdown of the monetary system was inevitable. The revolutionary government at first attempted to handle the situation by introducing widespread controls and rationing; and in order to obtain the goods it required, particularly food, it resorted to compulsory requisitioning from producers and attempted to set up a centralised system for collection and distribu-

[1] Dobb, op. cit., p. 35.

tion. The normal market link between town and country was abolished, and barter took the place of monetary exchange. These were the main features of the notorious period of war communism, which, however, according to one observer[1] were not so much the product of revolutionary theory as forced upon the revolutionary government by the breakdown of the monetary system and the dislocation of normal production and exchange facilities. At any rate, war communism did not last long, the government embarking on its New Economic Policy in 1921 and re-introducing, to a large extent, the market system. But the coercive measures used against the peasant during the period of war communism left a legacy of ill-feeling which was to continue for the next decade or so. The peasant did not willingly accept compulsory requisition and retaliated by reducing his output. The revolution began to founder on a shortage of food and only the introduction of the New Economic Policy saved it.

Some economic recovery followed, but it is fairly clear that the basic agricultural problem was not solved by the end of the 1920's, when the first Five Year Plan was introduced. Farming was still organised predominantly on small scale, individualistic lines, and methods remained primitive. Furthermore, the Land Reform legislation of 1917, which had dispossessed the larger landlords in favour of the small and middle-sized peasant, had the unexpected result of reducing the marketable surplus of food from the land. Before Land Reform, food entering urban markets had come mainly from the large farms which produced more than the landlord, his family and retainers consumed themselves. On the other hand the small peasant lived on a subsistence level, more often than not having too little rather than too much for his needs. The redistribution of land therefore increased the supply of food to the small peasant, but, since the latter and his family tended to increase their consumption at the same time, it reduced the marketable surplus. The Soviet government was thus faced with a twofold problem: first, to increase the productivity of both land and peasant; second, to ensure that the largest part of the increase in output went to the towns to satisfy the needs of the growing urban population. At the end of the 1920's the decision was taken to put agriculture on to a large-scale, scientific basis. Provision was made within the first Five Year Plan to increase the production of tractors

[1] Dobb, op. cit.

and other agricultural implements so that the farms could be mechanised. Indeed, within the State investment budget, provision was made to allocate a substantial proportion of investment resources to agriculture.[1] The institutional side of the problem was handled by the setting up of large State farms under the control of State managers: and the smaller peasants were encouraged and coerced into entering into collective arrangements with their neighbours. Once again the collection and distribution of the marketable surplus was organised on a centralised basis and delivery quotas were established for individual farms. All these steps suggest that Soviet planners had no intention of neglecting agriculture.

Even so, agricultural output did not come up to expectations. Labour was released from the farms to take up work in the new factories, but the output of food fell far short of what was necessary if real wages were to be kept constant, let alone increased. In part, this was due to the inefficiency of the State farms which were probably too large for good management: in part it was due to a mistaken policy of monocropping. But the most important cause of the new agricultural crisis was a further revolt by the Kulaks and middle-sized peasants who opposed the re-introduction of compulsory requisitioning. The revolt was more serious than that which had taken place during the period of war communism, and it led to widespread destruction of crops and livestock which was to inhibit agricultural development for the rest of the decade. The supply of food to the Russian worker fell during the period of the first Five Year Plan, at a time when money incomes in the towns were rising fast with the growth of industrialisation. Despite low collection prices paid by the State to the farms, the price of food in urban markets had repeatedly to be raised so as to equate supply and demand. Money wages of urban workers had to be allowed to rise in order to keep labour in the factories without employing extreme coercive measures; and cost inflation therefore spread into the industrial sector, adding to the other pressures there that were mentioned earlier.

The crucial part played by food prices in the Russian inflation of the 1930's is well illustrated by Jasny's price estimates given earlier. In ten years food prices to urban industrial workers rose by

---

[1] 20 per cent. See Kaplan, 'Capital Formation and Allocation', in *Bergson*, op. cit.

a thousand per cent, whereas the price level of industrial goods rose by no more than a third of this. The Soviet government succeeded, finally, in crushing the revolt of the peasant, and agricultural production began to revive after 1933. But although by 1938 output per farm worker had risen by about 28 per cent, total output barely kept pace with the rise in population: both rose by roughly 15 per cent.[1] Jasny argues that even at the high prices ruling in the 1930's, the demand for many necessities was not satisfied; and the agricultural problem remained with the Soviet people right up to the end of the 1930's. In the opinion of some observers it still does.[2]

In brief, the enormous rise in prices which took place in Soviet Russia in the 1930's was the consequence of the failure of agricultural output to rise in the early stages of rapid industrial growth. Severe excess demand for food and other agricultural products was therefore produced, causing their prices to rise steeply: in consequence, costs of production in industry were affected. We can thus account for the Soviet inflation in terms of *excess demand* in the agricultural sector plus *cost* inflationary pressures in the industrial sector — the type of inflation during growth that we analysed in some detail in Chapter III. In a private enterprise economy, steeply rising costs of production in the industrial sector would, at some stage, have brought the industrial expansion to a temporary halt, particularly if the quantity of money was fixed by an independent monetary authority. But the Soviet government was both industrial entrepreneur and monetary authority: hence it was able to ensure that aggregate monetary demand for industrial products kept pace with rising costs of production so that excess supply did not materialise. At the same time, it ensured that output was directed into capital formation and to satisfy defence needs.

It is obvious, therefore, that Soviet inflation cannot be cited as an example of inflation being conducive to economic growth in the sense of saving being forced. Japan's experience is a much better model for this. We have made it clear that the Japanese government was not reluctant to keep aggregate demand from pressing against aggregate supply; but at the same time it made sure that the

---

[1] For estimates of population growth see W. Eason, 'Population and Labour Force', *Bergson*, op. cit.; and for estimates of agricultural output see Jasny, 'The Socialised Agriculture of the U.S.S.R.', *Stanford University Food Research Institute, Misc. Publ. 11A*, October 1951.

[2] See, for example, V. P. Timoshenko, 'Agricultural Resources', *Bergson*, op. cit.

pattern of output kept in line with the pattern of demand as population and real income per head rose: in particular, it made sure that agriculture kept pace with industry. By avoiding serious excess demand in the food market, the Japanese government was able to minimise rising costs in industry. Hence the pressure of excess demand for industrial products more easily caused prices to rise relatively to costs; industrial profits were therefore inflated and saving and capital formation were successfully forced. Moreover, since the inflation which did take place was consequently very moderate, and gave rise to no danger of loss of confidence in money or in the monetary system, it proved compatible with the continued existence of a private enterprise system. Thus it is perhaps to the Japanese model of forced saving through inflation that under-developed countries must look if in the course of their development they wish to remain basically private enterprise.

Chapter IX

INFLATION AND GROWTH IN
LATIN AMERICA

So far, we have illustrated the arguments put forward in the early chapters of this book by drawing on the price and growth experience of a few already well-developed economies. We now consider an area of the world which, although still largely undeveloped, has in recent years experienced significant economic growth as well as severe inflation, namely Latin America.

The Latin American region comprises a large number of independent countries, so that it would clearly be impossible in a short chapter to survey the experience of each individually, even if we confined ourselves, as we shall, to the post Second World War years alone. But, apart from being members of the same region of world's surface, Latin American countries have a number of features in common which allows a rather general picture of the relation between growth and price behaviour to be drawn. This is not to suggest that all the countries have enjoyed similar advantages or disadvantages for economic growth, or that they have progressed at roughly the same rate, or that they have experienced roughly the same degree of price inflation. It can be seen quite clearly from Table I that whereas some countries, for instance, Brazil, Colombia, Peru and Venezuela, have developed at a rapid rate, others have lagged well behind. In particular, growth has been very slow and, indeed, only intermittent in two of the most important countries of the region, Argentina and Chile. Moreover, there is no close connection between growth and the amount of inflation. Prices rose at a rate of only about 3 per cent per annum in Venezuela, whilst they rose at over 20 per cent per annum in Peru and Brazil, whose rates of growth of real income per head were roughly the same. On the other hand, the rate of inflation was particularly high in those countries, Argentina, Chile, and Paraguay[1] in which growth was very slow, whereas moderate rates of

[1] Also in Bolivia, not included in Table I.

inflation of 3 to 5 per cent per annum generally seemed to go with moderate rates of growth.

Table I

Economic Growth and Inflation: Latin America, 1946–55

	Increase in Real Product per capita % p.a.	Rise in cost of living % p.a.
Argentina	0·5	44
Brazil	4·0	28
Chile	0·5	120
Colombia	3·5	13
Cuba	2·8	Prices fell
Dominican Republic	3·5	1
Ecuador	2·8	3
Guatemala	2·3	4
Honduras	2·0	5
Mexico	2·3	10
Paraguay	1·5	120
Peru	4·1	22
Venezuela	4·0	3

SOURCES: United Nations *Statistical Year Book*, 1957.
United Nations *Statistics of National Income and Expenditure* (Statistical Papers, Series H. No. 9).
United Nations *Economic Survey of Latin America*.

The most important feature common to nearly all the Latin American countries is the very great dependence of their internal economic development on external economic events. This is not so much due to exports being a high proportion of national product, although in some countries this proportion is very high indeed.[1] Rather it is due to the fact that export production, and sometimes even national product, is concentrated on a very few primary products. This emerges clearly even when we look at the region as a whole: three commodities, coffee, petroleum and sugar form about two thirds of the total exports of all countries together: but it is much more striking when we consider the individual countries

[1] In a number of countries exports are well over 20 per cent of national product; for instance, the proportion is over 30 per cent in Venezuela, 40 per cent in Panama, nearly 25 per cent in Honduras, and about 20 per cent in Colombia and Ecuador. In Argentina, Brazil and Chile, however, which are the most developed countries of the area, it is less than 10 per cent.

separately. Ninety per cent of Venezuela's exports in value goes out in the form of petroleum or petroleum products, and over one-third of Venezuela's national product is derived from this source. Sugar provides over 70 per cent of Cuba's exports and between one quarter and a third of its national product. Colombia derives about 15 per cent of its national product and two-thirds of its exports from the production of coffee, which also provides the Central American states (e.g. El Salvador, Guatemala, Costa Rica, Ecuador) with the bulk of their exports. Brazil of course is the largest coffee producer in the world, providing 50 per cent of the world's total. Being more developed than the Central American states, Brazil derives a much smaller proportion of its national product from coffee (about 5 per cent): nonetheless coffee comprises over 50 per cent of the value of its exports. The economy of Chile is based very substantially on the production of copper, not so much because copper production is a very high proportion of total national product,[1] or even because copper sales form 50 per cent of total exports, but mainly because a substantial part of government revenue is derived from this source. The exports of Argentina and Mexico are more diversified than those of most other Latin American countries: even so, over 90 per cent of Argentina's exports stem from the agricultural and livestock sector.

When a country's economy is geared so heavily to the production and export of one or very few major primary products, then its long-term rate of economic growth and its short-term monetary stability depends rather crucially on world demand for these products. A country may be fortunate in enjoying a long run expansion in world demand for its major export product, so that the price of it shows a persistent tendency to rise. We showed in Chapter III how favourable this could be for economic growth if it was accompanied by a long run improvement in the country's net barter terms of trade. Real income would then tend to rise at a faster rate than domestically produced output, and the country could, if it chose, undertake a higher rate of capital formation in relation to current national output without incurring further sacrifices of current consumption. Besides the *direct* effect of a favourable movement in the terms of trade on real income, a consequential higher rate of investment might also permit domestically produced output to rise at a higher rate. Moreover, provided

[1] It is about 4 or 5 per cent.

the volume of exports does not fall off as prices rise, the capacity to import would increase; and, since in the early stages of development imported capital equipment must figure quite prominently in total investment, this would facilitate the raising of the rate of investment. In choosing to use the increment of real income derived from the improvement in its terms of trade to raise its rate of investment, the country makes best use of its improved capacity to import. However, the rise in prices and incomes in the export sector is likely to spread into other sectors as well: hence a rise in prices as the terms of trade improve will usually become quite general throughout the economy as a whole. But, as we said in Chapter III, since this inflation is likely to be accompanied by a speeding up of economic growth, it may well be received with more equanimity than might otherwise be the case. On the other hand, a more serious form of monetary instability is introduced into the economy by short-term *fluctuations* in export prices. It is well known that, owing to inelasticity of both demand and supply, small changes in world demand can cause quite sharp changes in the prices of primary products. Not only are these short run fluctuations very disturbing to plans for long run economic growth, they also give rise to the danger of acute inflation, in the manner described in Chapter III.

We have seen that the economies of many Latin American countries are, in fact, tied to the production and export of one, or, at most, very few, primary products. Can we relate in any close way their differing rates of growth, and different experience as to inflation, to the movements of their export prices and their terms of trade? We shall try to answer this question by bringing together statistics of changes in export prices and the terms of trade, together with rates of growth and rates of inflation, for a number of countries to see what they reveal. But although we can expect to find that external factors will have been important, this does not mean that internal ones, such as the financing of domestic capital formation, public expenditure and taxation, and domestic agricultural development, can be ignored. Hence, we must refer to statistics relating to these matters as well. Furthermore, whilst a general picture of the sort attempted in the first part of this chapter may yield useful conclusions, it cannot throw much light on the actual process of inflation. We shall therefore conclude the chapter by describing in somewhat closer detail the actual development of inflation in two of the most important countries of the region, Argentina and Chile.

I

A GENERAL SURVEY

In Table II we bring together information concerning rates of growth, rates of inflation and changes in the terms of trade and in the capacity to import for the period 1947 to 1956. It is clear that expectations that larger gains in the terms of trade would go hand in hand with faster economic growth, and conversely, are only partly borne out.

Table II

The Terms of Trade, Capacity to Import and the Rate of Growth, Latin America, 1947–1956

	% change in terms of trade 1947/9–1954/56	Rate of Growth % p.a. 1946–55	Rate of Inflation % p.a.	% change in export prices 1947/8–1954/6	% change in capacity to import 1947/9–1954/6		Gross Fixed Investment coefficient 1955 % Gross National Product
I. Countries whose terms of trade improved by more than 50%					Current Values	Constant Values	
El Salvador .	+105	n.a.	n.a.	+106	+119	+117	n.a.
Guatemala	+ 86	2·3	4	+ 92	+ 72	+ 67	n.a.
Costa Rica	+ 70	n.a.	n.a.	+ 76	+ 88	+ 80	n.a.
Brazil	+ 68	4·0	28	+ 62	+ 36	+ 42	13·0
Ecuador	+ 68	2·8	·3	+ 46	+115	+147	n.a.
Colombia	+ 62	3·5	13	+ 84	+103	+ 78	23·4
II. Countries whose terms of trade improved by less than 50%							
Chile	+ 40	0·5	120	+58	+ 56	+ 44	10·0
Honduras	+ 30	2·0	5 (1950–5)	+41	+ 64	+ 52	n.a.
Dominican Republic	+ 7	3·5	1	+ 9	+ 75	+ 72	n.a.
Peru	+ 7	4·1	22	0	+103	+110	17·2
Venezuela	+ 1	4·0	3·5	+13	+ 97	+ 46	23·5
Mexico	Slight Improvement	2·3	10	Slight Rise	+ 85		13·7
III. Countries whose terms of trade worsened							
Argentina	− 37	0·5	44	− 24	− 23	− 35	22·4
Cuba	− 5	2·8*	Negative	− 10	0	+ 5	16·5

* In the case of Cuba, growth took place largely in the period prior to 1952.

SOURCE: United Nations: *Economic Survey of Latin America 1957*, Tables 69, 72, 81.

It will be seen that Brazil, Colombia, Ecuador, and Guatemala — all coffee producers whose terms of trade improved enormously in the post-war period — did in fact enjoy substantial economic development, whilst Argentina's failure to develop since 1948, and Cuba's lack of growth after 1952, went hand in hand with deteriorating terms of trade. But it is evident from the experience of Peru, Venezuela and Mexico that gains from the terms of trade have not been a necessary condition for economic development; and nor have they been a sufficient condition, if the experience of Chile and some of the Central American Republics is at all relevant. When the capacity to import is taken into account, however, the association between external factors and development becomes more decisive. Thus, the failure of Peru's or Mexico's terms of trade to improve was more than made up for by an expansion of export volume and inflow of foreign capital, and rapid economic development was made possible. Even so, the slow economic development of Chile, among others, remains to be explained.

Any expectation that prices would have risen most in countries whose export prices had experienced the largest rise — by virtue of the multiplier and accelerator effects that are likely to follow — is also not borne out. If the connection were close, then we should find that inflation would be greatest in the coffee producing countries, Brazil, Colombia, Ecuador, El Salvador, Costa Rica and Guatemala; and it is true that in some of them, Brazil and Colombia in particular, prices did rise quite considerably. But there was quite as much inflation in other countries whose export prices did not rise so much, for instance, Mexico and Venezuela, whilst in Argentina and Chile, inflation occurred at even greater rate. Thus, if inflation can be attributed to some extent to the pressure of overseas demand for exports, it is clear that the latter does not provide the whole explanation. But it might be argued that *fluctuations* in export prices and the terms of trade, as distinct from the long-term trend, are the more important inflationary factor. A sharp rise in export prices, followed by a sharp fall, can be more inflationary than a persistent long-term rise for the reasons we have analysed in Chapter III.[1] But nearly all Latin American countries experienced sharp rises and falls in export prices and the terms of trade. Brazil's export prices, for instance, rose by 100 per cent from 1948 to 1950, by a further 25 per cent in 1950–51, and then fell by 25 per cent in 1954–55. Ecuador's export prices rose 50 per cent in 1949–51, a further 20 per cent from 1951 to 1954, but then fell by 25 per cent in the following years. Similar experience can

[1] See pp. 45–50.

be recorded for other Latin American countries, as Table III makes clear, but no close connection between the extent of these fluctuations and the degree to which prices rose in the period *as a whole* can be observed. There is not much doubt, however, that some countries, for instance, Guatemala, Honduras, and Venezuela, were favoured to some extent by the absence of any significant

Table III

The Terms of Trade of selected Latin American Countries
(1953 = 100)

	1948	1949	1950	1951	1952	1953	1954	1955	1956
Bolivia									
Export Prices	92		88	131	123	100	98	97	104
Import Prices				not available					
Terms of Trade	90		100	128	121	100	99	97	100
Brazil									
Export prices	54	48	82	101	98	100	112	84	85
Import prices	102		80	98	108	100	86	87	101
Terms of Trade	53		102	103	91	100	130	97	85
Colombia									
Export prices	61	65	90	98	95	100	129	106	120
Import prices	101	96	103	108	105	100	100	102	104
Terms of Trade	60	68	87	91	90	100	129	104	115
Cuba									
Export prices	102	95	116	125	109	100	96	93	98
Import prices	109	100	87	104	103	100	92	99	
Terms of Trade	94	100	133	120	106	100	104	94	
Dominican Republic									
Export prices	105	84	104	130	109	100	119	101	97
Import prices				not available					
Terms of Trade	103	95	118	127	107	100	120	101	93
Ecuador									
Export prices	71	64	83	97	99	100	115	91	86
Import prices				not available					
Terms of Trade	70	65	94	94	97	100	116	91	84
Guatemala									
Export prices	59	62	87	102	101	100	121	112	127
Import prices	94	90	93	104	101	100	101	101	105
Terms of Trade	63	69	94	98	100	100	120	111	121
Honduras									
Export prices	74		90	95	101	100	108	109	111
Import prices	91		91	103	98	100	100	101	104
Terms of Trade	81		99	92	103	100	108	108	107
Peru									
Export prices			107	149	125	100	100	105	110
Import prices			94	111	112	100	97	105	112
Terms of Trade			114	134	112	100	103	100	98
Venezuela									
Export prices	94	94	96	99	98	100	108	108	104
Import prices	117	108	93	105	103	100	98	98	101
Terms of Trade	80	88	103	94	95	100	110	110	103

N.B. Where import prices for individual countries are not available, an import price index for Latin America is used to calculate the terms of trade.

SOURCE: International Monetary Fund: *International Financial Statistics.*

short run slumps in export prices, whilst it is clear that Venezuela's relative price stability over the whole period had something to do with the price stability of its main export. Moreover, as we shall argue later on in this chapter, a sharp fall in the export prices of both Argentina and Chile did contribute significantly to the intensification of inflation in these countries.

It seems, therefore, that external factors, working through the terms of trade and the capacity to import, do not by themselves explain Latin America's growth and inflationary experience: they obviously go some way, and more so for some countries than for others, but clearly they do not go all the way. We need in fact to look at internal factors as well.

An important role must have been played by government monetary and fiscal policies. In the past, the supply of money in Latin American countries was principally affected by external factors: variations in foreign trade and in the foreign exchange reserve almost automatically gave rise to expansions or contractions in the volume of money circulating. In the post-war period, these effects naturally continued, but increasingly, governments have intervened to offset the impact of external fluctuations, and, in many cases, to cause the supply of money to pursue an independent path. Indeed, in recent years, internal factors have begun to predominate, as governments manipulated the money supply to finance budget deficits and to stimulate private investment. Moreover, it is well known that in the post-war period, governments of many Latin American countries have played an active role in promoting economic development, very often being forced to take the initiative in investment and industrialisation owing to the absence of an experienced and active entrepreneurial class. In countries where this has been necessary, public expenditure on capital projects has been large and comprised an increasing proportion of total government expenditure. Then again, governments have expanded expenditure for the provision of current services for instance, on welfare and education. This is particularly true of the richer, more developed countries such as Argentina, Chile and Brazil. These measures have resulted very often in budget deficits and expansions in the money supply, which must have played an active or at least a permissive part in the inflationary process.

It is not easy to distinguish between the part played by external factors in promoting growth and inflation from that played by internal factors, such as government expenditure and capital formation. All that we can do is to look for an apparent connection between public expenditure and budget deficits etc. on the one hand and the rate of development and the rate of inflation on the other. We set out in the following tables some statistics relating to government expenditure, taxation and budget outcomes with a view to discovering such connections.

Table IV

Public Expenditure in Latin American Countries

	Public Expenditure as % gross national product			Percentage Increase in Public Expenditure at constant prices (Central Govt. only) 1947–1954
	1945	1950	1954	
Argentina	22	23	23	25 (1947-1953)
Brazil	16	19	19	64
Chile	17	16	17	45 (1947-1953)
Colombia	15	14	18	79
Ecuador	—	11	14	86
El Salvador (Central Govt. only)	9	10	11	97
Guatemala (Central Govt. only)	13	10	11	30
Honduras (Central Govt. only)	6	8	12	163
Mexico	11	12	15	63
Peru	14	14	15	94
Venezuela	16	22	21	97
	(Central Govt. only)		(Central + Local)	

SOURCE: United Nations: *Economic Survey of Latin America 1955*. Part II. Tables 2 and 5.

The first table (i.e. Table IV) gives an idea of the claims made by the public sector on the national product of various Latin American countries. It measures these claims both in terms of the proportion of public expenditure to gross national product, and in terms of the increase in public expenditure in real terms over the post-war period. The ratio of public expenditure to national product does not seem crucial in determining the extent to which countries suffered from inflation. The ratio was certainly highest, in each case over 15 per cent, in Argentina, Chile, Brazil and

Colombia where inflation, particularly in the first three countries, was very severe. But we have Peru with a much lower ratio yet also severe inflation; and Venezuela with one of the highest ratios but only very moderate inflation. Nor does the increase in government expenditure over the post-war period seem vital: compare, for example, Argentina, Chile and Brazil with Colombia, Mexico and Venezuela. Public expenditure in real terms grew substantially in all countries but probably less so in Argentina and Chile where inflation was most severe.

Public expenditure includes ordinary expenditure (i.e. expenditure for the provision of administrative services and health, social welfare, educational and defence services), transfer payments (which include contributions to social welfare funds, retirement and old age pensions, subsidies and interest on the national debt) and capital expenditure, namely, fixed capital equipment in basic industries etc. Table V shows how total expenditure was distributed among these categories.

Table V

Distribution of Public Expenditure within the
Central Government: Latin America

(Percentages)

	Current Expenditure			Transfer Payments			Investment		
	1945	1950	1954	1945	1950	1954	1945	1950	1954
Argentina	40	38	44	25	35	35	35	27	21
Brazil		47	48		26	26		27	26
Chile	49	54	54	22	26	27	29	20	19
Colombia	47	50	52	27	20	18	26	30	30
Ecuador		48	57		19	26		24	26
El Salvador	65	67	65	6	5	5	29	29	30
Guatemala	56	59	59	5	6	3	39	35	38
Honduras	76	72	60				24	28	40
Mexico	43	43	34	16	19	27	35	34	38
Peru	81	61	59	12	24	18	7	15	23
Venezuela	58	48	54	13	12	13	28	39	33

SOURCE: United Nations: *Economic Survey of Latin America, 1955*. Part II, Table VI.

Again, it is not clear that this table throws much light on the cause and extent of inflation. It is certainly true that three countries which experienced most rapid inflation, Argentina, Brazil, Chile, devoted an increasing proportion of total expenditure to the provision of 'ordinary' services and to transfer payments; but even by 1954, the proportion devoted to 'ordinary' expenditure was lower than for most other countries. In fact, of course, the increase in the 'ordinary' expenditure *proportion* in Argentina and Chile was the consequence of deliberate, if unsuccessful, anti-inflationary policies, pursued by these countries, the main plank of which was a cut in public investment expenditure. Thus in both countries the proportion of investment expenditure to the total fell sharply. It is also probable that the relatively high expenditure on transfer payments in Argentina, Brazil and Chile reflected the higher stage of economic and social development of these countries, although in Chile it also reflected the system of exchange rates which entailed massive subsidisation of imports by the government (see later).

But, of course, if the distribution of public expenditure does not help much to explain the extent of inflation in Latin American countries, it may go a substantial way towards explaining the comparative rates of growth. It is significant, that those countries which enjoyed very substantial post-war growth — Colombia, Ecuador, Mexico, Peru and Venezuela, for example — devoted an increasing proportion of an expanding total expenditure to investment. The case of Peru is indeed very striking: whereas total public expenditure increased by over 90 per cent in real terms from 1947 to 1954, the proportion devoted to investment rose from 7 to 23 per cent. This suggests that public investment expenditure rose more than five-fold during this period. Indeed, given the absence of external factors creating inflation, there is not much doubt that public investment expenditure was the cause of inflation as well as growth; and Peru's experience possibly provides the clearest case of internal monetary policy being aimed at growth — even to the extent of permitting rapid inflation — and being successful. Moreover, the part played by the public sector in promoting growth is even more clearly brought out if we take note of the increase in public investment expenditure *per capita* over the post-war period. Considering the most important countries, we find that from 1945 to 1954 *per capita* investment expenditure increased by 81 per cent in Brazil, by 82 per cent in Venezuela, by 233 per cent in Peru — all countries which developed significantly

R

— whereas the increase was only 6 per cent in Argentina; and in Chile there was even a net fall.[1]

The effect of public expenditure on the rate of inflation should not of course be considered in isolation. We need to take into account the revenue side of the public sector, and, in particular, the balance between expenditure and taxation. Table VI brings out the change in public current expenditure in relation to the change in public revenue for the post-war period, and brings out also the change in public saving in relation to the change in public investment. From this can be inferred the extent to which public revenue contributed, if at all, towards saving for private investment.

Table VI

Public Saving and Capital formation, 1946–54: Latin America
(Current Prices)

	Ordinary Revenue % increase	Ordinary Expenditure % increase	Public Saving % increase	Public Investment % increase	Gross National Product % increase
Argentina (1947–53)	262	326	(*)	246	219
Brazil (1947–55)					
Central	290	343	55	421	300
Local	415	454	948	348	300
Chile (1945–54)	821	1085	(*)	572	1025
Colombia (1945–54)	553	490	1072	581	321
Mexico (1945–54)	321	290	428	341	221
Venezuela (1945–53)	276	185	684	208	166
Honduras (1946–53)	132	157	70	438	—
El Salvador (1947–54)	211	185	285	200	—
Guatemala (1946–53)	116	91	118	88	120

(*) Saving was negative at end of period.

SOURCE: United Nations, *Economic Survey of Latin America 1955, Part II*.

A rough contrast can be made between Argentina, Chile and perhaps Brazil, on the one hand, and, on the other, Colombia, Mexico, Venezuela, and some of the Central American Republics for which information is available. In Argentina and Chile we find that ordinary expenditure increased more than ordinary revenue, so that public saving tended to fall rather than to rise.[2] In the

[1] See United Nations, *Economic Survey for Latin America 1955*, Part II, Table 12.

[2] It should be noted that public saving is defined as the difference between current expenditure and revenue, whilst the budget balance is defined with reference to the difference between public saving and public investment expenditure.

case of Argentina, both ordinary expenditure and ordinary revenue increased faster than gross national product, which suggests that the government was attempting to obtain a larger share of total production for current purposes. Investment expenditure also rose somewhat faster than gross national product, but of course at a much faster rate than public saving. Hence, throughout most of the post-war period, the overall budget was in deficit, in some years even to the extent of more than 50 per cent of ordinary revenue (see Table VII). In the case of Chile, also, the budget tended to be in large deficit most years and to become increasingly unbalanced over time. Here, the cause seems to have been a failure of revenue to keep pace with either current expenditure or gross product, so that although public investment also rose less than gross product, it nevertheless rose faster than public saving. In Brazil, current expenditure (including local as well as central government) and revenue kept pace with each other and rose at a somewhat faster rate than gross national product. Although public saving rose substantially it was only just sufficient in some years to cover the very substantial rise in public investment, and in most years the overall budget remained in deficit. These countries just referred to experienced very severe inflation, and it is at least significant that

Table VII

Budget Balances as a Percentage of Ordinary Income
Latin America

	Argen-tina	Brazil		Chile	Colom-bia	Mexico	Vene-zuela
		Central Govt.	Local Govt.				
1945	−65·1	−	−	−14·3	−20·6	−20·1	−18·1
1946	−57·0	−	−	−19·2	−23·9	2·2	10·5
1947	−16·8	3·2	−18·7	−14·8	−15·5	−16·7	5·9
1948	−50·5	0·2	−12·7	4·8	−22·9	−21·6	− 2·2
1949	−38·6	−14·0	− 4·8	7·7	−11·3	6·4	0·9
1950	−34·3	−19·7	−15·9	−13·2	− 1·0	4·1	− 3·7
1951	−31·6	9·5	− 5·2	− 7·4	− 2·5	11·7	− 4·1
1952	−25·7	6·7	−22·5	−23·7	− 0·9	0·3	0·6
1953	−31·0	− 6·8	−14·6	−30·3	−13·3	− 9·6	8·1
1954	—	− 5·2	−11·7	−28·1	−13·3	−16·4	—
1955	—	−13·3	− 4·5	—	—	—	—

SOURCE: United Nations: *Economic Survey of Latin America 1955*, Part II, Table 35.

inflation was less in those countries, such as Colombia, Mexico, Venezuela and the Central American Republics, in which revenue rose more than current expenditure. The consequential large expansion in public saving in these countries did not necessarily result in budget surpluses. Colombia, for example, had a continual budget deficit which did not significantly diminish over the period. The reason, of course, was the enormous expansion in public invest-ment which was a major factor underlying Colombia's growth. Public investment also rose substantially in Mexico and Venezuela, but not so much as to absorb all public saving. The budget was roughly in balance in some years, and over the whole period accumulated surpluses about offset accumulated deficits. It is significant that inflation was less severe in Mexico and Venezuela than it was in Colombia, and less severe in Colombia than it was in Argentina or Chile or Brazil.

One factor of quite considerable importance has not yet been brought out. This is the fact that the revenue of public authorities, and therefore their ability to save, was subject to very considerable fluctuations. These fluctuations arose, first because government revenue in most Latin American countries is highly dependent on external receipts, and second, because external receipts have fluctuated. Pretty well all Latin American countries make sub-stantial use of taxes on exports and imports and on the trading profits of the major exporting companies, and these make the most significant contribution to public revenue. Venezuela, for example, raises 75 per cent of its total revenue from taxes on the external sector of the economy. Comparable figures for other countries are: Chile, 45 per cent, Ecuador, 38 per cent, Peru 29 per cent, Mexico 28 per cent and Colombia 25 per cent. Only in the case of Argen-tina (6 per cent) and Brazil (11 per cent) can the dependence be said to be small.[1] The contribution of the external sector to national finances has of course been very welcome: 'it has been the decisive factor in determining the evolution of public saving in Latin American countries which have been favoured by growing or relatively high saving coefficients.'[2] No doubt, countries like Venezuela, Mexico and Colombia, with reasonably high investment coefficients and satisfactory rates of growth, owe much to the generally favourable trend in the external sector. But instability has

---

[1] United Nations, *Economic Survey of Latin America 1955*, Part II, Table 16.
[2] Ibid., p. 157.

also been introduced into the monetary system of some countries by the very fact that external receipts and therefore public revenue have not been under the control of governments. It is easy to see that sharp fluctuations in export receipts and in the tax revenue obtained from them can provoke considerable inflation: when receipts and revenue are rising, governments often enter into commitments of a current or capital nature from which they find it very difficult to disengage themselves when receipts and revenue subsequently decline. They are forced into budget deficits and credit creation, often at a time when the real income of the community has suffered a check from worsening terms of trade. Later, we shall illustrate from Chile's experience how sharp contractions in export receipts can lead to the intensification of inflation when government revenue and the system of exchange rates are intimately linked. Whilst there is no doubt that instability is introduced by fluctuations in the export sector and by the dependence of revenue on exports, nevertheless the extent of inflation suffered by various countries cannot be directly linked with it. In Argentina, for example, where fluctuations in export receipts have not been so important, although the long-term downward trend has, and where public revenue is only but slightly linked to the external sector, inflation has been extreme.

It is convenient at this point to summarise the conclusions so far. It is clear that both external and internal forces have played a part in Latin America's growth and inflationary experience. The former have been important, not only because of the direct effect that external receipts and the terms of trade have had on demand and on available supply in the economy, but also because they have had an indirect effect working through public finances. Internal factors, largely government fiscal and credit operations, have increased in importance over time as governments began to pursue independent (i.e. independent of external factors) policies to promote growth. In some countries, government operations have added to the pressures introduced by the external sector, and in others, they have offset them or taken their place. Apart from stressing the external factors as being the prime mover, however, little further generalisation is possible. Argentina's development was hindered by external forces whilst, for a number of reasons, government promotional activities resulted more in inflation than growth. Chile's development suffered somewhat from external factors, but less so than Argentina's, whereas inflation in part resulted from the fact that internal finances were very precariously dependent on external receipts (see later). Brazil, Colombia, Mexico, Venezuela and others all benefited greatly from external factors. Inflation was also introduced by these factors, but whereas in the case of Mexico and Venezuela, moderate internal policies were pursued with a view to keeping down inflation, governments in Brazil and Colombia took more risks and promoted a very high rate of investment, producing more extreme inflation as well as faster growth.

But if no sweeping generalisation is possible at this point, one factor of considerable, perhaps primary, significance remains to be considered. We argued in Chapter III that one of the major causes of inflation in under-developed countries is the failure of the agricultural sector to develop at a rate appropriate to the growth of the economy as a whole, and it seems certain that Latin American experience in the post-war period provides a good illustration of this.

On the face of it agricultural production in Latin America seems to have shown a very satisfactory growth, both since pre-war days and in the post-war period itself. Table VIII sets out the

Table VIII

Agricultural Production in Latin America

(1934–38 = 100)

	Total	Food-stuffs	Non Food-stuffs	Per capita		
				Total	Food-stuffs	Non Food-stuffs
1946/7	111	115	89	91	94	73
1947/8	114	120	86	92	96	69
1948/9	116	121	89	91	94	70
1949/50	119	122	98	91	94	75
1950/1	125	130	98	93	97	73
1951/2	121	125	100	88	91	73
1952/3	131	135	107	93	96	76
1953/4	132	136	104	91	95	72
1954/5	135	139	109	92	94	74

SOURCE: United Nations: *The Selective Expansion of Agricultural Production in Latin America*. Chapter III, Table 15.

facts. Total production in 1954/5 was about 35 per cent greater than in pre-war days and the production of foodstuffs 39 per cent greater. But when population growth is taken into account the picture is not so rosy: *per capita* production of foodstuffs was about 6 per cent lower than pre-war, and does not seem to have risen at all in the post-war period. Non foodstuff production *per capita* fared worse, being 26 per cent below the level of pre-war.

These figures are very much affected by the production of some important products — coffee, meat and wheat — the total production of which fell sharply as against pre-war; and the performance of Latin America as a whole is dragged down by the poor agricultural record of two countries, Argentina and Brazil, the main producers of these commodities. In Argentina, for example, agricultural production *per capita* in 1954/5 was some 30 per cent below pre-war and was even 9 per cent lower than at the end of the war.[1] There was a slight rise in agricultural production *per capita* in Brazil during the post-war period, but even so in 1954/5 it remained 10 per cent below pre-war level. Hence, if the figures for Latin America as a whole are adjusted to exclude the results in these two countries, they indicate a substantial rise in *per capita* production since 1938 (27 per cent) and some rise (12 per cent) since 1946. Nonetheless, the relative failure of agriculture to develop in Argentina and Brazil cannot be ignored in assessment of the performance of the area as a whole, and neither can the effects on growth and inflation in the area be ignored, since, pre-war, these two countries were an important source of supply to other Latin American countries.

The supply of agricultural output *in toto* of a country depends not only production but also on exports and imports. A feature of post-war development in Latin America has been the increasing concentration on production for domestic use. It is commented on in successive Economic Surveys of the area.[2] From the end of the war to about 1955/6 production for export rose by only 3 or 4 per cent whereas production for domestic use rose by more than 20 per cent.[3] On a *per capita* basis, production for export *fell* by 10 per cent and for domestic use rose by 5 or 6 per cent. Moreover, Latin America as a whole, and Brazil, Colombia, Mexico, Venezuela and

[1] United Nations, *Selective Expansion of Agricultural Production in Latin America*, Chapter III, Table 16.
[2] For instance, the *Economic Surveys of Latin America* for 1953, 1956 and 1957.
[3] United Nations, *Economic Survey of Latin America 1953*, Table 116.

(to a somewhat lesser extent) Chile, in particular, have become increasingly dependent on agricultural and foodstuff imports. In other words, the area as a whole and most countries within it, have taken advantage of improved terms of trade to export less and import more of their primary products and foodstuffs. A notable exception is Argentina which, not benefiting from a favourable move in its terms of trade, had to cut its imports of food in the post-war period. The combined effect of the relative decline in exports and increase in imports, however, was not great enough to offset the failure of production to rise with population and *per capita* real income. It would not be expected, of course, that food output *per capita* would rise in the same proportion as real income *per capita*: but, if an estimate of 0·6 for the income elasticity of demand for food is accepted as reasonable,[1] it is evident that *available food supplies* (i.e. taking into account the change in exports and imports) in Latin America as a whole did not rise sufficiently to match the rise in demand, at *unchanged relative prices of food and other goods*, brought about by the rise in real income. It is estimated that whereas income *per capita* in the area as a whole was about 45 per cent higher than pre-war, food supply *per capita* was only about 8 per cent higher.[2] In other words, to avoid undue pressure on food prices relative to other prices, the income elasticity of demand would have to have been less than 0·2. Even if meat, the production *per capita* of which fell greatly since pre-war, is excluded — which properly speaking it should not be, given its importance in pre-war Latin American diet — the *required* income elasticity of demand (i.e. that required to avoid a relative rise in food prices) would have to have been less than 0·4. It is clear, in other words, that a large change in relative prices was required to produce balance in the demand and supply of food, and this could hardly be achieved, if at all, except in the context of a substantial rise in the general price level: hence it is not surprising that food prices led the way in the great inflations experienced by many Latin American countries.

If we look at individual countries for which we have reliable data, the result is quite revealing (see Table IX). We find, in Argentina, for example, that whereas disposable income *per capita*

---

[1] See United Nations, *Selective Expansion of Agricultural Production in Latin America*, p. 21.
[2] Ibid., Table 26.

in 1952/3 was about 20 per cent above pre-war, food supply *per capita* was 7 per cent lower (if meat is excluded, food supply *per capita* is roughly unchanged). Income in Brazil was more than 60 per cent higher than pre-war as against a rise in food supplies of only 5 per cent, although, admittedly, the picture is much better when milk and meat are excluded. The expansion of food supply in Chile, relative to income growth, seems more satisfactory, although during the later part of the post-war period, food supply ceased to grow with real income. Colombia's position seems highly satisfactory, but food supply in Mexico seems to have lagged well behind income unless milk is excluded from the comparison. In all cases, except Colombia, the *required* income elasticity of demand to avoid pressure on food prices would have had to have been lower than in fact was likely to be the case in these countries.

Table IX

Per capita Real Income and *per capita* Food Supply
Pre- and Post-War: Latin America

	Available food supply per capita			Disposable gross income per capita *		
	1934/8	1949/51	1952/3	1934/8	1949/51	1952/3
Argentina	100	97	93	100	135	121
Argentina (*excluding meat*)	100	100	101	—	—	—
Brazil	100	105	105	100	150	162
Brazil (*excluding meat and milk*)	100	128	128	—	—	—
Chile	100	113	113	100	122	133
Colombia	100	134	134	100	135	149
Mexico	100	113	114	100	177	180
Mexico (*excluding milk*)	100	125	127	—	—	—

* Defined as *per capita* consumption of all available goods and services.

SOURCE: United Nations, *The Selective Expansion of Latin American Agriculture.* Chapter IV.

The relationship between food supplies and income growth in Argentina is obviously very unbalanced, and it will be remembered that inflation in this country has been quite extreme. However, inflation was also extreme in Chile where the relationship, although unbalanced, is not as bad as that of Argentina. But the important factor in this country is perhaps the post-war development itself, rather than the comparison with pre-war, for it is estimated that *per capita* food supplies in the period 1951/5 were 3 or 4 per cent *below* those of 1942/5.[1] In contrast, Mexico's food supplies in relation to real income seem much less favourable, comparing post-war with pre-war, than is the case for Chile, but here again, post-war development may be more pertinent than pre- and post-war comparison. The rise in food supplies seems to have taken place only *since the end of the war*, not, as is apparently the case in Chile, during the war itself.[2] This may explain why Mexico's post-war inflation has been very much less. Colombia's position seems satisfactory in all respects except that the most substantial contribution to increased food supply came from imports. Whilst this must mean that food supply is to some extent precarious, it seems likely that lagging food supplies played less part in Colombia's inflation than they did in the case of the other countries we have considered.

Similar detailed information for other Latin American countries does not exist, but it seems reasonably clear that in most instances food supply played an important part in inflation. For instance, Cuba's lack of inflation, despite substantial growth at least up to 1952, must be partly due to the satisfactory expansion of food output in the early post-war period, whilst at the other end of the scale, the almost hyper-inflations of Paraguay and Bolivia were largely connected with the shortage of food. Bolivia,[3] indeed, provides a very striking illustration of the two-way connection between inflation and backward agricultural development, as well as of the problem of growth and inflation which confronts countries whose economics are dependent on the production of one or very few primary products, and whose terms of trade and capacity to import are liable to extreme fluctuations. The solution to the latter problems clearly lies in diversification, largely through industrialisation; but, paradoxically, if this carried out too far or too fast in relation to the development of agriculture the danger of inflation becomes acute and the problem of growth more complicated.

[1] United Nations, *Economic Survey of Latin America, 1957*, pp. 283/4.
[2] Ibid., Table LXVIII, p. 291.
[3] See United Nations, 'The Economic Development of Bolivia', in United Nations, *Economic Bulletin for Latin America*, Vol. II, No. 2.

It is clear that most Latin American countries have been confronted with this dilemma.

This survey of post-war Latin American experience does not permit us to come to any conclusion regarding the beneficial effects — or otherwise — of inflation on growth, a question that has aroused some interest among economists in recent times. A number of Latin American countries pursued policies, aimed at promoting industrialisation, which clearly resulted in inflation but not much growth. Argentina seems to present the clearest instance of the lack of success of such policies, although it has to be borne in mind that external factors were generally unfavourable. Peru, on the other hand, although not particularly favoured by external factors, seems to have achieved rapid growth through domestic government policies which were very inflationary. Mexico is perhaps another, although more moderate, example. In the main, however, countries which made the most development, for instance, Brazil, Colombia and Venezuela, were the most favoured by external factors, which also contributed to inflation; but the latter was incidental rather than causal. Thus if any lessons can be drawn from Latin American experience these are perhaps negative rather than positive. Two seem to stand out. First, it seems clear that if under-developed countries do not solve their agricultural problems in the early stages of development then severe inflation is difficult to avoid: it can in fact only be avoided if the growth of other sectors of the economy is slowed down, that is, if overall development is slowed down. Second, the experience of some Latin American countries, in particular some of the Central American Republics, seems to suggest that if anti-inflationary policies of a monetary nature are pursued too firmly then growth also suffers. These countries did their best to offset the inflationary effect of improving terms of trade and booming external receipts on their internal monetary situation. They seem to have countered the multiplier and accelerator effects arising from the external sector, and used their increased capacity to import to add to their foreign exchange reserves. In consequence, domestic capital formation did not benefit and growth was held back. Thus although it may not be clearly argued that the deliberate promotion of inflation promotes growth, it can be argued that efforts *to prevent* inflation when this is being introduced through the external sector, are also likely to check growth at the same time. Whether this is an argument for permitting inflation depends on the circumstances confronting individual countries: certainly no general answer can be given.

We have thus far reviewed on a brief comparative basis the various factors that contributed to inflation and growth in Latin America. It will be instructive, however, to look somewhat more closely at the experience of one or two countries individually so as to emphasise what appear to be the more important of these factors. We shall finish this chapter, therefore, by highlighting some aspects of the connection between growth and inflation in Argentina and Chile; and in particular we shall attempt to bring out the crucial importance of the unbalanced nature of development in these two countries for the process of inflation.

II

ARGENTINA

A closer look at the process of inflation in Argentina is valuable because it brings out very clearly the relationship between inflation, the external terms of trade, forced industrialisation and lagging agricultural development. We find very well illustrated:

(1) the character of inflation and growth when external forces are proving favourable, and *per capita* real income is rising;

(2) the severe inflationary consequences that follow a worsening in these external factors, particularly when the earlier favourable effects have been directed largely to the promotion of industrialisation, to the neglect of agriculture;

(3) the difficulty of checking these inflationary consequences without at the same time checking growth; and, finally;

(4) the rather paradoxical result that steps that eventually have to be taken to alter the fundamental imbalance of the economy tend, at first, to accelerate rather than dampen inflation.

Two phases may be discerned in the process of inflation in Argentina.[1] The first phase extends from the end of the Second World War until 1948 or 1949, during which time external factors were proving favourable to growth. The second phase extends from 1948/9 until the present, during which time external factors operated against growth. For the purpose of analysis, however, it is useful to sub-divide this later period into three: namely, the period

[1] United Nations, *Economic Survey of Latin America 1957*, p. 115.

of acute inflation that followed the worsening of external forces, which extended up to 1952: the period during which efforts were made to bring inflation to an end; and finally the period of the New Economic Policy, introduced in 1955, which aimed at correcting the fundamental imbalance of the economy.

From the end of the war until 1948, Argentina's export prices rose substantially, thereby causing an improvement in the terms of trade of more than 50 per cent. Argentina, at this time, had the further advantage of emerging from the war with ample reserves of foreign exchange, but for political reasons a substantial part of these were used to expatriate foreign debt and to buy out the foreign owners of many public service industries.[1] Despite this, and despite the further fact that export volume declined during these years,[2] Argentina was able to double the volume of its imports. A considerable volume of investment was therefore made possible — the ratio of gross fixed capital formation to gross national product was probably around 25 per cent — and as a result the development of the economy was able to proceed at a very rapid rate. It is estimated that between 1945 and 1948 gross product *per capita* rose by something like 6 per cent per annum, and if the direct effect of improved terms of trade is taken into account, the rise in income *per capita* works out at about 8 per cent per annum (see Table X).

Rapid growth was not without its inflation, and prices rose by about 30 per cent from 1946 to 1948. But money wages rose faster than prices and the rise in real wages was substantial (40 per cent). Indeed, the rise in real wages was greater than the rise in production which was of the order of 20 per cent;[3] and, despite the improvement in the terms of trade, the gain in real wages must to some extent have been at the expense of other sectors of the economy. The losers seem to have been public sector employees, on the one hand, and, more important, farmers, on the other.

The extent of the loss of agriculture is best brought out by the accompanying table (Table XI) taken from the Economic Survey of Latin America 1957.[4] It shows that whereas net industrial prices

---

[1] United Nations, *Economic Bulletin for Latin America*, Vol. I, p. 27, 'The Economic Situation in Argentina'.

[2] The purchasing power of exports, taking into account the change in the terms of trade, declined somewhat from 1946 to 1948. See ibid., Table 3, p. 30.

[3] United Nations, *Economic Survey of Latin America, 1957*, Table 115.

[4] Ibid., Table 117.

Table X

Argentina: Gross National Product and Income 1945–54

	Gross National Income (Millions of Pesos at 1950 prices)	Gross National Product (Millions of Pesos at 1950 prices)	Per Capita	
			Gross National Income (Pesos at 1950 prices)	Gross National Product (Pesos at 1950 prices)
1945	48,983	48,836	3210	3200
1946	55,198	53,197	3557	3428
1947	63,253	59,114	4007	3744
1948	65,961	62,353	4097	3873
1949	62,829	61,544	3803	3725
1950	62,291	62,291	3673	3673
1951	64,219	64,222	3686	3686
1952	59,740	59,986	3346	3360
1953	63,010	63,225	3457	3469
1954	65,987	66,091	3555	3561

SOURCE: United Nations: *Economic Bulletin for Latin America*, Vol. I, No. 1. Page 26/7, Table 1.

rose by something like 80 per cent between 1945 and 1948, agricultural prices rose by only 65 per cent; so that whilst the *external* terms of trade of agricultural exports against imports (largely industrial goods) were showing substantial improvement, the *internal* terms of trade were worsening.

This development was the result of deliberate policies on the part of the government, which, by employing a combination of price controls over many basic agricultural products (e.g. cereals — wheat, maize, barley, oats, etc.) and over-valuation of the exchange rate, prevented the farm sector from obtaining the benefit of high world prices of agricultural products. On the other hand, industrialisation was promoted by these policies, particularly by the effective subsidisation of capital equipment and industrial raw material imports. Price controls encouraged labour to move from the land into industry, but since this was not 'surplus' labour and since it was not offset by the introduction of new techniques or replaced by capital, agricultural output tended to fall. The effects of this were hidden up to 1948 by the fact that the needs of expanding population at home were met by a decline in exports; but when the terms of trade ceased to move in a way that could offset export decline, the inevitable imbalance of the economy became apparent.

Table XI

Argentina: Internal and External Terms of Trade of Agricultural Export Products

Year	Internal Prices (1938-39 = 100)			External Terms of Trade	Ratio of Internal and external terms of Trade
	Prices of Agricultural Production for export	Net Industrial Prices	Price Relationship		
1939	96·1	109·1	88·1	79·0	111·5
1945	135·2	194·6	69·5	81·7	85
1946	215·2	244	88·2	112·0	78·7
1947	203·2	300·8	67·8	133·9	50·6
1948	222	372	59·7	131·7	45·3
1949	267	486·8	54·8	109·7	50·0
1950	343·2	574	59·8	93·1	64·2
1951	545·0	737·1	73·9	101·9	72·6
1952	597·5	906·4	65·9	70	94·2
1953	734·7	947·8	77·5	93	83·4
1954	743·6	1000	74·4	83·8	88·7
1955	842·5	1124·6	74·9	81·9	91·5
1956	1127·3	1268·6	88·9	74·5	119·3
1957	1343·9	1598·2	84·1	68·0	123·7

SOURCE: United Nations, *Economic Survey of Latin America 1957*, Table 115.

From 1948 on, the terms of trade began to move unfavourably for Argentina — apart from the temporary boom at the time of the Korean War. The volume of exports could not rise sufficiently to offset this adverse price effect, partly because of the needs of the population at home, partly because agriculture was suffering from the neglect of earlier years. Foreign exchange reserves were drawn on and use was made of international credit; but even so imports had to be contracted. The effect was to diminish the ability of Argentina to add to its capital equipment, and the investment coefficient, which in the early post-war years was above 25 per cent, fell to 23 per cent. More important, however, was the limitation on the supply of fuel and industrial raw materials, which prevented the full exploitation of the productive capacity that had been built up in previous years.[1] The growth of the economy was consequently checked (see Table X) and indeed, both product *per capita* and income *per capita* began to fall. By 1957 they were both lower than they had been in 1948. But the halt in development was not

[1] See United Nations, *Economic Bulletin for Latin America*, Vol. I, No. 1, Table 5, p. 33.

accompanied by a halt in inflation: on the contrary, the latter now accelerated. The wage-price spiral, which had been a feature of inflation of the earlier years, now, in contrast, operated in an environment in which real income *per capita* was falling: the terms of trade were worsening and productivity in the domestic economy was declining. In other words, the various bargaining groups of the economy were no longer operating in a situation where relative income gains could be made without *absolute* loss to others: instead, all groups were faced with absolute declines in their standards, and relative advantages could only be obtained at increased absolute cost to others. Hence the psychological pressure behind the wage-price spiral intensified. The government itself constituted an important body that was reluctant to reduce its absolute claims on the economy: indeed, public expenditure, formerly running at a little less than 20 per cent of natural product, now rose to more than 20 per cent.[1] Public saving fell when public capital expenditure didn't and the budget became increasingly unbalanced (see Table VII). The gap was financed by credit creation, as indeed were the needs of private enterprises in the face of an acute wage-price spiral. By 1952, prices had risen by more than 200 per cent above their 1948 level.[2]

Inflation at this rate could not for long be tolerated, and the government was eventually forced into taking steps to bring it to an end. Stabilisation controls were applied to prices and wages in 1952 and the Government imposed restrictions on the creation of credit by the banking system. Public expenditure was also contracted, falling from about 22 per cent of national product in 1951 to 19 per cent in 1952, and to below 15 per cent in 1953. Thanks to credit restriction there was no offsetting rise in private investment, and the overall rate of fixed capital formation to national product fell to its lowest post-war level (20 per cent). These measures were strikingly successful in checking inflation: prices in 1953 were only about 4 per cent above 1952, and rose only another 4 per cent in 1954. But the effect on output was also severe: manufacturing output fell by some 6 per cent from 1951 to 1952 and remained at this level in 1953. Industry was forced to work well below capacity — at the 50 per cent level in some cases[3] — and bankruptcies were widespread. Hence the government was not anxious to maintain

---

[1] United Nations, *Economic Survey of Latin America, 1953*, Table 12.
[2] A poor harvest in 1952 also made matters worse.   [3] See ibid., p. 75.

its restrictive policy at such a cost; this, plus the fact of an opportune good harvest in 1953, led to some relaxation in 1954. Public
expenditure rose again and credit restrictions were eased. But the
fundamental imbalance in the economy remained, so that as output
began to recover, prices began to rise as well. Whereas the rise in
prices in each of the two previous years had been no more than
4 per cent, in 1954 they rose 12 or 13 per cent.

The government had in fact taken some steps in 1952/3, and
later, to correct the structural deficiencies of the economy. The
exchange rate was devalued and, more important still, better
exchange rates were applied to agricultural exports (e.g. cheese,
butter, wool, wheat). Devaluation was accompanied by import
restrictions which, in conjunction with credit restriction, were the
prime cause of the decline in industrial output. It was soon
evident, however, that these steps were insufficient and new
measures were introduced in 1955. The principal purpose of the
1955 measures was to stimulate agricultural output, which despite
the adjustments of 1952/5, was still discouraged by the existing
system of exchange rates. Not only this, the low exchange rate[1]
involved the government in heavy losses in its centralised purchases
of agricultural crops, since the peso price obtained for exports was
lower than the price paid to the farmer by the government. These
losses had to be financed by credit creation. Hence an important
measure of the new policy was the standardisation of the exchange
rate at a much higher level[2] which was to apply to most foreign
trade transactions. Furthermore, minimum guaranteed prices of
many important crops were raised, and a development fund was set
up to promote technological progress in agriculture.[3]

The essential purpose of these measures was, therefore, to shift
the distribution of income and investment towards agriculture. It
is too soon to say how far these measures have proved successful.
Agricultural production rose substantially in 1955 and 1956,[4]
although in 1957 there was some fall. It is clear, however, that the
measures succeeded in improving the terms of exchange between

[1] The multiple exchange rate system gave a higher peso price for dollars in the
case of minor exports, and non-essential imports than it gave to the main or
priority exports and priority imports, cf. *Economic Bulletin*, Vol. I, No. I, p. 35.
[2] 18 pesos to the $.
[3] The fund was to be financed by the retention of proceeds from the sale of
some agricultural products not requiring such a large devaluation, and by
receipts from surcharges and duties on imports.
[4] See United Nations, *Economic Survey of Latin America, 1957*, Table 105.

S

agricultural products and industrial products. Between 1955 and 1956 agricultural prices rose about 20 per cent more than industrial prices, and for the first time since the beginning of the war the *internal* terms of trade of agriculture were more favourable than the external. Unfortunately, but inevitably, the improvement in the exchange position of agriculture was accompanied by intensification of inflation. Given the need to raise agricultural prices relatively to industrial prices, and given the fact that the latter could hardly be forced down without severe dislocation of industry, the general price level had to rise. The government, at the time of introduction of its new policies, had estimated that devaluation would raise the cost of living by 10 per cent. In fact, however, it could not prevent money wages from rising in sympathy with prices — which was, of course, necessary if the internal monetary situation was to be kept under control. As a result, the wage-price spiral once again got under way. By December 1956 retail prices were 17 per cent above the level at the end of 1955, and the rise accelerated in 1957.

It is obvious that the post-war experience of Argentina brings out in clear relief the unpleasant consequences of unbalanced growth. The Economic Commission for Latin America summarises the situation in the following terms: 'It . . . constitutes a typical instance of the promotion of development without the balance and integration which are essential if the growth achieved is to prove strong and lasting.'[1] And again: 'Between the stagnation of primary activities and the later decline in industry there was obviously a relationship of cause and effect.'[2] These consequences could be hidden when the terms of trade were moving favourably, but the subsequent worsening of the external factors, although making the situation more difficult to handle, was not responsible for it. By 1955 the Argentinian economy had reached a position where further inflation was inevitable before a stage of more orderly and stable growth could be attained.

III

CHILE

Inflation in Chile was even more explosive than in Argentina, particularly after 1953/4; but whilst the situation had character-

[1] United Nations, *Economic Bulletin fot Latin America*, Vol. I, No. I, p. 34.
[2] Ibid., p. 30.

istics peculiar to Chile, making a separate account worthwhile, at bottom lay the unbalanced nature of Chile's economic development.

The problem of achieving growth in Chile is somewhat complicated by the fact that the economy is very dependent on one commodity — copper — both for its supply of foreign exchange and for its national revenue. Productivity in the copper industry is eleven times greater than it is in the economy as a whole, thirteen times greater than in industry and twenty times greater than it is in agriculture.[1] It is not surprising therefore that the government draws a substantial proportion of its revenue from this source. Furthermore, copper exports form more than 50 per cent of total exports and make the most substantial contribution to Chile's capacity to import. In further contrast to Argentina, Chile's government seems to have been less active in promoting growth (although, apparently, still more active than its own private sector) — at least, if public expenditure on capital formation is any guide. Indeed, the government seems to have used a substantial proportion of potential export proceeds to finance consumption rather than investment, and the exchange system has been used to subsidise imports for personal consumption. Finally, and still in contrast to Argentina, the distribution of income in Chile seems far more unequal than in Argentina. Whilst this has tended to narrow the industrial market, it does not seem to have led to large saving and investment in the private sector. On the contrary, the propensity to consume of the upper income groups appears to be high, and the industrial structure has therefore come to reflect this. In general, Chile seems to have fared better than Argentina in respect of world demand for its export products: the terms of trade and the capacity to import have shown significant improvement over the post-war period. It is true that inflation in Chile accelerated after a break in copper prices in 1953, in the same way that Argentina's difficulties were made worse by external factors in 1948/9; but Chile's terms of trade recovered in the following two years and made a substantial contribution to gross income. Even so, the expansion of Chile's gross product ceased in 1953, and *per capita* income fell in the following years: and this development provides yet a further illustration that anti-inflationary measures cannot work without having serious adverse effects on growth,

[1] See ibid., 'Some aspects of the inflationary process in Chile', Table I.

unless the basic causes of inflationary growth are removed at the same time.

In the first few post-war years, 1947 to 1952, the Chilean economy expanded under the influence of a substantial rise in the dollar value of its exports and in its capacity to import. The government was encouraged by the increase in its revenue to expand its own expenditure. Indeed, current expenditure rose more than ordinary revenue which itself trebled from 1947 to 1952, and capital expenditure also showed a large rise. In fact, in real terms public expenditure rose by more than 40 per cent, and though this increase was greater than that of the private sector, the latter also grew significantly. In consequence, imports rose at a very fast rate which, despite the improvement in export receipts, proved excessive. Pressure on the balance of payments mounted and continual exchange rate depreciation was resorted to. By 1952 the rate of exchange was 62 pesos to the dollar as against 30 pesos to the dollar in 1947. Depreciation of this magnitude was obviously very inflationary and contributed greatly to the wage-price spiral of the period. Real product *per capita*, however, rose, probably by 10 to 11 per cent, but the gain was not distributed very equitably. Wages just about kept pace with prices which suggests that the distribution of income must have shifted considerably in favour of the upper income groups. The fact that such a distributional change did not affect the rate of inflation — prices rose by about 200 per cent in the five years — is a reflection of the high propensity to consume of the upper income groups. Hence capital formation did not benefit by as much as it might: instead the structure of production began to reflect the consumption demand pattern associated with income inequality,[1] a development which was to add to inflationary pressure as time went on.

An abrupt fall in copper prices occurred in the second half of 1953, but the consequential fall in export receipts, far from producing deflationary effects on the domestic level of income — as multiplier theory would lead us to expect — set up forces which more than doubled the rate of inflation. These forces arose on account of two important features of the Chilean economy, the first being the heavy dependence of public finances on copper sales, and the second being the system of exchange rates which was used to subsidise imports, particularly of consumption goods.

[1] See p. 267.

Subsequent fiscal and credit policies served to accentuate these forces and help produce the rapid rate of inflation.

The exchange rate system played such an important part in inflation at this time that some brief description of its operation is necessary. As we have seen, the copper industry was the major source of fiscal revenue and foreign exchange receipts in the economy. The government obtained its revenue by means of a 50 per cent (later raised to 60 per cent) direct tax on copper income, the base being the difference between the price of copper in the New York market and the cost of delivering copper in that market. In addition to other customs duties and special sales and surtaxes, there was also a so-called 'implicit tax' on the production costs of the industry, arising out of a difference between the rate of exchange at which the government sold pesos to the copper companies in order to enable them to cover their costs in Chile [i.e. the *'returned value'* rate] and the rate at which the government sold the dollars so obtained from the companies to importers. Taxes on the copper companies amounted to well over 50 per cent *of their gross value* added,[1] and contributed between a quarter and a third of all government revenue. Moreover, the exchange rate system and its associated 'implicit tax' on production costs operated to give a substantial subsidy to imports. Between 1950 and 1953 the subsidy as a proportion of import prices amounted to over a third on average, and to over 40 per cent on imported consumer goods. Capital goods were less favoured, the subsidy running out at the rate of about 25 per cent. How this subsidy was achieved is shown by the following example.

Let us suppose that in a free exchange market the rate would be 30 pesos to a dollar, but suppose also that the government maintains an official exchange rate of 20:1 at which it sells dollars to importers: that is, the government converts the dollars it receives from the copper companies in payment of tax into pesos at this official rate. Suppose, however, that in selling pesos to the copper companies, to enable them to cover their expenses in Chile, the government fixes a rate (i.e. the 'returned value' rate) of 15:1. Now assume that the taxable income (or net value added on sales) of the copper companies is $24,000. Government receipts of direct tax, if the tax rate is 50 per cent, amounts to $12,000 or, when sold to importers, 240,000 pesos. If the companies' expenses in Chile, to be

[1] In one year it amounted to over 74 per cent. See ibid., Table 3.

covered in domestic currency, amounts to 150,000 pesos, then the Chilean government would receive a further $10,000 for providing this currency (the returned value rate is 15:1). When sold to importers however the dollars would yield 200,000 pesos. Hence total government revenue from the copper companies amounts to 290,000 pesos (i.e. 240,000 pesos from the direct tax, 50,000 pesos from the implicit tax on production costs). At the same time $22,000 will have become available for imports. The element of import price subsidy arises because the official rate of exchange is over valued, the more so for official sales than for official purchases of domestic currency. If the government had to deal at the free market 'parity' rate in all transactions then the government would receive 360,000 pesos in direct tax, there being no 'implicit tax' on production costs; but only $17,000 would become available for imports. In effect therefore the government is subsidising imports to the tune of 70,000 pesos,[1] and the subsidy in relation to import price is about 30 per cent. But this subsidy is evidently very precarious. Suppose that copper sales fall off, reducing the taxable income of the companies to $20,000 and therefore the direct tax receipts to $10,000 or 200,000 pesos. If the copper companies' expenses in Chilean currency fall to 120,000 pesos then the government receives a further $8,000 which it is able to sell to importers for 160,000 pesos. Hence the *net* revenue receipts of the government are now 240,000 pesos instead of the 290,000 formerly; only $18,000 become available for imports. Thus if other government expenditure is fixed, then an immediate budget deficit results.[2] If sufficient foreign exchange reserves exist then imports can be maintained and the budget deficit can be covered by sales of dollars. If, however, reserves are inadequate to finance the same volume of imports and if the government must get rid of its budget deficit, then importers must be made to buy less dollars but to pay more pesos for them. Rationing of dollars solves the first problem but clearly not the second. A solution to both problems is only provided by devaluation of the exchange rate, i.e. raising the peso price of dollars to importers, which however must have repercussions on the peso price of imported goods.

[1] In the fiscal accounts the whole operation can be represented *either* as a *net* receipt of revenue of 290,000 pesos, there being no corresponding expenditure item, *or* as a gross revenue receipt of 360,000 pesos with a corresponding expenditure item of 70,000 pesos. The latter alternative seems to be adopted in Chile.
[2] Assuming balance beforehand.

It was this process that led to the acceleration of inflation in Chile in 1953. A fall in copper sales produced a 26 per cent fall in government revenue from copper, and a 10 per cent fall in total government receipts. The exchange rate was devalued sharply, by more than 70 per cent, thereby reducing import subsidies, but even so, the budget deficit rose to 20 per cent of total expenditure.[1] This, of course, was inflationary in itself, but more important was devaluation and the reduction in the subsidy component of import prices: the cost of living rose 70 per cent. Consumer goods, being the most heavily subsidised, rose the most in price, and consequential adjustments in the salaries of public employees, and, later, wages in private industry, added further pressure. Because of this, and on account of rising raw material and fuel costs, the production costs of the copper companies rose. The 'returned value' rate therefore had to be raised, so that in order to prevent further adverse effects on government revenue which would result from this, the official rate to imports had also to be raised again. Hence a further twist was given to the inflationary spiral. At the same time government revenue from other sectors of the economy was tending to fall,[2] although government current and capital expenditure continued to rise. Hence a combination of growing budget deficits and repeated adjustments to the exchange rates brought about a self sustaining rise in prices. At any rate, from 1952 to 1955, when inflation reached its climax, prices rose by more than 270 per cent.

Gross domestic product rose by 8 per cent in 1952 and by 6 per cent in 1953: in the following year however it fell, and despite some recovery in 1955, was still below its level of 1953. The stagnation from 1953 to 1955 was not due to a fall in the capacity to import: in fact the latter rose, partly as a consequence of falling dollar import prices. Private investment in fixed capital equipment was running at a very low level, no more than 5 per cent of the gross national product, but this cannot have been due to lack of financial incentive or inability of the upper income groups to save. The distribution of income in Chile is very inequal[3] and taxes on industries other than copper are very low. It appears however that Chile presents a very clear example of the distorting effects of rapid

---

[1] At first, the selling rate of dollars to importers was raised whilst the 'returned value' rate of copper companies was left unchanged — hence the 'implicit' tax on production costs was raised.

[2] Explained by rigidity in the tax system and widespread evasion.

[3] See *Economic Survey of Latin America, 1957*, Table 183.

inflation on the distribution of investment.[1] Resources tended to flow into speculation in real estate and into the erection of luxury type residential building: in 1955 the latter absorbed more than 45 per cent of fixed investment.[2] This type of investment was of course of a very low productivity nature. To some extent this was no new phenomenon, but had been characteristic of private investment throughout much of Chile's economic development; in 1954/5, however, it got worse. Public sector investment had played the major role in producing growth in the past, but in efforts to check inflation this was seriously cut back, particularly in 1956, and whilst inflation was thereby somewhat checked, a further decline in national product became apparent.

The most effective check to inflation, applied in 1956, was however the regulation of wages and salaries in both the public and private sectors. These were adjusted so that they rose less than prices, thereby reducing the real income of the wage and salary earning sector. The distribution of income moved yet further away from the lower income groups, and in consequence the demand for industrial consumer goods declined. There was also less pressure on industrial costs. As a result the rate of inflation in 1957 was only half that of 1956, and a third of that in 1955, but still reached the formidable rate of 30 per cent. The need to bring about a regressive shift in income distribution in order to check inflation, even then with only partial success, throws considerable light on the more fundamental causes of Chile's economic difficulties. It should be considered in conjunction with two facts: first, that the distribution of income in Chile was already very unequal before the 1956 stabilisation measures were introduced;[3] and second, that despite considerable income inequality the level of private investment, in relation to national product, was very low. In other words, it seems doubtful that the shift of income could be explained by expected favourable effects on saving, since the propensity to save of the upper income groups was very low. Rather it must be explained by a lack of balance between the pattern of consumption demand, which would result from a more equitable distribution of income, and the structure of production which had arisen over the war and post-war periods.

[1] See Chapter II, pp. 34–5.
[2] See United Nations, *Economic Survey of Latin America, 1957*, p. 208.
[3] Workers and salaried employees who comprised over two-thirds of the population received only 44 per cent of national income. Ibid., p. 197.

If we look at the change in the structure of production from the early 1940's to the mid-1950's three things stand out quite clearly: first, a decline in the share of agriculture from 17 to 15 per cent; second, a rise in the share of industry from about 15 to 19 per cent; and third, a very striking increase in the share of personal services and trade. Indeed, whereas the share of services had amounted to 43 per cent in 1940, it had risen to 57 per cent in 1955. Three quarters of the 60 per cent increase in national product since 1950 took the form of services. Since demand for services constitutes a more important component of the expenditure of upper income groups, it is clear that the distribution of income must have moved accordingly, and in fact it is certain that it did become more inequitable.[1] It is also clear, however, that there is a lower limit to the level of real consumption of the poorer sections; and when, as in 1953, external factors tended to bring about a fall in total real income, steps have to be taken to prevent a fall in the absolute standards of these lower income groups. Thus, when prices rose in 1953 and 1954, as a result of devaluation, the compensation of workers and employees was adjusted proportionately. But, of course, the attempt to maintain the real income of the employee sector, *at a time when total real income was falling*, necessarily involved a shift of income distribution towards it. In fact, this was not possible without a substantial change in the structure of production to bring it more in line with the pattern of demand arising out of a more equal distribution of income. In particular, a substantial relative rise in food production was required which clearly was not possible in any short period of time. It is not surprising, therefore, that prices of food and other essentials began to rise sharply. But inflation did not help to bring about the desired pattern of production; quite the contrary, investment was increasingly directed into speculative activities. Even when, as in 1956, the attempt to maintain the real income of the lower income groups was abandoned, the reduction in their incomes did not bring about a proportionate reduction in the demand for food, although the demand for some industrial products was reduced. Hence, food prices continued to rise rapidly in 1956 and 1957 even though the total rate of inflation was reduced.

In short, Chile's experience is yet another and indeed striking illustration of the severe inflationary consequences of unbalanced

[1] Ibid., Table 183.

growth. In many ways it is of more significance than that of Argentina. Whereas in Argentina, in addition to the potent factor of agricultural stagnation, there also seemed to be present the general pressure associated with an excess of investment, private plus public, over saving (or at least so we can infer from the fact that (1) the investment coefficient, (2) the ratio of public expenditure to national product, and (3) the share of wages and salaries in national income, were all very high) — this pressure seemed to be absent in Chile. As we have seen, the investment coefficient was very low, public expenditure in relation to national product was not excessive, and the distribution of income was such that private saving could have been made. Yet inflation in Chile was even greater than in Argentina. The root cause seems to have been, not the pressure of investment over saving, but rather the pressure of the wage-earning sector to raise its share of the national product, and at times, even, to prevent a fall in its absolute real income, which, however, could not be successful provided the pattern of production remained unchanged. The income elasticities of demand for food and other necessities of the wage-earning class were such that any tendency for a rise in the real incomes of the wage earners immediately put pressure on the prices of these goods. In fact, the wage-earning class was fighting a battle it had to lose. It could, of course, be objected at this point that the relatively strong trade union organisation in Chile lay at the bottom of the whole process, for without organised pressure money wages would not have risen so much or so fast. But it is also important to point out that if the structure of production had been such that this pressure could have had some success in improving the relative position of labour — and this did not necessarily involve a cut in investment — inflation, similarly, would have been less. In other words it cannot be argued that trade unions produced inflation *because* they made it impossible for saving to match investment: it is quite clear that they were not successful in altering the distribution of income in their favour, in fact it moved against them. Rather, they made apparent the consequences of a severe imbalance in the structure of production of the Chilean economy. The Economic Commission for Latin America[1] aptly summarised Chile's dilemma in the following terms: '. . . the Chilean economy is faced with a choice between two alternatives: on the one hand, the removal of the structural

[1] Ibid., p. 197.

obstacles to more rapid development with stability; and on the other, either inflation, or stagnation and increasing unemployment together with relative internal stability.' We may place the emphasis somewhat differently: if inflation is to be prevented, either the supply of agricultural products and foodstuffs in particular must be increased, or the power of employees to force up their money wages must be removed: in the former case, economic growth becomes possible, whilst in the latter case it will probably prove impossible.

IV

CONCLUSIONS

The important conclusion of this survey of Latin American experience can be put shortly and simply. It is that analysis of inflation in under-developed countries in terms of the relation between investment and saving, or in terms of expansive credit and fiscal policies, is not always appropriate. It is clear, for instance, that because the economies of many under-developed countries are built around the production of one or very few primary products, the demand for which tends to fluctuate sharply in the short run, they are open to external pressures that create inflationary pressures independent of purely domestic policies. Furthermore, such inflationary pressure is difficult to counteract with purely monetary policies without adversely affecting growth. Perhaps of more importance, however, is the inflationary pressure produced by unbalanced development. No matter how firmly governments control their money and financial systems, no matter how careful they are in keeping the rate of capital formation in balance with private and public saving, they will find it difficult to achieve growth without inflation if investment is directed largely towards the expansion of industry to the neglect of agriculture. Obversely, anti-inflationary policies in such circumstances can only work if they contain as an integral part a policy of agricultural promotion which, of course, takes time to produce results. There can be little doubt that considerable evidence for this conclusion can be drawn from Latin American experience, and no doubt from the experience of other under-developed countries as well.

Chapter X

SUMMARY AND CONCLUSIONS

In the first part of this book the attempt was made to examine in a purely theoretical fashion the nature and effects of the forces likely to bear on the price level in the course of economic growth: in the second part, the historical experience of a few countries was reviewed, albeit rather briefly, partly with the aim of seeking confirmation of the theoretical reasoning appearing earlier, partly with a view to establishing empirically some connection between the rate of economic growth and the behaviour of the price level. It is perhaps not too much to claim that the brief historical surveys do in fact provide some empirical confirmation of the theoretical analysis put forward in the earlier chapters, but this is not as reassuring as it might sound. It is, of course, inevitable that economists must rely on historical evidence for confirmation or rejection of their theories, simply because of their inability to conduct controlled experiments; but, unfortunately, history is seldom able to provide conclusive tests. The mere collection and organisation of historical facts usually have to be undertaken with some theoretical interpretation or mould in mind: indeed, without some such hypothesis the historian runs the risk of not recognising or appreciating pertinent historical facts. Hence it may not be surprising, but nor will it be very reassuring, to find historical fact and theory very often in accord. The biggest difficulty, however, is that historical facts are frequently capable of being interpreted in a number of different ways which, although competing with one another in many vital respects, are, nonetheless, all equally plausible. In other words, historical evidence can seldom be relied upon to reject conclusively one hypothesis in favour of another. It is in the light of considerations of this sort that the conclusions seeming to emerge from the combination of theoretical and historical analysis attempted here must be judged.

In the course of this book, considerable emphasis has been placed on the relative rates of growth of agriculture and industry. It has been argued that unless an appropriate relationship exists between the growth rates of these two important sectors of the economy, the terms of exchange between them must alter. Since agricultural prices typically tend to respond more rapidly than do the prices of industrial products to changes in the balance between supply and demand, their behaviour determines in large part the behaviour of the general price level. Thus in a situation where agricultural growth is tending to lag to an inappropriate extent behind both the growth of industrial output and the growth of real income, excess demand pressures tend to appear in the agricultural product market. Whether excess demand or excess supply pressures exist in the industrial market depends on the balance between investment and saving; but, in either case, if agricultural prices are more flexible than industrial prices, then the required improvement in the terms of exchange of agriculture tends to be brought about by an absolute rise in agricultural prices, rather than by a fall in industrial prices. This is not just an immediate or short run effect, for the rise in agricultural prices tends to generate consequential pressures on costs of production in industry, partly through a direct effect on raw material costs in industry, and partly, perhaps, through an induced effect on industrial money wages. Industrial prices may therefore be prevented from falling, even in a market where there tends to be excess supply; and indeed, if the cost pressures are substantial enough, they may even begin to rise. In this way, the improvement in agriculture's terms of exchange produces a rise in the general price level. Such a development is more likely to take place as the result of a spontaneous slowing down in the rate at which agricultural output is growing, relatively to other output; but it may also occur if the improvement in agriculture's terms of exchange is being produced by an acceleration in the rate of growth of industry. For opposite reasons, an acceleration in the rate of growth of agricultural output can produce a fall in the general price level.

Under-developed countries are particularly prone to inflationary pressures generated by a strong improvement in agriculture's terms of exchange. At bottom, lies an excessive rate of industrialisation. It is, of course, easy to understand why many under-developed countries feel the need to industrialise at all costs. Industrialisation appears an attractive solution for a country which, either because it has a very large population relatively to its supply of land, or because of unpropitious natural or sociological conditions, is not likely to be able to feed a growing population at rising standards of living. The development of an export trade in manufactures, which will enable it to purchase food and other agricultural materials from abroad, seems to be the only way out. Even where agricultural supply conditions are not unfavourable, so that the development of agricultural or other primary product exports would be possible, industrialisation may still seem preferable. The international demand for primary products seems to lag behind the growth of manufacturing output and real income in the main importing countries: hence for a country to develop its economy on the lines of becoming a predominantly primary product exporter implies that its rate of growth is likely to be lower than that of the more advanced countries, and/or that its international terms of trade are likely to show a long-term tendency to worsen.[1] Industrialisation for export, however, may also run up against considerable difficulties. Newly developing countries usually have to start by producing and exporting the simpler and cruder types of manufactures, such as textiles; the possession of more advanced capital equipment and technical knowledge, and of more highly skilled labour, gives the older, more advanced industrial countries an overwhelming comparative advantage in the production of the more complex kind. Unfortunately, world demand for many of the simpler kinds of manufacture is not expanding rapidly, certainly not as fast as the demand for the more complex kind. Hence if the newly industrialising countries are significantly to expand their exports of manufactures, they must usually displace existing high cost producers in the already developed countries. As desirable as this is on grounds of economic efficiency, it is by no means an easy matter to bring about. It requires very liberal commercial policies on the part of the already developed countries, and a willingness to see domestic producers and labour suffer, at least temporarily, until they can be absorbed elsewhere in the economy. Experience does not suggest that the older countries are particularly liberal in this respect; and, in any case, resources are not so mobile that the displacement of high cost producers can take place at a rapid rate. It is not surprising therefore that many under-developed countries may seek to industrialise, either with domestic markets in mind, or with the aim of exporting the simpler manufactures to each other,

[1] See R. Nurkse, *Patterns of Trade and Development* (Wicksell Lectures, Stockholm 1959).

rather than to attempt to break into the markets of the more advanced industrial countries.

But if this policy is to succeed, the under-developed areas must not ignore their agricultural sectors. If industrial output is to be directed mainly towards domestic markets, then domestic agriculture must be developed sufficiently to supply the necessary foodstuffs for continuing economic growth: if it is directed towards the markets of other under-developed countries, then somewhere within the 'under-developed' trading group, there must exist a country or countries which are able to produce a surplus of food, above what is required for their local needs.[1] Failing this, industrialisation is likely to lead to severe excess demand for food and a consequential rapid rise in food prices. Money wages in industry, almost certainly, are bound to be affected, and before long severe cost inflationary pressures spread throughout the economy.

In some circumstances, such as those outlined in Chapter II, inflation can, of course, prove favourable for economic growth. When, as is often the case, an under-developed country runs up against the difficulty of mobilising sufficient voluntary saving by employing orthodox fiscal and institutional means, then it may feel constrained to create credit and run budget deficits so as to place purchasing power into the hands of potential entrepreneurs and to raise the rate of investment above what it would otherwise be. But it is important to note that the sort of inflation we have just been considering, in which excess demand for food forces up prices in industry, is not an efficient mechanism for forcing saving since industrial profits do not necessarily benefit from the rise in prices. Moreover, there are other dangers associated with a rapid rise in prices, the most important being that confidence might be lost in the value of money: if this happens, the monetary and financial system would soon break down, and speculative rather than productive investment would thrive. The experience of Japan in the early stages of its development, however, shows that this latter danger can be avoided: if this is a guide, governments can pursue liberal financial policies without inflation becoming more than very moderate. But it must be emphasised that important conditions underlay Japan's success in this direction. The elasticity of supply

---

[1] Unfortunately, it seems to be the case that the largest food surpluses in the world are to be found in the developed areas of the world, particularly in North America.

of labour to her growing industries was very high, and political opposition to the formation of trade unions was strong: the combined effect of these factors was to keep money wages relatively stable. Moreover, the distribution of income was very unequal and was encouraged to remain so by the policies of government: thus the propensity to save was high. In addition, Japan successfully developed the export of an important product, silk, which had small import content and made use of her abundant labour: thus she was enabled to have a high marginal propensity to import which served to check inflationary booms. The most important restraining factor in Japan's long inflation, however, was her success in promoting agricultural development in the early stages of growth. Although real wages in terms of industrial products were held back, in terms of food there was a substantial rise in the first twenty-five or thirty years of growth. Food prices never got out of hand, hence money wages were more easily stabilised with consequential favourable effects on industrial prices.

The moral is that, whilst under-developed countries may be well advised to court the risk of some inflation in the interests of growth, there is better chance that inflation will be useful in this direction if agriculture is encouraged to develop at a rate appropriate to the growth of industry.

Fundamentally, the same price raising forces may operate in the more developed countries as well. Usually however the inflation of prices is much less violent. This is partly because agricultural products figure much less prominently in total production, so that fluctuations in agricultural prices affect the general price level much less. It is also true that the supply of agricultural products to the advanced countries is more assured than it is to the poorer ones. If an advanced country relies on domestic farm production for the bulk of its food supplies then its agricultural sector is usually highly developed, and is able to expand production without much difficulty in the course of growth. If, on the other hand, the developed country relies on imports of foodstuffs to feed its population then its trading position is usually strong enough to enable it to call on many sources of supply when the need arises. Nonetheless, the growth of agricultural as well as primary product supply can, for long periods, fail to keep pace with demand, as determined by the growth of the economy as a whole, in which case there is a tendency for primary product prices to rise. The rise may be slow and gentle enough not to have significant effects on costs in industry; but even if industrial prices remain stable, the gradual rise in primary product and food prices pushes the general price level upwards. If costs in industry are significantly affected as well, then the inflation of prices becomes more rapid and extensive.

An explanation of this sort has been held to account for the *secular* upturn in prices throughout the trading world in the late 1890's.[1] An extension of manufacturing production in a number of countries (not necessarily an acceleration in the rate of growth of manufacturing production in any *one* country) in the last quarter of the nineteenth century led to a rise in the rate of growth of demand for primary products, the supply of which did not respond. Also, there was a sharp fall in the rate of growth of agricultural output in the United States after 1900, this country for the first time becoming a *net* importer of food. Farm and primary product prices therefore rose strongly after 1900 and with them, although less steeply, the price level of industrial products as well. In the 1870's and '80's, the mechanism probably worked the other way: an enormous extension of the world supply of agricultural and primary products, relative to the growth of manufacturing, produced a fall in the price level of primary products and therefore a fall in prices in general.

It should be noted that many agricultural and other primary product prices are largely determined in international markets; that is, their long run behaviour does not depend closely on policies pursued in any one country, or even on the rate of growth of agricultural and primary product supply in any one country. Thus the general price level of any one country is subject to pressures not easily under the control of domestic authorities. It is fairly clear, for instance, that the price level in Britain has been greatly influenced through much of its modern development by the behaviour of world primary product and agricultural prices. In addition, we have argued that the rates of growth of many countries, particularly if 'specialised' in the production of primary products or in the production of industrial products, are likely to be affected by any long-term changes in the terms of exchange between these products; and we concluded that, *all other things being equal*, specialised industrial countries were likely to experience faster rates of growth when primary product prices were

[1] See Chapters VI and VII.

T

falling[1] and lower rates of growth when they were rising. Conversely in the case of the specialist primary producer. In turn, it follows that industrial countries are likely to be growing faster when their price level is stable or falling than when it is rising, whilst the opposite is true for the primary producers. Although in illustration of this argument we examined the experience of Britain and the United States alone, there is reason to believe that the experience of other countries does not refute it. Germany in the nineteenth and early twentieth centuries, for instance, seemed to grow faster when prices were falling, as did the United Kingdom, whereas Sweden and Denmark, both primary producers and exporters in the early stages of growth, seemed to grow faster when their prices were rising.[2]

Apart from an appropriate balance between the growth of industry and the growth of agriculture, a further necessary condition for the general price level to remain stable during growth is that *aggregate* demand for goods and services should rise at the same rate as the *potential* growth of *aggregate* supply.[3] If the former is rising at a faster rate than the latter, then prices tend to be drawn up by excess demand or pushed up by rising costs of production; if the reverse is true, downward pressure on prices appears. However, in this latter case, the result is likely to be a slowing down in the *actual* growth of supply as well as, if not instead of, a fall in prices. Hence control over demand for the purpose of maintaining price stability must not be managed in such a way that the actual growth of supply suffers.

There is a further aspect to the problem. The potential growth rate of supply is not independent of the *composition* of the aggregate demand for goods and services, since, in large part, it depends on continual additions to, and replacement of, capital equipment. Thus, part of the economy's available output must be 'demanded' for investment purposes, and the larger the proportion of total output directed towards the satisfaction of this demand, the faster will the potential output grow over time. Hence, control over demand for goods and services must be operated in such a way that

[1] Provided the fall was produced by an autonomous acceleration in the growth of supply of primary products. See Chapter IV.

[2] See S. Kuznets, 'Quantitative aspects of the Economic Growth of Nations, I', *Economic Development and Cultural Change*, Vol. V, No. 1, October 1956.

[3] By 'potential' growth, we mean growth as determined by the growth of population, capital, technical knowledge, etc.

whilst it prevents actual demand from rising at too fast a rate relative to the potential growth of supply, it does not lower the latter relative to what it might be, given the increase in population, technical knowledge, and other factors, that also determine the rate of growth.

Our survey of price and growth behaviour in Britain, America and Japan shows that demand in these countries, at least, was not in fact typically regulated in such a way that prices were kept stable: prices both rose and fell in the course of development. Apart from wars, the explanation of short run fluctuations in prices lies in the unstable nature of investment in private enterprise economies. Capital accumulation did not, and does not, typically take place at an even rate through time: rather, investment decisions, and consequential increases in demand for capital goods, tend to be lumped together at certain points of time. Consumption plus investment expenditure then becomes larger than what the economy can currently meet, and prices therefore tend to rise. Nonetheless, the rise in investment expenditure normally results in an increase in *real* capital formation: in other words, rising prices do tend to divert resources away from consumption to investment, at least in a relative sense, and, therefore, it might be said that inflation has successfully forced saving.

But in the course of development in Britain and America, and to a lesser extent in Japan, inflation during the investment booms never became very serious. Usually investment expenditure began to decline before the fact of inflation became an important element in consumers' and producers' decisions, in other words, before inflation began to produce its own dynamic. It is not clear why investment booms did come to an end in Britain and America at this point. It may have been because of an increasing shortage of money and credit in the later stages of the boom. If so, this was not the result of deliberate action on the part of governments. In the nineteenth century, the operation of the international Gold Standard perhaps tended to serve somewhat as an automatic check to a continual rise in prices, except when the world output of gold was increasing.[1] When banks began to lose gold from their reserves, because of an internal or external drain, interest rates began to rise

---

[1] This is not to say, of course, that an increase in the world output of gold *caused* the rise in prices, or that prices tended to fall *because* there was insufficient supply of gold.

and bank credit tended to become scarcer. Entrepreneurs may therefore have found it more difficult and more costly to obtain finance for further investment, so that their expenditure began to fall. Some economists,[1] however, have played down the monetary factor, emphasising instead *real* factors, such as the full employment ceiling, as being the proximate cause of the collapse of the boom. We, however, are not concerned with this problem, which is essentially a matter for trade cycle theory: instead we are interested in how prices behaved.

With the collapse of the investment boom, aggregate demand declined, very often to below the capacity of the economy to produce. As a result, output fell, and with it, prices as well. This was the mechanism through which *secular* or long-term stability in the value of money was maintained in Britain and America in the course of the nineteenth century; in the slumps, prices very often fell as much as, and sometimes more than, they had risen in the preceding boom. Moreover, it is sometimes argued that the slump, as well as the boom, was a crucial and vital stage in the process of growth, since it enabled the previous burst of real capital formation both to be assimilated and to produce a rise in productive efficiency. It should be noted, however, that this mechanism did not operate in Japan. Indeed, the reason why the price level in this country rose as much as it did in the course of its long run economic development, was not so much that prices rose more strongly in any short period of time, but rather that they seldom fell. The argument, sometimes advanced, that Japanese governments promoted inflation in order to accelerate the rate of growth is thus somewhat misleading. It is truer to say that governments did not allow significant slumps to develop, being ready to create credit freely and to take the initiative in promoting investment, whenever private enterprise tended to languish. As a result, Japan enjoyed what amounted to an almost perpetual boom, with prices rising almost continuously. It must be noted too that economic growth did not suffer from the absence of slumps, as the argument we have just referred to might suggest: indeed the rate of development in Japan after 1860 was much higher than had typically been the case in Britain and America during the comparable stage of their growths.

[1] For example, J. R. Hicks, see *A Contribution to the Theory of the Trade Cycle* (Oxford 1950).

The fact that slumps were sometimes associated with severe declines in production and employment as well as a fall in prices made them undesirable on economic and social grounds; and after the particularly severe slump of the 1930's, governments of most mature capitalist countries came to accept the responsibility of checking them. Moreover, since the 1930's, knowledge of the workings of a private enterprise economy has increased, so that governments are now better able to deal with slumps than they once were. The maintenance of full employment is therefore a primary objective of government economic policy. The implication is, however, that downward pressure on prices is now likely to occur much less frequently in the developed capitalist countries than it once did. Furthermore, there are clear signs that prices are much less flexible in the downward direction than they were when the economy was less developed, and industry was less complex. We explored the reasons for this in Chapter V and in parts of the chapters on Britain and America dealing with their post-Second War development. One obvious reason is the decline in the relative importance of agricultural and primary product production in total output, the prices of such commodities generally being more flexible in the short run than are the prices of commodities produced in the industrial sector. In addition, price flexibility in the downward direction has probably declined in the industrial sector itself, owing to the growing preference of producers to compete through advertising, product differentiation and the like, rather than through price. In consequence, slumps probably have to be deeper and more prolonged to get the same fall in the general price level, the more developed and industrialised an economy becomes.

In these circumstances, when prices do not readily fall, secular price stability seems to require that they should never rise. One step towards the achievement of this aim would be to even out the rate of capital accumulation over time; in other words, to prevent large-scale investment booms. Such a policy of course would also contribute to the prevention of slumps. Most governments of advanced capitalist countries have moved in this direction; and the fact that in many such economies a large part of total investment is typically carried out by government departments or by institutions, such as nationalised corporations, directly under their control, is an important element in a policy of stabilising investment over time.

Moreover, governments increasingly conduct their monetary and fiscal policies with the object of influencing private investment decisions. Post-war experience in Britain and America, however, does not suggest that such stabilisation policies are likely to be one hundred per cent successful, partly because investment decisions in the private sector are by no means highly sensitive to fiscal and monetary measures, and partly because it is both difficult and costly to regulate public investment so as to offset cyclical fluctuations in private investment. Thus, if the economy is normally kept operating at or very close to the full employment output, it is likely that excess demand pressures will sometimes appear and prices will therefore rise.[1]

An alternative possibility is of course not to run the economy *normally* at full employment level of output. Instead, it might be possible to keep some excess capacity, both of labour and equipment, in hand, large enough to satisfy a temporary increase in demand whenever private investment booms. Naturally, demand would have to be allowed to rise over time, as the capacity to produce rose, but at no time would it be as great as the maximum output that could be produced.[2] Once again the objective is more easily stated than achieved. For one thing, it is obviously not an easy matter for governments to judge the rate at which productive capacity is likely to rise: the rate at which physical capital accumulates is by no means a reliable indicator since other factors, such as the growth of the labour force and technical progress, may also vary over time. And demand must not be allowed to fall too low, otherwise potential output is being wasted. Moreover, unnecessary unemployment of labour raises problems of a social nature which are not necessarily less than those raised by some secular price inflation; and, in any case, the reserve of labour would have to be paid much higher rates of unemployment pay than are customarily paid in most countries, since, according to the terms of the policy, its presence is just as vital to stable growth as is employed labour. Perhaps the most significant objection to the 'reserve capacity' policy is, however, that it might well slow down the long-term rate

---

[1] Consumption demand, particularly for consumers' durables, may also be subject to independent fluctuations, and therefore may require controlling.

[2] The rate at which both demand and output is allowed to rise over time may of course depend on the rate at which the capacity to import increases over time; but this raises further questions of policy with which we are not explicitly concerned.

of growth. The greatest inducement to an entrepreneur to add to his capital equipment is existence of excess demand for his product. Generally, too, profits are very high at this time, not so much because profit margins over direct costs are necessarily high, but because overhead costs per unit of output are very low, probably lower than originally planned for when the plant was installed. Thus finance for expansion tends to be readily available. In any case, the mere fact that machinery is working at or close to maximum capacity probably means that maintenance costs are high, so that there is an incentive to replace old equipment with new, which may technically be capable of a higher flow of output. Hence, in choosing to work the economy normally at a lower level of output than it is in fact capable of, the government may be 'buying' price stability with a somewhat lower rate of growth.

Unfortunately, this is not the most acute form this dilemma may take. Even if aggregate demand could be stabilised over time so that excess demand never appeared, it would not follow that prices would not rise over time. An advanced industrial economy is subject to *secular* price raising forces independent of the effect of short-term booms. We have already referred to the way in which the price level can be affected by a failure of primary production to keep pace with demand, but pressures operating on the price level in the same manner can be produced more generally. Thus, changes in the *composition* of demand, which are bound to occur in a dynamic economy, tend to produce excess demand for the products of some industries and excess supply of others. For reasons discussed in some detail in Chapter V, prices tend to rise more easily and quickly in the former industries or sectors than they fall in the latter ones: statistically, therefore, the *general* price level tends to rise. Nor is this just a statistical phenomenon: the rise in prices (and incomes) in the former sectors often affects costs in the latter sectors, thereby causing prices to rise in these sectors as well, despite deficient demand. The implication is that regulation of aggregate demand, although a *necessary* condition for secular price stability, is not a sufficient one.

Differing productivity growths in various sectors of the economy, operating in an environment in which downward flexibility of prices is relatively low and in which there is persistent pressure for comparable increases in money incomes in all sectors, produce similar effects on the general price level. When productivity increases are not easily or quickly reflected in falling prices, but rather in rising money incomes, then prices are bound to rise in some sectors where productivity growth is relatively low. There is, for instance, a constant tendency for 'service' prices to rise relatively to the prices of manufactured goods, owing to the faster rate of growth of productivity in manufacturing industry; but if manufactured good prices do not fall very much, service prices must rise. Once again, the net result is a rise in the general price level. Hence, a policy which aims at relating wage increase generally to the '*average*' rate of productivity growth in the economy — the alternative of allowing wages in each sector to rise in sympathy with productivity growth in *each sector*, not really being politically possible or socially desirable in the long run — is no guarantee that the general price level will not rise.

The secular price-raising effect of these pressures can, of course, be checked by periodic slumps, deep enough and prolonged enough to force some prices down: but, as we have said, such slumps are undesirable both on economic and social grounds, and would inevitably result in a lower rate of growth over time.

In brief, there are a number of forces bearing on the price level in the course of economic growth; and, as far as economic policy is concerned, it is evident that governments are bound to be faced very often with a policy dilemma, namely the choice between faster economic growth and price stability. But it must be emphasized that governmental concern with price stability is as new in the history of the democratic industrial countries as is concern with full employment. It is perfectly true that the major democratic industrial powers, for example, the United Kingdom and the United States, achieved their growth in the nineteenth century, at least, with very little persistent inflation. The price level in Britain was probably lower at the end of the nineteenth century than it was at the beginning, even if the Napoleonic Wars are discounted. But as we have stressed, prices did rise at times, both in the short run, during the upswing of the trade cycle, and in the long run, in the upswing of the secular movement of prices, for instance in the 1850's and again in the two decades before the First World War. Furthermore, the overall relative price stability was not the result of deliberate government policy: governments were not explicitly concerned with price movements as such, any more than they were with the rate of economic growth. Only in so far as they caused balance of payments difficulties could governments be said to be worried. The reason for this is that the operation of the nineteenth century International Gold Standard was expected to take care of it. Thus, if prices in one country rose, causing imports to rise and exports to fall, gold would soon flow out. This would soon check prices, perhaps even reverse them,[1] which in turn would reverse the movement of gold. International flows of gold in other words, ensured reasonable price stability. Following the rules of the gold standard game would certainly prevent serious or prolonged inflation in one country alone; on the other hand, it is clear that the gold standard did not prevent inflation on a world-wide scale, as the secular movements of world prices in the nineteenth century prove. Provided rising prices did not involve a decline in the gold reserves, governments did not seem to concern themselves explicitly with prices, and certainly did not closely watch the movements of a 'price index', which many seem to do to-day. And perhaps it was a good thing they did not, or the progress of growth would probably have been less.

In the twentieth century, however, the international Gold Standard seemed to produce unwelcome effects on employment and production; and in consequence it was abandoned in the 1930's. Instead, governments became concerned with the level of employment: many of them, indeed, accepted explicit employment targets. World War II forced on them even greater responsibility for the conduct of economic affairs, and this did not greatly diminish when the war was over. In particular, the cold war and Soviet economic competition have forced democratic countries to accept the need for faster economic growth, again fostered by government action. The benefits of high employment have undoubtedly been real, and pre-occupation with further economic development has been no bad thing. But the post-war gains seem to have been made at the expense of price stability, both in the short and the long run, for reasons that we have explored in some detail. As time passed, political awareness of and opposition to inflation have grown in many countries, forcing governments to become more concerned with prices. Indeed, it can be truthfully said that if the events of the 1930's forced democratic governments to concern themselves with employment, the 1940's and 1950's have forced them to accept responsibility for prices as well; and perhaps the

---

[1] Prices were probably more flexible at this time.

policy of absolute price stability seems to have become accepted as firmly as the policy of full employment once was.

What conclusions may we draw? The facts suggest that one or other of two broad solutions have to be adopted. The first is obvious: policy objectives must not be stated or pursued in absolute terms. Thus, whilst governments should be concerned with maintaining economic growth they should not explicitly aim at *maximum* growth. Whilst being concerned with employment they should not insist that unemployment never rises above some absolute minimum level, below which it would be almost impossible to make it fall. Whilst looking for reasonable price stability they should not tie their objective to some given maximum figure in a price index. In very recent years, it is clear, in fact, that countries are beginning consciously to compromise; many have become less concerned with full employment than price stability, and are fixing their minimum employment targets at lower levels than formerly. The more contemporary danger is perhaps that the objective of stability in the value of money will be pursued with the determination that full employment once was, giving rise to dangers that are no less and may be worse. As we have said, when prices do not easily fall, stability in the value of money requires that they never rise; and it is difficult to see how the latter can be ensured, at least in open economies such as the United Kingdom, exposed to autonomous fluctuations and secular trends in the price level of imported raw materials and foodstuffs, without unduly restricting the rate of economic growth. Indeed, if the choice between lower production, lower employment and slower growth, on the one hand, and some gradual rise in prices, on the other, has to be made, then there is much to be said for accepting the latter rather than the former, for it is on the production of goods and services that our wellbeing depends, not on prices.[1] It might be an advantage for government not to admit that prices must sometimes rise — or to forecast that they will rise in specific economic circumstances —

[1] It might be argued here that a persistent rise in prices might itself force a slower rate of economic growth than could be achieved with price stability. This would happen if a rising domestic price level caused exports to grow more slowly than otherwise, thereby restricting imports of raw materials and food-stuffs. But this need not be a serious danger. In the first place it is likely that all mature industrial countries will experience similar price raising forces, hence there is no need for the competitive position of any one of them to suffer; and in the second place, the secular price raising forces we have referred to bear more on the price level of *services* than on the price level of manufactured goods, and the former, of course, do not normally enter into international trade.

for the best way to keep inflation 'creeping' or moderate, is to remove expectation that it will continue. Indeed, it may be advisable for the government to ensure that prices do stabilise at times, taking advantage when they can of periods when primary product prices are falling. But governments should have no doubt in their own mind about the priority to be given, within reason, to production and employment over prices.

The alternative solution is for the government to intervene very much more than it does at present in present-day democratic and free enterprise economies: the difficulty in pursuing policy absolutes arises as much from the limitations of policy measures considered to be conventional, desirable or permissible, as it does from the policy absolutes themselves. The government, for instance, might be prepared to use indirect taxes and subsidies to stabilise prices in the face of changes in factor and raw material costs,[1] whilst using direct taxes, interest rates, physical controls and the like to regulate production and employment;[2] or it may go further, as in collectivised economies, by fixing prices and wages by administrative decree, and by controlling investment and the distribution of resources to maximise production and growth. Provided the ends of policy are consistent in terms of resources available, policy absolutes could presumably be achieved; but such measures would imply less political and economic freedom than is customarily thought desirable in democratic societies: indeed, some people would deny that such a society could remain democratic at all.

A more acceptable form of intervention open to governments of democratic countries would be aimed at increasing the degree of price competition in manufacturing industry: as we have said, it is the reluctance of many manufacturers to reduce their prices when their costs would enable them to do so that tends to produce the secular rise in the price level. The current attack on monopoly in Britain and America is obviously a step in this direction, but it is clearly not enough, since it is not only the large-scale producer or monopolist who behaves in this way. One possibility might be to increase the relative advantage of price competition as against advertising by raising the cost of the latter, for instance, through a tax. Alternatively, tax rebates might be given to firms which can

[1] i.e. insulating the domestic economy from the world economy.
[2] See B. Hansen, *The Economic Theory of Fiscal Policy* (Allen and Unwin).

show that they have lowered prices in the course of the fiscal year. Or the government itself might even set up in production in order to act as a price leader. In whatever manner it is achieved, it is clearly necessary that some prices should be made to fall, since it is inevitable that other prices will have to rise. Only in this way can a serious secular price raising force be avoided.

It is obvious that policy decisions involve compromise between many objectives: rapid economic growth, full employment, maximum production, price stability, political and economic freedom are all desirable, but it is doubtful whether they can all be obtained in a 100 per cent way at the same time. Choice has to be made, and priorities must be established. Compromise, however, is no new thing for any society. But what is desirable — and this is where economic analysis must play a part — is that the nature of the compromise should be made clear: governments should be made aware of what they necessarily reject when they decide in favour of something else. Sometimes a choice is not involved, at other times it certainly is; but until we know the reason why, rational choice is hardly possible. Thus the contribution, if any, of this book lies in this direction: in outlining some of the pressures that operate on prices during the course of economic growth, it attempts to make clear what is involved in the choice between faster economic growth and price stability.

INDEX OF SUBJECTS

INDEX OF AUTHORS

PRINTED IN GREAT BRITAIN BY ROBERT MACLEHOSE AND CO. LTD
THE UNIVERSITY PRESS, GLASGOW